Insurgent Public Space

From parking spaces being transformed into temporary parks, to metal pigs being deposited on sidewalks, to "sleep-in" protests, public spaces around the world are often utilized in unconventional and unusual ways. Frequently going against their traditional uses, citizens and activists are reclaiming and creating places for temporary, informal gathering in urban sites across the globe.

Challenging how we define public spaces, nearly twenty such guerrilla and everyday projects are illustrated here with photographs and insightful commentaries. Often used to make serious statements, but sometimes just for fun, these insurgent spaces question the ways in which we each use our city and how we define public space.

Jeffrey Hou, as editor, has carefully chosen authors who have firsthand experience in researching and implementing these insurgent public spaces. Their expertise has created a unique cross-disciplinary book looking at how public adaptation of spaces can affect the social and spatial relationships within our urban environments. Appealing to citizens, professionals, and students interested in urbanism, these valuable and fascinating insights focus on a subject and practice that has, up until now, been largely ignored.

Jeffrey Hou is Chair and Associate Professor of Landscape Architecture at the University of Washington, Seattle. His research and practice focus on design activism and engaging marginalized social groups in the making of public space.

D1566780

Insurgent Public Space

Guerrilla urbanism and the remaking of contemporary cities

Edited by Jeffrey Hou

Routledge
Taylor & Francis Group

LONDON AND NEW YORK

This edition published 2010
by Routledge
2 Park Square, Milton Park, Abingdon, Oxon, OX14 4RN

Simultaneously published in the USA and Canada
by Routledge
270 Madison Avenue, New York, NY 10016

Routledge is an imprint of the Taylor & Francis Group, an informa business

Typeset in Frutiger by Prepress Projects Ltd, Perth, UK
Printed and bound in Great Britain by The Cromwell Press Group, Trowbridge, Wiltshire

British Library Cataloguing in Publication Data
A catalogue record for this book is available from the British Library

Library of Congress Cataloging-in-Publication Data
Insurgent public space: guerrilla urbanism and the remaking of the contemporary cities/edited by Jeffrey Hou.
p. cm.
1. Urbanization—Case studies. 2. Public spaces—Case studies. I. Hou, Jeffrey, 1967–
HT361.I48 2010
307.76 – dc22   2009041890

ISBN10: 0–415–77965–0 (hbk)
ISBN10: 0–415–77966–9 (pbk)
ISBN10: 0–203–09300–3 (ebk)

ISBN13: 978–0–415–77965–4 (hbk)
ISBN13: 978–0–415–77966–1 (pbk)
ISBN13: 978–0–203–09300–9 (ebk)

Contents

Notes on contributors

Shin Aiba is Associate Professor at the Tokyo Metropolitan University. He received his PhD in Engineering from the Department of Architecture at Waseda University. He is a co-founder of "Alice Center," a pioneer of intermediary organizations for NPOs/NGOs. His research focuses on city planning, local governance, and citizen participation.

Giorgia Aiello is Lecturer in the Institute of Communications Studies at the University of Leeds and co-director of the Urban Archives project at the University of Washington. She is a 2008 recipient of the National Communication Association Critical and Cultural Studies Division's Outstanding Dissertation Award.

Caroline Chen is a PhD candidate in Landscape Architecture and Environmental Planning at the University of California, Berkeley. Her research examines how people improvise and use designed spaces in unexpected ways to find joy in urban China. She holds an MLA from the Harvard University Graduate School of Design.

Hung-Ying Chen works at ARENA (Asian Regional Exchange for New Alternatives) based in Seoul, South Korea. She graduated from the Graduate Institute of Building and Planning in National Taiwan University. Her research interest covers different social issues related to spatial planning and social activism.

Yung-Teen Annie Chiu is Assistant Professor at the Praxis University in Taipei. She received her PhD from the National Taiwan University. She is project co-coordinator for the Center on Globalizing Asian City: People, Place and Identity. She has developed an integrated research/design/construction method involving construction, installation art, and documentary film.

Tom Dobrowolsky co-directs the Urban Archives, holds an MLIS from the University of Washington, and is pursuing a PhD in the Program in the Built Environment. Research interests include urban history, digital archives, and phenomenology of public spaces. Tom's digital media experiments explore their technical, academic, artistic, and ethical dimensions.

Irina Gendelman received her PhD in Communication from the University of Washington. She currently works as an Assistant Professor of Instructional Design and Adjunct Professor of Anthropology at Saint Martin's University in Lacey, Washington. She is the founder of CROW mural projects and co-director of Urban Archives.

Yasuyoshi Hayashi is a community designer engaged in Machizukuri since the 1970s. In the 1980s, Hayashi concentrated on citizen participation, Machizukuri ordinances and workshops. In the 1990s, he worked with citizens to expand Machizukuri. With the New NPO Law established in 1998, he focuses on new social infrastructure to support future communities.

Jeffrey Hou is Chair and Associate Professor of Landscape Architecture at the

University of Washington, Seattle. His research and practice focus on design activism and engaging marginalized social groups in the making of public space. He received his PhD in Environmental Planning and M.Arch. from University of California, Berkeley.

Min Jay Kang is Associate Professor at the Graduate Institute of Building and Planning, National Taiwan University. He was a project director of several highly controversial conservation projects in Taiwan, including Taipei's Treasure Hill and Skin-peeling Alley, and conducted a comprehensive field survey of Taipei's cultural landscapes.

Isami Kinoshita is Professor of Landscape Architecture at Chiba University, where he teaches city planning and environmental management. Since 1980, his work has focused on participation of citizens and children in the design and making of urban open space. He received his PhD from Tokyo Institute of Technology in 1984.

Michael A. LaFond directs id22: Institute for Creative Sustainability in Berlin. He is involved in networking initiatives emphasizing relationships between culture, creativity, communication, art, education, housing, and cultures of sustainable development, and public and university projects dealing with self-organized, civil society-initiated redevelopments of vacant properties, and democratizations of urban planning processes.

Laura Lawson is Associate Professor of Landscape Architecture at the University of Illinois, Urbana-Champaign. She received her PhD in Environmental Planning and MLA from the University of California, Berkeley. She currently serves as Director of the East St. Louis Action Research Project.

Jia-He Lin is an activist in Taiwan. He has a master's degree from the Graduate Institute of Building and Planning at National Taiwan University. His main concern is the social rights of transmigrants in contemporary Asia. He is currently a board member of the Trans-Asia Sisterhood Association, Taiwan (TASAT).

Teresa Marie Mares is a doctoral candidate in Sociocultural Anthropology at the University of Washington. She intends to complete her dissertation in 2010, with the generous support of the American Association of University Women American Dissertation Fellowship and the University of Washington Stroum Dissertation Fellowship.

Blaine Merker is a landscape architect and public artist based in San Francisco. He co-directs the art and design studio Rebar and is a founder of Park(ing) Day. In his work, he explores the intersection of design and community activism in the subtle socio-spatial cues that create the collective environment.

Osamu Nishida is Assistant Professor at the Yokohama National University where he also studied from 1995 to 1999. He was Assistant Professor at the Tokyo Metropolitan University from 2002 to 2007. He established ON Design Partners in 2004. His research and practice focus on city planning and design.

Mima Nishiyama is Associate Professor at Chiba University in Japan. Her teaching and research interests include local agrofood movements, community development, rural family life, and gender studies. She has recently conducted research on local agrofood movements in the US and Japan as they relate to community development and sustainability.

Sawako Ono is Professor of Landscape Architecture at Chiba University. Her research field is the cultural history of gardens. She is especially interested in the opening mechanisms of gardens, which are primarily enclosed. Her principal publications include *Flower-viewing in Edo* and *We Want a Park Like This*.

Andrew Pask is Director of the Vancouver Public Space Network (VPSN), a non-profit organization based in British Columbia. Trained as an anthropologist and urban planner, Pask has worked on urban issues, community-based research, design and planning projects in cities across Canada. Information on the VPSN can be found at http://www.vpsn.ca.

Devon G. Peña is Professor of Anthropology and American Ethnic Studies at the University of Washington, and is Founder/President of the Acequia Institute. He is the author of several books, the most recent being *Mexican Americans and the Environment: Tierra y Vida*, published by the University of Arizona Press.

Jeannene Przyblyski is Associate Professor of Interdisciplinary Studies at the San Francisco Art Institute and Executive Director of the San Francisco Bureau of Urban Secrets, a public art studio and think tank dedicated to exploring the multiplicity of urban pasts and charting the manifold futures of cities (http://www.bureauofurbansecrets.org).

Michael Rios is Assistant Professor in the Department of Environmental Design at the University of California, Davis. Previously, he taught in the School of Architecture and Landscape Architecture at The Pennsylvania State University, where he was inaugural director of the Hamer Center for Community Design from 1999 to 2007.

James Rojas is a nationally recognized urban planner who examines Latino cultural influences on urban design. His influential Massachusetts Institute of Technology thesis on the Latino built environment has been widely cited. For the past eighteen years Mr. Rojas has lectured extensively and written on this subject.

Ryoko Sato is Associate Professor at Ehime University in Japan. She teaches tourism and community development in the faculty of law and literature. Her main research interests include partnerships between urban and rural areas and community development with farmers' markets. She worked as a journalist until spring 2009.

Janni Sorensen is Assistant Professor in the Department of Geography and Earth Sciences at the University of North Carolina, Charlotte. She received her PhD in Urban and Regional Planning from the University of Illinois, Urbana-Champaign. She worked with the East St. Louis Action Research Project at the University of Illinois.

Erick Villagomez is a founding editor at *re:place* magazine. He is an educator, independent researcher, and designer with interests in human settlements at all scales. His private practice, Metis Design Build, is dedicated to a collaborative and ecologically responsible approach to the design and construction of places.

Pina Wu graduated from the Graduate Institute of Building and Planning, National Taiwan University. She also received a master's degree in Public Policy and Urban Planning at Harvard University. She likes to walk around in the city, observe, and enjoy life in the public spaces.

Preface

This book came to being in a way that was not unlike the stories of ad-hoc, informal, incremental, and yet purposeful actions that you are about to read. In 2007, Isami Kinoshita and I put together a panel, titled "Variations on the Public Realm," at the 6th Conference of the Pacific Rim Community Design Network, which produced the initial set of working papers. The Pacific Rim Community Design Network is a loosely connected group of community-based activists and scholars around the Pacific Rim who meet every two years or so to exchange and debate the practice of community design. Conceived by Taichi Goto, with support from Randy Hester, the network was formally launched in 1998 at a working conference at the University of California, Berkeley, followed by consequent meetings in Japan, Taiwan, Hong Kong, Seattle, and China. I am indebted to my colleagues from the network for the inspirations and lessons over the years in engaging citizens and communities in grassroots planning and design. The discourse of insurgent public space could not have emerged without the generous sharing and exchanges of ideas among those within the network. Specific thanks go to Dan Abramson for spearheading the organization of the 2007 conference in Quanzhou that snowballed into this project.

Following the 2007 conference, I was invited by Min Jay Kang and other colleagues at the Organization for Urban Re-s (OURs) to lead a working group as part of the "Do-It-Yourself, Design in Yangminshan Charrette" in Taipei, Taiwan. The design charrette brought together ten faculty members and over fifty students from different universities in Taiwan and the University of Washington. The five-day workshop examined ways to transform the former American military housing quarters in Sanzihou, one of the last green spaces in the dense metropolis, into a space for communities and citizens. The experimentation and discussion during the charrette that centered on the making of Do-It-Yourself (DIY) urban spaces solidified the concept of insurgent public space and the motivation to turn the initial set of 2007 conference papers into a book.

To expand the scope of the book, I initiated a call for papers to those outside the network, several of whom in turn introduced others to join this collaborative effort. My sincere thanks go to Blaine Merker and David Hohenschau, whom I got to know respectively at the Design Activism symposium at Berkeley organized by Randy Hester and the 5th Conference of the Pacific Rim Community Design Network that I organized in Seattle. Both put me in touch with their respective colleagues in San Francisco and Vancouver. The additional contributors have immensely widened the breadth and perspectives of this project. With each new author and new chapter that tells a story from a different social and cultural context, we further articulate and capture the wide-ranging instances of insurgent public space in the increasingly interconnected global villages. I am grateful to the contributing authors, whose intense passion and interest in the work of insurgent public space has kept this project going. I hope this book is only the beginning of our collaboration.

There are many other individuals and institutions that were also critical in making this book a reality. Specifically, the book could not have been completed without the Johnston/Hastings Publication Support from the College of Built Environments at the University of Washington in Seattle. I thank Dean Daniel Friedman for his generosity and support of this project. I am also indebted to Mark Francis and Sergio Palleroni who assisted me early on in seeking funding support for this project. During the many years of teaching at the University of Washington, my colleagues in the Department of Landscape Architecture have provided me with an engaging and supportive environment that enables me to pursue this work. Thank you, JoAnne Edwards, Kristina Hill, Julie Johnson, Lynne Manzo, Kelley Pagano, Vicky Reyes, Iain Robertson, Nancy Rottle, Luanne Smith, Ben Spencer, David Streatfield, Nhon Troung, Fritz Wagner, Thaisa Way, Daniel Winterbottom, and Ken Yocom.

The initial manuscript of this book was completed during my sabbatical leave in Taiwan in fall 2008. I am grateful to Professor Chao-Ching Yu for hosting me in the Department of Landscape Architecture at the Chung-Yuan University. Special thanks also go to Shenglin Elijah Chang and Jingyong Wu at National Taiwan University for sharing with me their office (and humor) where I edited many of the chapters – a much needed relief from having to work on crowded planes, trains, buses, subways, and other forms of true and pseudo public spaces during my travel. Immense thanks go to Alex Hollingsworth, my editor at Routledge, and the anonymous reviewers for recognizing the value of this work. Upon returning to Seattle, my research assistant Sarah Ferreter was instrumental in assembling the final manuscript and in bringing the project to the finish line. For my own chapter in this book, I am grateful to Stella Chao and Joyce Pisnanont for the opportunity and rewarding experience of working with the youths of the WILD program in Seattle's International District and in making me a part of the community.

This book is a collective effort. It is a space for us to share our stories, lessons, ideas, and critical perspectives. With this book and its many narratives, we intend to inform, instigate, and enable other instances of insurgent placemaking.

Jeffrey Hou, Seattle

CHAPTER 1

(Not) your everyday public space

Jeffrey Hou

With a sixteen-foot statue of Vladimir Lenin standing in a street corner, a salvaged rocket sitting on top of a building, a car-eating troll crawling under a bridge, Fremont is undoubtedly one of the most eccentric neighborhoods in Seattle. One day in 2001, the neighborhood (a.k.a. the Center of the Universe) welcomed yet another addition to its treasured collection – an eight-foot-long metal pig that was anonymously planted on a sidewalk overnight.

The pig became an instant celebrity. Neighbors wondered who left it there. The local press followed the news for months – trying to identify the instigator(s), how the pig was erected without permission, and then why it mysteriously vanished two months later, just one day before it was to be moved to a new location following complaints by several business owners. It turned out that the pig was the work of two anonymous artists. The artwork was meant as an anti-consumerism statement, mocking the official "Pigs on Parade," an art and fundraising event that featured decorated pig sculptures in malls and streets of Seattle.

Planted on a public sidewalk, Fremont's pig was not only a social and artistic statement, but also an attack on the official public sphere in the contemporary city. Although the pig did not physically alter the space except for its footprints, its unauthorized presence challenged the norms of public space by defying the city's requirement for a deposit to put art on a sidewalk. Although its actual production did not involve the so-called public process, the work engaged the public through the media and everyday conversation. Through the space it occupied and the debates it engendered among neighbors, citizens, and the media, the pig renewed the discursive instrumentality of public space as a forum for open discussion. It gives meanings to the full notion of publicity in a public space.

In cities around the world, acts such as the pig installation in Fremont represent small yet persistent challenges against the increasingly regulated, privatized, and diminishing forms of public space. In Portland, Oregon, activists from the group City Repair painted street intersections in bright colors and patterns, and involved neighbors in converting them into neighborhood gathering places. In Taipei, citizens frustrated with rocketing housing costs staged a "sleep-in" in the streets of the most expensive district in the city to protest the government inaction. In London, Space Hijackers, a group of self-proclaimed "anarchitects," has performed numerous acts of "space hijacking," from "Guerrilla Benching" – installing benches in empty public space – to the "Circle Line Party" in London's Underground (till they were stopped by the police).

Rather than isolated instances, these acts of insurgency transcend geographic boundaries and reflect the respective social settings and issues. In cities from Europe to Asia, residual urban sites and industrial lands have been occupied and converted into new uses by citizens and communities. From coast to coast in North America, urban and suburban landscapes have been adapted and transformed by new immigrant groups to support new functions and activities. In Japan, suburban private homes have been transformed into "third places" for community activities.[1] From Seattle to Shanghai, citizen actions ranging from gardening to dancing have permanently and temporarily taken over existing urban sites and injected them with new functions and meanings.

These instances of self-made urban spaces, reclaimed and appropriated sites, temporary events, and flash mobs, as well as informal gathering places created by predominantly marginalized communities, have provided new expressions of the collective realms in the contemporary city. No longer confined to the archetypal categories of neighborhood parks, public plaza, and civic architecture, these *insurgent public spaces* challenge the conventional, codified notion of public and the making of space.

What can we learn from these acts of everyday and not-so-everyday resistance? What do they reveal about the limitations and possibilities of public realm in our contemporary city? How do these instances of insurgency challenge the conventional understanding and making of public space? How are these spaces and activities redefining and expanding the roles, functions, and meanings of the public and the production of space? These are the questions we intend to address in this book.

Public space: democracy, exclusion, and political control

Public space has been an important facet of cities and urban culture. In cities around the world, urban spaces such as plazas, markets, streets, temples, and urban parks have long been the centers of civic life for urban dwellers. They provide opportunities for gathering, socializing, recreation, festivals, as well as protests and demonstrations. As parks and plazas, urban open spaces provide relief from dense urban districts and structured everyday life. As civic architecture, they become collective expressions of a city as well as depositories of personal memories. As places where important historical events tend to unfold, public spaces are imbued with important, collective meanings – both official and unofficial.

Serving as a vehicle of social relationships, public discourses, and political expressions, public space is not only a physical boundary and material setting. Henaff and Strong (2001: 35) note that public space "designates an ensemble of social connections, political institutions, and judicial practices." Brill (1989: 8) writes that public space comes to represent the public sphere and public life, "a forum, a group action, school for social learning, and common ground." In the Western tradition, public space has had a positive connotation that evokes the practice of democracy, openness, and publicity of debate since the time of the Greek agora. Henaff and Strong (2001) further argue that the very idea of democracy is inseparable from that of public space. "Public space means simultaneously: open to all, well known by all, and acknowledged by all. . . . It stands in opposition to private space of special interests" (Henaff and Strong 2001: 35). Landscape architecture scholar Mark Francis (1989: 149) writes, "Public space is the common ground where civility and our collective sense of what may be called 'publicness' are developed and expressed." Fraser (1990) argues that, as a public sphere, public space is an arena of citizen discourse and association. Furthermore, I. M. Young (2002) sees public space in a city as accessible to everyone and thus reflecting and embodying the diversity in the city.

However, contrary to the rhetoric of openness and inclusiveness, the actual making and practice of public space often reflect a different political reality and social biases. Agacinski (2001: 133) notes that, before the French Revolution, "the public" in the Western tradition referred to the "literate and educated" and "was never thought to be the same as the people." Even in recent Western history, some have argued that, "despite the rhetoric of publicity and accessibility," the official public sphere rests on a number of significant exclusions, based on gender, class, and race (Fraser 1990: 59). The gender division of public and private, in particular, has been a powerful instrument of exclusion as it relegates women to the private sphere and prevents them from fully participating in the public realm (Drucker and Gumpert 1997). By delineating what constitutes public and private and by designating membership to specific social groups, the official public space has long been exclusionary, contrary to Young's (2002) notion of a public space that embodies differences and diversity.

Aside from the practice of exclusion, public space has also been both an expression of power and a subject of political control. Under medieval monarchy in the West, public space was where political power was staged, displayed, and legitimized (Henaff and Strong 2001). In the totalitarian societies of recent times, large public spaces serve as military parade grounds – a raw display of power to impress citizens as well as enemies. In modern democracies, as the power has shifted to the people, public spaces have at last provided a legitimate space for protests and demonstrations – an expression of the freedom of speech. But such freedom has never come without considerable struggles and vigilance. In the post-9/11 world of hyper-security and surveillance, new forms of control in public space have curtailed freedom of movement and expression and greatly limited the activities and meanings of contemporary public space (see Low and Smith 2005).

Across the different cultural traditions, the functions and meanings of public space have varied significantly, illustrating the varying means and degrees of social and political control. In recent Western democracies, public space and the formation of public opinion have been important components of the democratic process. Through opportunities of assembly and public discourses, political expressions in the public space are important in holding the state accountable to its citizens. This distinction between the public and the state has been an important ingredient in democratic politics. By contrast, in countries influenced by Confucianism in the East, social and individual life is dictated predominantly by obligations to state and family, with little in between. The official public space is traditionally either non-existent or tightly controlled by the state.

A useful illustration is Edo-era Tokyo. Under the rule of the Tokugawa shogunate, the city was spatially divided between *Yamanote* (consisting of large private estates occupied by ranking officials in the upland) and *Shitamachi* (the compact and tightly regulated quarters for the commoners in the flatland). In Shitamachi, gated streets and waterfront markets served as the only recognizable form of public gathering space. To escape from the gated quarters and regimented pattern of everyday life, one had to go to the pleasure grounds that lay outside the official quarters of the city (Figure 1.1).

In many Asian cities, public space has been synonymous with spaces that are representing and controlled by the state. In contrast, the everyday and more vibrant urban life tends to occur in the back streets and alleyways, away from the official public domain. Seoul's *Pimagol* ('Avoid-Horse-Street'), narrow alleys that parallel the city's historic main road Jong-ro, serve as an example (Figure 1.2). To avoid repeatedly bowing to the noble-class people riding on horses on Jong-ro, a requirement back in the days of feudal power, the commoners turned to the back alleys, away from the main road. Over time, restaurants and shops began to occupy the back alleys, which became a parallel universe and an important part of the vibrant everyday life in the city.

The development and design of public parks in America provides yet another illustration, showing how public space has long been an ideologically biased and regulated enterprise contrary to the rhetoric of openness. In the United States, Cranz (1982: 3, 5) argues that early parks were built from "an anti-urban ideal that dwelt on the traditional prescription for relief from the evils of the city—to the country." The emergence of reform parks in the United States further demonstrated this bias. Located in mostly dense, immigrant and working class neighborhoods, they were designed to move children and adults from the streets (Cranz 1982). With the goal of social and cultural integration, and provisions for organized play, the parks and

Figure 1.1 Popular with tourists today, the Asakusa temple district was once one of Edo-era Tokyo's pleasure grounds that lay outside the city quarters. Photograph by Jeffrey Hou.

Figure 1.2 Seoul's disappearing Pimagol was once an important passage and gathering space for commoners and the city's unofficial public space. Photograph by Jeffrey Hou.

palygrounds were also designed to assimilate immigrants into the mainstream American culture (Cranz 1982). Today, although multiculturalism is more widely acknowledged, the historic bias continues, as Low, Taplin, and Scheld (2005: 4) found that "restrictive management of large parks has created an increasingly inhospitable environment for immigrants, local ethnic groups, and culturally diverse behaviors." Observing how different cultural groups use the neighborhood parks in Los Angeles, Loukaitou-Sideris (1995: 90) writes that, contrary to the notion of inclusiveness, the "contemporary American neighborhood park does not always meet the needs of all segments of the public."

Erosion of public space and public life

In the literature on public realm in recent decades, the erosion and decline of public space and public life have been a predominant theme. In *The Fall of Public Man*, Sennet (1992/1978) argues that public life has become a matter of formal obligation in modern times. More importantly, the private and personal have taken precedence over the public and impersonal, as society became less interested in public matters and more driven by private interests and personal desires. He further states, the "unbalanced personal life and empty public life" are manifested in the dead public space of modern architecture, with few opportunities for social interactions (Sennet 1992/1978: 16). More recently, Putnam (1995) uses the metaphor of "bowling alone" to characterize the decline of civic engagement in American society. Using evidences in decreased voter turnout, attendance in public meetings, and memberships in traditional civic organizations, including labor unions and church groups, he argues that such decline undermines the working of democracy (Putnam 1995).

In the last few decades, a number of practices have further challenged what is left of public space in both its physical and political dimensions. Most notably, the growing privatization of public space has become a common pattern and experience in many parts of the world where downtown districts as well as suburban lands are transformed into themed malls and so-called festival marketplaces. To emulate successful urban spaces of the past, neo-traditional streetscapes and town squares are reproduced but segregated from the rest of the city to create a supposed safe haven for shoppers and businesses. Whereas the physical form and appearance of the spaces may look familiar to the traditional public space in the past, their public functions and meanings have become highly limited.

Increasingly, to spur economic development, public funds are used to subsidize development of private venues, while developers are generously rewarded for providing spaces with limited public use. As streets, neighborhoods, and parks become malls, gated communities, and corporate venues, public space becomes subjected to new forms of ownership, commodification, and control. Davis (1992: 155) observes, "The 'public' space of the new megastructures and supermalls have supplanted traditional streets and disciplined their spontaneity." Loukaitou-Sideris and Banerjee (1998: 278) further write, "American downtown is a product of purposeful design actions that have effectively sought to mold space according to the needs of a corporatist economy and to subordinate urban form to the logic of profit."

The control of public space is now a worldwide phenomenon that shows how form follows capital. From Los Angeles's Bunker Hill to Sandton in Johannesburg, private interests have created fortified downtowns and urban sub-centers, protecting an increasing array of pseudo-public and private properties against the possible intrusion of the "undesirables" (Whyte 1980). In addition to the limited public functions, the privatization of public space has important implications for the political sphere of contemporary cities. Kohn (2004: 2) writes, "When private spaces replace public gathering space, the opportunities for political conversation are diminished." Mitchell (2003: 34) also argues that, "in a world defined by private property, the formation of public sphere that is at all robust and inclusive of a variety of different publics is exceedingly difficult." Barber (2001: 203) notes that the privatization and commercialization of space have turned our "complex, multiuse public space into a one-dimensional venue for consumption." He further writes, the "malling of America has sometimes entailed the mauling of American civil society and its public" (Barber 2001: 201).

Insurgent public space: momentary ruptures and everyday struggles

Given all the historic limitations and contemporary setbacks, is it still possible to imagine a public space that is open and inclusive? Mitchell (2003) offers an important argument that the making of public space and its associated freedom and openness always requires vigilance and actions. He writes, "[The idea of public space] has never been guaranteed. It has only been won through concerted struggle" (Mitchell 2003: 5). Similarly, Watson (2006: 7) argues, "public space is always in some sense, in a state of emergence, never complete and always contested." Mitchell (2003: 5) further argues that struggle "is the only way that the right to public space can be maintained and only way that social justice can be advanced." To him, it is through the actions and purposeful occupation of a space that it becomes public.

Today, even as more and more public spaces have become heavily regulated and privatized, there are attempts by individuals and communities at greater freedom. These acts, despite their momentary nature, defy what Sorkin (1992) characterizes as the "end of public space." In San Francisco, throngs of cyclists form Critical Mass to reclaim public streets from cars. The movement now has a presence in over 300 cities around the world where cyclists engage in regular acts of civil disruption. In Beijing (where cyclists once inspired their counterparts in San Francisco), even after the crackdown on the pro-democracy movement in Tiananmen Square, the square remains a tense political stage, ruptured periodically by individual acts of dissent that recall the massacre of 1989 and the continued political oppression. In Taipei, students demonstrating against police brutality under the Kuomintang government during a recent protest camped out in the city's Liberty Square in 2008. To show their determination to stay and to demand a government response, the students began building a village on the square, complete with a kitchen, classrooms, a vegetable garden, a webcast station, and tents for sleeping (Figures 1.3 and 1.4). In Hong Kong, Filipina guest workers occupy the ground floor of Norman Foster's signature HSBC building (an icon of global capital) every Sunday, and transform it from an anonymous corporate entrance to a lively community gathering space where migrant workers picnic, chat, and reunite (Figure 1.5).

On a different front, while new technologies in telecommunication and media have undermined the importance of place-based public space, they have also enabled new types of actions and means of public dissent. Since 1994, the Zapatista Army of National Liberation has built strong international support for its struggle against the Mexican state, using the Internet as a means of communication. Starting with the anti-WTO protest in Seattle in 2000, anti-globalization activists have relied on globalized technology to communicate with each other around the world

Figure 1.3 Students of the Wild Strawberries Movement occupied the Liberty Square in Taipei to protest against police brutality and a law that restricts the freedom of assembly and demonstration. Photograph by Jeffrey Hou.

Figure 1.4 A temporary memorial built by the students to mourn the loss of democracy, mocking the memorial of the former Nationalist Chinese dictator Chiang Kai-Shek in the background. Photograph by Jeffrey Hou.

and stage protests at the gatherings of world leaders and international financial institutions. More recently, in the coastal Chinese city of Xiamen, text messaging enabled thousands of citizens to gather instantaneously in a street protest against the building of a chemical complex. The large turnout forced the local government to reject the development. Lately, social networking tools such as Twitter have been linked to mass mobilization and communication in protest events in Iran and Moldova (Cohen 2009). Together, these examples testify to Mitchell's argument that the end of public space argument is "overly simplistic in that it does not necessarily appreciate how new kinds of spaces have developed" (Mitchell 2003: 8).

On a more everyday level, citizen initiatives and informal activities have created other new uses and forms of public space. They include spontaneous events, unintended uses, and a variety of activities that defy or escape existing rules and regulations. These everyday practices transform urban spaces into what Watson (2006: 19) calls, "a site of potentiality, difference, and delightful encounters." A case in point is the community garden movement in North America and elsewhere in which hundreds and thousands of vacant or abandoned sites (including both public and private properties) have been transformed into productive plots and as places for cultivation, recreation, gathering, and education by communities (Lawson 2005, Francis *et al.* 1984; Figure 1.6). These and other forms of community open spaces have emerged as an alternative park system in cities and towns (Francis

Figure 1.5 Every Sunday, Filipina workers transform the ground floor of the HSBC building in Hong Kong into a community gathering place. Photograph by Jeffrey Hou.

Jeffrey Hou

et al. 1984). Through personal and collective uses that provide both private and public benefits, these community gardens function as "hybrid public spaces" that are distinct from their conventional and official counterpart (Hou *et al.* 2009).

Although these everyday expressions of public space activism might not have the appearance of radical insurgency, it should be noted that many of the outcomes would not have been possible without extensive grassroots struggle. For instance, in the Mount Baker neighborhood of Seattle, gardeners and community activists joined to defend a well-used community garden from being sold by the city for private real estate development. Teaming up with supporters and open space advocates around the city, they petitioned the City Council to pass an ordinance that requires the city to compensate sale of park property with an equivalent amount of open space in

Figure 1.6 Community gardens such as the Danny Woo Garden in Seattle's International District were created by residents and community organizers and are distinct formally and socially from the typical public open space. Photograph by Jeffrey Hou.

the same neighborhood. The ordinance effectively saved not only their garden plots but also all other similar park properties in the city (Hou *et al.* 2009). Across the Pacific, in the Shilin Night Market in Taipei, one of the largest and most popular evening markets in the city, illegal vendors find ways every night to escape police enforcement. The vendors develop their own monitoring protocols, make-shift apparatus, and temporary storage sites so that, when the policemen approach the market from a distance, they can easily detect them, signal each other, disappear in a matter of seconds, and then converge again once the cops go away (Figure 1.7). The informal mechanism and the drama that unfolds several times in a night enable the vendors to create one of the liveliest and most dynamic marketplaces in the city, bypassing regulations and enforcement.

Figure 1.7 Vendors in Taipei's Shilin Night Market can disappear with their merchandise in a matter of seconds to escape law enforcement, adding drama to the already colorful night market. Photograph by Jeffrey Hou.

This book

This book is an attempt to better understand such everyday and not-so-everyday making of public space that defies the conventional rules, regulations, and wisdom. It focuses on alternative spaces, activities, expressions, and relationships that have emerged in response to opportunities, constraints, and transformation in contemporary society. The rubric of "insurgent public space" provides a way for us to define and articulate these expressions of alternative social and spatial relationships. Rather than bemoaning the erosion of public realm, this collective body of work focuses on the new possibilities of public space and public realm in support of a more diverse, just, and democratic society.

This edited volume represents the voices of individuals who have been active in realizing such possibilities through their practice, research, teaching, and civic involvement. They are anthropologists, communication scholars, and geographers, as well as architects, artists, community organizers, landscape architects, and planners. All of the essays focus on actual struggles and examples. They offer lessons and explore further possibilities based on experiences and encounters on the ground. To provide a comparison of the parallel and widespread occurrences around the world, this book takes on a deliberately cross-cultural approach and includes diverse cases from the different geographic regions and social contexts.

Some recent publications have addressed or informed aspects of our investigation. The phenomenon of unintended uses of urban public space in particular is a subject of growing academic interest represented by the publication of *Loose Space* (Franck and Stevens 2006) and *Everyday Urbanism* (Chase et al. 1999). Franck and Stevens (2006: 4) argue that unintended uses "have the ability to loosen up the dominant meanings of specific sites that give rise to new perceptions, attitudes, and behaviors." They define loose space as "a space apart from the aesthetically and behaviorally controlled and homogenous 'theme' environment of leisure and consumption where nothing unpredictable must occur" (Franck and Stevens 2006: 3). In *Everyday Urbanism*, Crawford (1999) presents a similar concept. She writes, "everyday space stands in contrast to the carefully planned, officially designated and often underused public space that can be found in most American cities" (Crawford 1999: 9). It represents "a zone of social transition and possibility in the potential for new social arrangement and forms of imagination" (Crawford 1999: 9).

In *The Ludic City*, Stevens (2007: 196) explores the playful uses of urban spaces that are often "non-instrumental, active, unexpected, and risky." Yet they provide new experiences and produce new social relations (Stevens 2007: 196). Similarly, in *City Publics*, Watson (2006: 7) focuses on "marginal, unpretentious, hidden and symbolic spaces" and "often forgotten subjects." In *The Informal City*, Laguerre (1994: 2) explores urban informality "as site of power in relation to external discipline and control power." In contrast to the formalized spaces and practices, "urban informality is the expression of the freedom of the subject" (Laguerre 1994: 24). In the field of design and planning, a number of recent publications reflect the resurging practice of design activism (see Architecture for Humanity 2006, Bell 2003, Bell and Wakeford 2008, Bloom and Bromberg 2004, Palleroni 2004). The work often involves professionals working with citizens and communities in transforming spaces for community and public use. In *Design for Ecological Democracy*, Hester (2006) envisions the human stewardship of an even greater public space – the planet and its social and ecological systems. Finally our conceptualization of insurgent public space is indebted to the notion of "insurgent citizenship" or "insurgent space of citizenship" from John Holston (1998: 39). Similar to the opposition to the state's legitimization of the notion of citizenship, the insurgent public space is in opposition to the kind of public space that is regulated, controlled, and maintained solely by the state.

This volume seeks to build upon these investigations and interpretations of alternative urban practices and forms of activism to imagine a different mode of production in the making of public space, a public and a space that are heterogeneous, fluid, and dynamic.

The stories

The book is organized around a typology of actions and practices that shape the different stories of resistance. This typology is not meant to be exhaustive or categorical but rather is a way to highlight the specific characters and purposefulness of the actions.

Appropriating represents actions and manners through which the meaning, ownership, and structure of official public space can be temporarily or permanently suspended. Here, three case studies examine ways through which citizens transform the public realm by repurposing the existing urban landscapes. From Beijing, Caroline Chen examines how local residents cope with rapid urbanization and make use of existing urban infrastructure and residual spaces for their everyday recreation and socialization. From Los Angeles, James Rojas examines how Latino immigrants improvise and reinvent the notion and practice of public space in the city through new use of streets, sidewalks, vacant lots, and other spaces. From San Francisco, Blaine Merker describes how the artist and designer group Rebar has identified "niche spaces" within the framework of public and quasi-public spaces and claimed them as sites for social and artistic discourses.

Reclaiming describes the adaptation and reuse of abandoned or underutilized urban spaces for new and collective functions and instrumentality. From Berlin, Michael LaFond describes the work of eXperimentcity, which turns vacant lots in the city into venues for cooperative, ecological housing, and youth projects. From Tokyo, Shin Aiba and Osamu Nishida present work from their Re-city project, which reutilizes the existing building stocks in the Kanda district and transforms them into new neighborhood public spaces. From Vancouver, Erick Villagomez examines strategies to incrementally enhance and diversify the existing urban fabric through the exploitation of residual and neglected spaces.

Pluralizing refers to how specific ethnic groups transform the meaning and functions of public space, which results in a more heterogeneous public sphere. Michael Rios considers the prospects for a distinctive Latino Urbanism in the United States and the different ways Latinos make claims to public spaces in the city. Jeffrey Hou examines how the making of a Night Market in Seattle's Chinatown-International District has engendered a physical, social, and cultural reconstruction of the public realm in the neighborhood. From Taiwan, Hung-Ying Chen and Jia-He Lin examine how Southeast Asian immigrants negotiate their identities and place through the making of their own collective space. Using ChungShan as a case study, Pina Wu examines how Filipino guest workers in Taipei find refuge in the streets, alleys, shops, restaurants, and offices of an alienating city.

Transgressing represents the infringement or crossing of official boundaries between the private and public domains through temporary occupation as well as production of new meanings and relationships. Here, three case studies from Japan explore the potentiality of a new public space that straddles the public and private realms. Using cases in the Setagaya Ward of Tokyo, Yasuyoshi Hayashi considers the network of community-based non-profit organizations as the basis of a "new public" in Japan. Isami Kinoshita examines how the concept of *niwa-roju* (Garden Street Trees) transforms the boundaries between private properties and the public streets and the social relationships inside the community. Sawako Ono, Ryoko Sato, and Mima Nishiyama describe the conversion of private farmhouses both for new quasi-public uses and as an intermediary between city and country.

Uncovering refers to the making and rediscovery of public space through active reinterpretation of hidden or latent meanings and memories in the urban landscapes. From Seattle, Irina Gendelman, Tom Dobrowolsky, and Giorgia Aiello of Urban Archives present how their project uses the city as a laboratory to research diverse and often unconventional forms of urban expression that address the complex relationships of power. Jeannene Przyblyski presents three projects by the San Francisco Bureau of Urban Secrets that engage citizens to experience cities as "sites of recovered memory and a repository of competing histories." From Taipei, Annie Chiu examines how a movement to preserve a brothel as a city historic landmark challenges the mainstream historic preservation discourse and conservative social values, as well as the boundaries between private sites/bodies and public memories. Also from Taipei, Min Jay Kang investigates the potentiality of fallow or underused spaces for a different imagination in the making of an urban landscape.

Finally, with *Contesting*, the book returns to the theme of struggle over rights, meanings, and identities in the public realm. From Canada, Andrew Pask looks at how growth of public space activism has unfolded in Vancouver and Toronto to challenge the privatization and surveillance of public space. Teresa Mares and Devon Peña examine two cases of urban farms in the United States, as illustrations of the insurgent uses of public space for food production and community organizing. In East St. Louis, Laura Lawson and Janni Sorensen describe the long-term struggles that the community has to endure to reutilize abandoned vacant land to address flooding, expand community services, and spur economic development.

Guerrilla urbanism: towards smaller yet grander urban public space

The stories in this book represent struggles by communities and individuals to find their place and expressions in the contemporary city and in doing so redefine the boundaries, meanings, and instrumentality of public sphere. The individuals and groups include activists, architects and landscape architects, community organizers, graffiti artists, homeowners, immigrants, parents, planners, sex workers, squatters, students, teachers, and urban farmers. The list goes on. As the variety of cases in this collection suggests, there are diverse means through which individuals and groups can engage actively in the contestation and remaking of public space, and the city by extension. From conversion of private homes into community third places to the occupation of streets for alternative uses, each of these acts may seem small and insignificant. But, precisely because these acts do not require overburdening investment or infrastructure, they enable individuals and often small groups to effect changes in the otherwise hegemonic urban landscapes. Although the actions may be informal and erratic, they have helped destabilize the structure and relationships in the official public space and release possibilities for new interactions, functions, and meanings.

Because of the scale and mode of production, the making of this alternative public space is more participatory and spontaneous, and therefore more open and inclusive. The insurgent public space that they have created is therefore both a smaller and a grander public space. These smaller yet grander public spaces reflect the subjectivity of its multiple actors and the broader instrumentality of space as a vehicle for a wider variety of individual and collective actions. Although these individuals and groups do not all fit the likely descriptions of what Fraser (1990: 67) calls the "subaltern counterpublics," by resisting against the hegemonic regulations of the contemporary public space and the notion of an undifferentiated public they become active participants in "a widening of discursive contestation" in the public space and public sphere of the contemporary society.

The making of insurgent public space suggests a mode of city making that is different from the institutionalized notion of urbanism and its association with master planning and policy making. Unlike the conventional practice of urban planning, which tends to be dominated by professionals and experts, the instances of insurgent public space as presented in this book suggest the ability of citizen groups and individuals to play a distinct role in shaping the contemporary urban environment in defiance of the official rules and regulations. Rather than being subjected to planning regulations or the often limited participatory opportunities, citizens and citizen groups can undertake initiatives on their own to effect changes. The instances of self-help and defiance are best characterized as a practice of guerrilla urbanism that recognizes both the ability of citizens and opportunities in the existing urban conditions for radical and everyday changes against the dominant forces in the society.

As cities and their social, economic and political dimensions have continued to change, the functions, meanings, and production of public space have also evolved over time. As urban populations and cultures become more heterogeneous, a growing presence and recognition of cultural and social differences have made the production and use of public space a highly contested process. Reflecting the current cultural, economic, and spatial changes of cities, insurgent public space represents a growing variety of actions and practices that enable and empower such contestation. If public space is where identities, meanings, and social relationships in cities are produced, codified, and maintained, it is through insurgent public space that alternative identities, meanings, and relationships can be nurtured, articulated, and enacted. Through the variety of actions and practices, insurgent public space enables the participation and actions of individuals and groups in renewing the city as an arena of civic exchanges and debates. Through continued expressions and contestation, the presence and making of insurgent public space serves as barometer of the democratic well-being and inclusiveness of our present society.

Note

1 The concept of "third place" was introduced by Ray Oldenburg (1989) to describe the places that anchor community life between home and work place.

Bibliography

Agacinski, S. (2001) 'Stages of Democracy', in Henaff, M. and Strong, T. B. (eds.) *Public Space and Democracy*, Minneapolis: University of Minnesota Press.

Architecture for Humanity (ed.) (2006) *Design Like You Give A Damn: Architectural Responses to Humanitarian Crisis*, New York: Metropolis Books.

Barber, B. R. (2001) 'Malled, Mauled, and Overhauled: Arresting Suburban Sprawl by Transforming Suburban Malls into Usable Civic Space', in Henaff, M. and Strong, T. B. (eds.) *Public Space and Democracy*, Minneapolis: University of Minnesota Press.

Bell, B. (ed.) (2003) *Good Deeds, Good Design: Community Service through Architecture*, New York: Princeton Architectural Press.

Bell, B. and Wakeford, K. (eds.) (2008) *Expanding Architecture: Design as Activism*, New York: Metropolis Books.

Bloom, B. and Bromberg, A. (eds.) (2004) *Making Their Own Plans/Belltown Paradise*, Chicago: WhiteWalls.

Brill, M. (1989) 'Transformation, Nostalgia, and Illusion in Public Life and Public Place', in Altman, Irwin and Zube, Ervin H. (eds.) *Public Places and Spaces*, New York: Plenum Press.

Chase, J., Crawford, M., and Kaliski, J. (eds.) (1999) *Everyday Urbanism*, New York: Monacelli Press.

Cohen, N. (2009) 'Twitter on the Barricades', *New York Times*, 21 June. Online. Available HTTP: http://www.nytimes.com/2009/06/21/weekinreview/21cohenweb.html?_r=1&sq=iran%20twitter&st=cse&scp=1&pagewanted=print (accessed 22 June 2009).

Cranz, G. (1982) *Politics of Park Design: A History of Urban Parks in America*, Cambridge, MA: MIT Press.

Crawford, M. (1999) 'Introduction', in Chase, J., Crawford, M., and Kaliski, J. (eds.) *Everyday Urbanism*, New York: Monacelli Press.

Davis, M. (1992) 'Fortress Los Angeles: The Militarization of Urban Space', in Sorkin, Michael (ed.), *Variations on a Theme Park*, New York: Hill and Wang.

Drucker, S. J. and Gumpert, G. (eds.) (1997) *Voices in the Street: Explorations in Gender, Media, and Public Space*, Cresskill, NJ: Hampton Press.

Francis, M. (1989) 'Control as a Dimension of Public Space Quality', in Altman, I., and Zube, E. H. (eds.) *Public Places and Spaces*, New York: Plenum Press.

Francis, M., Cashdan, L., and Paxson, L. (1984) *Community Open Space: Greening Neighborhoods through Community Action and Land Conservation*, Washington, DC: Island Press.

Franck, K. A. and Stevens, Q. (eds.) (2007) *Loose Space: Possibility and Diversity in Urban Life*, London: Routledge.

Fraser, N. (1990) 'Rethinking the Public Sphere: A Contribution to the Critique of Actually Existing Democracy', *Social Text*, 25/26: 56–80.

Henaff, M. and Strong, T.B. (eds.) (2001) *Public Space and Democracy*, Minneapolis: University of Minnesota Press.

Hester, R. T. (2006) *Design for Ecological Democracy*, Cambridge, MA: MIT Press.

Holston, J. (1998) 'Spaces of Insurgent Citizenship', in Sandercock, L. (ed.) *Making the Invisible Visible: A Multicultural Planning History*, Berkeley: University of California Press.

Hou, J., Johnson, J. M., and Lawson, L. J. (2009) *Greening Cities, Growing Communities: Learning from Seattle's Urban Community Gardens*, Seattle: University of Washington Press.

Kohn, M. (2004) *Brave New Neighborhoods: The Privatization of Public Space*, New York: Routledge.

Laguerre, M. S. (1994) *The Informal City*, Berkeley: University of California Press.

Lawson, L. (2005) *City Bountiful: A Century of Community Gardening in America*, Berkeley: University of California Press.

Loukaitou-Sideris, A. (1995) 'Urban Form and Social Context: Cultural Differentiation in the Uses of Urban Parks', *Journal of Planning Education and Research*, 14: 89–102.

Loukaitou-Sideris, A. and Banerjee, T. (1998) *Urban Design Downtown: Poetics and Politics of Form*, Berkeley: University of California Press.

Low, S. and Smith, N. (eds.) (2005) *The Politics of Public Space*, New York: Routledge.

Low, S., Taplin, D., and Scheld, S. (2005). *Rethinking Urban Parks: Public Space & Cultural Diversity*, Austin: University of Texas Press.

Mitchell, D. (2003) *The Right to the City: Social Justice and the Fight for Public Space*, New York: Guilford Press.

Oldenburg, R. (1989) *The Great Good Place: Cafés, Coffee Shops, Community Centers, Beauty Parlors, General Stores, Bars, Hangouts, and How They Get You through the Day*, New York: Paragon House.

Palleroni, S. (2004) *Studio at Large: Architecture in Service of Global Communities*, Seattle: University of Washington Press.

Putnam, R. (1995) 'Bowling Alone: America's Declining Social Capital', *Journal of Democracy*, 6 (1): 65–78.

Sennett, R. (1992/1978) *The Fall of Public Man*, New York: W. W. Norton.

Sorkin, M. (ed.) (1992) *Variations on a Theme Park,* New York: Hill and Wang.

Stevens, Q. (2007) *The Ludic City: Exploring the Potential of Public Space*, London: Routledge.

Watson, S. (2006) *City Publics: The (Dis)enchantments of Urban Encounters*, New York: Routledge.

Whyte, W. H. (1980) *The Social Life of Small Urban Spaces,* Washington, DC: Conservation Foundation.

Young, I. M. (2002) 'The Ideal of Community and the Politics of Difference', in Bridge, G. and Watson, S. (eds.) *The Blackwell City Reader*, Malden, MA: Blackwell Publishing.

PART ONE

APPROPRIATING

CHAPTER 2

Dancing in the streets of Beijing

Improvised uses within the urban system

Caroline Chen

Underneath a freeway overpass, on a vacant concrete traffic island in the middle of bustling Beijing, forty Chinese women in their sixties and seventies, dressed in silk brocaded jackets and padded silk pants, slowly waved lime-green handkerchiefs and fluttered hot pink, white, and green striped fans above their heads (Figure 2.1). They followed an undulating and circulating pattern, dividing into two rows, then reuniting to form one big group. They danced alongside one another, without partners, moving to the rhythm of five male musicians playing drums, cymbals, and horns at the head of the makeshift city stage. Dressed in dark winter overcoats, knit caps, and heavy woolen scarves, the musicians stood somberly nearby. Sometimes watching the dancers, sometimes nodding at each other, they enveloped the space within their percussionist sphere.

It was 7 a.m. in deep December in northern China. Mingguang Qiao, a concrete pad underneath a freeway overpass, belonged to *yangge* dancers for the moment, despite the passing rumbling buses, honking taxis, and sweeping street cleaners. At

Figure 2.1 "Big" *yangge* dancers celebrating twelve years of dancing underneath Mingguang Qiao, a residual space under the third ringroad in Beijing. Photograph by Caroline Chen.

9 a.m., the dancers abruptly stopped dancing and moved off in a flash, disappearing into the city in different directions, some hardly pausing to say goodbye to one another. Except for a few watermelon seeds from an intersession break, the dancers left no trace behind of their gathering on the concrete pad. The traffic sounds increased as rush hour approached, enfolding the stage back into its default setting, a silent and unexceptional space, within the formal city. These kinds of temporary performances happen every morning and night.

Beijing's urban landscape does not stand still. With an official population of 15 million inhabitants and a burgeoning community of foreigners, Beijing is witness to a vision reminiscent of New York or London, erupting overnight from the body of a historic Chinese city. Narrow courtyard alleys are vanishing and large green parks are appearing. Active Beijing residents are finding new spaces for their activities as the city densifies, limiting public open space. They are still practicing *taichi*, dancing *yangge*, and playing chess along with incorporating new activities such as rollerblading, jogging, and old-person disco dancing. Only now they are taking part in these activities in residual spaces: busy street median strips, concrete areas between highway flyovers, parking lots, sidewalks, grounds just outside the gates of parks, stadiums, and schools, as well as spaces inside parks. Beyond their original design intent, Beijing residents are adapting new urban spaces for past functions, turning to what Michel de Certeau (1984) characterizes as tactics. As they appropriate spaces to support their old habitats and practices, they are unintentionally but effectively developing new typologies of hybrid use, missed opportunities for conceptual and programmatic innovation by foreign designers, and headaches in the minds of Chinese city planners.

Many long-time residents of Beijing have seen their everyday landscapes transformed in a blink of an eye. But they are not leaving quietly. Just like the aging *yangge* dancers at Mingguang Qiao, the Chinese elderly are defending what spaces are left available to them after witnessing how former dancing places have become roads, large green parks that require admission fees, new subway stops, new business districts, opera houses, or apartment buildings populated by newcomers. These new neighbors often complain about their loud music and lively dancing, wishing that they had quiet grass and trees from Beijing's city greening campaign as neighbors instead.

Loosening

Anyone interested in understanding how Beijing residents use urban space must necessarily turn their attention to what Karen A. Franck calls "loose space": what results when residents liberate designed public spaces such as parks, plazas, and parking lots from the limits of the original, intended program and piggyback new and foreseen functions of their own choosing on the space (Franck and Stevens 2007). The sheer number of residents who appropriate these unofficial spaces within the urban fabric – spaces underneath freeways, unused sections of parking lots after stores close, construction zones in the evening, and widened sidewalks – gives one reason for pause. Is the variety of activities articulated in the city a tribute to the flexibility and creativity of residents or an implicit critique of existing city design?

Leanne G. Rivlin differentiates the qualities of these resulting "found spaces" from pre-programmed, "designed" spaces:

> [Found spaces] constitute a large portion of the outdoor urban places used by children and adults . . . [they] are "found" in the sense that users locate and appropriate them for uses that they serve effectively but which they were not originally designed to serve . . . Found spaces offer alternative places for public life since their uses spring from a complex matrix of needs brought to them by users . . . these activities do not differ dramatically from those occurring in spaces designed for leisure activities, but they do differ in their origins, their diversity and often in the physical qualities of their sites.
>
> (Rivlin 2007: 39)

Looseness in a city expresses the desires of users – such as the elderly – that may otherwise be overlooked by designers and planners. Not only do these "loose spaces" provide a forum for residents to articulate their spatial needs for daily *taichi* and *yangge*, they also allow others have little access to the planning process to appropriate the open-endedness of these spaces for their own needs.

But, although we may draw a distinction between "loose (or 'found') spaces" and "designed" spaces for the sake of convenience, there is one further distinction here that we wish to note. As Rivlin pointed out, "found" and "designed" spaces differ in their intent and origins. Likewise, the origins of many seemingly "designed" parks and plazas in Beijing differ from those in Europe or the United States. Whereas these latter parks were originally intended to provide an arena for socializing rural workers to city life and restoring the physical and psychic faculties of industrial workers (Cranz 1982), many of the large, green parks in Beijing came from a different lineage: they were former imperial gardens and temples, converted into public parks to beautify the city as part of the regional "greening program" (Cranz 1979).

From this perspective many of Beijing's large green parks are "found" as well – they are existing green areas that originally served imperial uses, but the state has now appropriated them to become "public." Here I place "public" in quotation marks because, in a strict sense, many such parks are not free for residents to use: these parks require an admission fee. Although annual, discounted park passes are available for students and the elderly, many residents opt to find their own, more accessible spaces elsewhere in the city.

Tourists, however, often unconstrained by these fees, arrive at these destinations by the busload. Locals wishing to avoid these crowds visit the parks in the morning, or choose to "loosen" parts of the city, claiming their own grassroots space, away from the tourists, unconstrained by opening and closing times, free of charge.

Everyday life on the ground

In order to begin understanding what matters to regular Beijing residents, what they choose to do in public space and how they define – on their own terms – what a public space is, we divert our gaze from the pyrotechnics of high-profile, overnight transformation of the city skyline to focus our attention on the daily activities of the person on the ground.[1] From 2004 through 2007, we researched several types of urban spaces in Beijing that residents used to pursue everyday outdoor leisure activities.[2] In this paper we will discuss findings from four sites: (1) Yiheyuan, a large park on the Northwest fringes of Beijing; (2) Beihai, a small urban park in the center of Beijing; (3) Deshengmen, a hybrid space consisting of a large plaza and enlarged traffic rotary, now surrounded by a maze of freeways; and (4) Mingguang Qiao, a paved area underneath a freeway overpass on the western side of the city. Although the typologies of "large park," "plaza," and "urban park" are familiar to the designer repertoire, the hybrid rotary-park and freeway overpass spaces are less obvious choices for everyday use.

Site one: Yiheyuan (The New Summer Palace), a large park in suburban Beijing

Over 700 acres in area and located in the northwest outskirts of Beijing, Yiheyuan is a former private imperial retreat. After the founding of the People's Republic of China in 1949, the park was opened to the public and is now a regular tourist destination and World Heritage Site. Slightly smaller than New York's Central Park, Yiheyuan is characterized by the still, reflective surface of its iconic, 540-acre man-made Kunming Lake. Small pavilions, strategically placed for admiring the landscape, dot the perimeter of the lake. Paved paths connect these small stations, winding skyward to a prominent hill that overlooks the park. Man-made islands, bridges, and covered corridors adorn the largely naturalistic landscape. An entry fee is required and the park is closed at night.

Many local residents stated their preference for using the park in the morning because of the influx of noisy tour groups beginning at noon and continuing through the afternoon. Amongst the users of the park are groups of residents engaged in relatively quiet activities such as sword-dancing and taichi underneath groves of trees near Kunming Lake. These groups at Yiheyuan consist of ten or fewer participants – much smaller numbers than we later observed in sites closer to the the city center. The resident users we interviewed all live within one mile of the park and arrive mostly on foot, with the exception of one retired woman who rides a public bus three times a week for over an hour to arrive at the park. She told us the solitude, quiet, and long views were worth the effort; such experiences were impossible to find anywhere else in the city.

Site two: Beihai, an urban park in central Beijing

A former imperial garden, this 170-acre park includes a ninety-six-acre lake and is situated in the city center. Now a public park, it is one node along a wider network of parks in the imperial chain of lakes. Like Yiheyuan, Beihai also features a large water body as a central attraction, encircled by architectural pavilions that are connected by paved paths. Rockeries, temples, bridges, and an island in the lake are popular gathering spots.

Beihai was far more crowded than the more suburban large park, Yiheyuan. There, we encountered residents organized in groups of up to thirty members, engaged in a variety of activities from modern dance to *taichi*. We interviewed some *yangge* dancers who were practicing in the park. One dancer expressed satisfaction with the park's design, but others pointed out that there was not enough space in the park for everybody who wished to use it. "There are too many visitors and the park lacks supervision," one dancer complained, pointing to the parade of tour groups passing by, waving brightly colored flags. When asked where else residents can dance without competing with tour groups for space, they named neighborhood parks, such as the Purple Bamboo Garden.

In Beihai, we also encountered "bird walkers," elderly men who took their pet birds for a walk to give them "fresh air."[3] The men transported their pet birds inside blue, cloth-covered birdcages by foot, or by bicycle to the park, where they then attached the uncovered cages on low-hanging branches of nearby trees. Then, crouching or standing quietly in the vegetation, singly or in small groups, the men listened to their pets sing.[4] Like the dancers, "bird walkers" also complained to us about the number of tourists in the park, wishing for increased security and less crowding in the park. When asked which alternative sites would suit them, they suggested Xiangshan Park, a popular park with steep terrain located on the outskirts of Beijing, close to Yiheyuan. The "bird walkers" spoke of experiencing joy when listening to their pet birds sing. The men also appeared to enjoy observing other park users passing by while unnoticed, crouching from their lookout within vegetated cover. As we approached the men to ask them questions, they at first seemed disturbed by our presence and attention to their activity and some even declined to talk to us.

Site three: Deshengmen, a hybrid rotary-plaza

At Deshengmen an enormous fortified tower looms over a tripartite space consisting of a bus parking lot, paved plaza, and landscaped park. This mulitfunctional space is located at the junction of the Badaling Expressway and the second Ring Road, which was formerly Beijing's defensive city wall. Flanked on one side by the gate and watchtower, and surrounded by multiple lanes of high-speed traffic on the remaining three sides, an unceasing whoosh of passing traffic saturated the plaza, despite the visual adornment of lawns, trees, and flower beds on the northern part of the enlarged rotary-plaza.

During the daytime, the watchtower is a minor stop for some tour groups. Behind this structure is a parking lot for the motley tour buses park behind the structure. Chest-high bollards separate the lot from the plaza. Tourists arriving in buses paused to enjoy a view of the city atop Deshengmen, to visit a coin museum and gift shop inside the gate, and then depart. Local Beijing residents come to Deshengmen during the day, too, but for other activities. Elderly "bird walkers" like the ones at Beihai come, dressed in blue military-style suits that Mao Zedong popularized. We observed them running across the expressway in front of trucks, buses, and cars with birdcages in hand to arrive at the enlarged rotary, their goal: the trees with low-hanging branches on the northern end of the site. The birdsongs,

Figure 2.2 Musicians at
the foot of Deshengmen
warm up for "big"
yangge. Photograph by
Yunke Xiang.

sharp and startling, were surprisingly audible over the unremitting roar of the passing traffic.

Later in the evening, tour buses parked for the night at Deshengmen and the "bird walkers" returned home. Slowly, between 6 and 7 p.m., a wide cross-section of Beijing's popuation began to appear at the rotary – from mothers with toddlers to the elderly, from long-time residents to migrant workers from the countryside, from the spry to those in wheelchairs. Various representatives from Beijing's diverse community began assembling at the rotary-plaza on foot, by bicycle, and by public bus, all crossing multiple lanes of traffic like the "bird walkers" earlier in the day. They carried with them brightly colored fans, rainbow scarves, and handkerchiefs. Car, truck, and bus drivers blared their horns. Finally, the drum bearer for the first *yangge* group arrived, set up her drum, and began pounding. Soon after, the drummer for the second group arrived. Undocumented migrant workers from the countryside followed the others, also running across traffic to join: the audience had arrived. They squatted on the ground or perched atop the same chest-high bollards that served to keep tour buses off the plaza for a better view, they pulled their shirts over their midsections to cool off, and with arms crossed across their knees, awaited the start of their free evening entertainment (Figure 2.2).

The acoustic environment of Deshengmen is ideal for *yangge*, one dancer explained. Pointing up at Deshengmen watchtower, she pointed out how the massive structure catches the beating of the drum and reflects the booming sounds back downward onto the dancers, to their great delight. Deshengmen is shared by two dance groups that used to be one. The original group became too large and bifurcated into two separate groups of fifty members each. When both groups are drumming and dancing, the vibration from the percussion instruments is not only heard by the ears, but felt by the body; the traffic noise, so prevalent during the day, dissipated in the wake of total immersion in deafening drumming and smashing cymbals: music for the *yangge* dance.

Site four: Mingguang Qiao, *a concrete pad underneath a freeway overpass*

Like Deshengmen, it provides an ideal acoustic space for *yangge* dancers who enjoy loud and live percussion accompaniment. Large concrete columns support the freeway overhead, while doubling as a backdrop for musicians and dancers at this wide, flat space. Near the concrete pad is the Yuan Dadu Relics Park, a linear park that runs along the footprint of a section of Beijing's former city wall. While teeming with exercise groups practicing sword-dancing and taichi, the *yangge* dancers pointed out the size of their group precludes them from dancing there: the space within the park are either already occupied or too small.

In the morning, from 7 to 9 a.m., retired Beijing women meet to dance *yangge* together here. After they finish dancing, this space is slowly reoccupied by mobile barbers and retired chess players who linger here through the afternoon. Later in the evening, from 7 to 10 p.m., middle-aged and young couples arrive on the north side of the concrete columns to dance tango, while younger men and women gather at the south side of the concrete columns, dancing to Chinese pop music. At 3 a.m., a middle-aged couple arrives by bicycle at the deserted site. There is a portable stove and large steel pot affixed to the back of one bicycle. When parked the bicycle becomes a late-night dumpling kiosk for taxi drivers on their night shift. Taxi drivers carry their own short-legged stools so they may squat and eat steaming bowls of dumplings, while protected by the elements, underneath the overpass at Mingguang Qiao.

Migrant thresholds

The loud music and colorful fans of the *yangge* always seem to draw an audience. During the course of research, we identified four components of *yangge* dance in the city that frequently co-occurred: (1) a dance leader, (2) music, (3) an appropriate space for dancing, and (4) an audience. Here, we will briefly examine the audience.

Beijing witnessed a significant influx of undocumented migrants from the countryside in the years leading up to the 2008 Olympics. According to anthropologist Li Zhang (2001), even though the city needed labor to build the Olympics facilities, workers were often excluded from participating in daily city life. Taxi cab drivers often spoke disparagingly of migrants, refusing them service, fearing they would soil the upholstery. Restaurant owners often refused them service, and some long-time Beijing residents we interviewed regarded them with suspicion.

Yangge dancing appeared to allow migrants temporary participation in city life. Although we did not observe many migrants joining the dance itself, migrants often stood nearby, watching. *Yangge* was free of charge and took place outdoors in public spaces. Although at least one dancer voiced her dislike of "the strange people who stare at us when we dance," there were many more cases – such as the *yangge* group at Deshengmen – that allowed migrants to join, identified by their sunburned, bare upper torsos. In all our sites that did not require an admission fee, migrants were present in the audience.

Stavros Stavrides describes how walking and watching can create "threshold spaces," opportunities that create the possibility of new relations, rather than reinforcing standing orders of separation and hierarchy:

> Thresholds mark occasions, opportunities for change. Thresholds create or symbolically represent passages towards a possible future, already existing in the past. Recognizing such thresholds, the flâneur, and the inhabitant as flâneur, can appreciate the city as a locus of discontinuities, as a network of crossroads, turning points. In the unexpected connections realized by these thresholds, otherness emerges, not only as a threat but also as a promise.
>
> (Stavrides 2007: 177)

In this way, *yangge* dancing creates a threshold environment for the newest arrivals to the city. Building the city for the Olympics by day, migrants participate as *yangge* audiences at night. Here, they blend in and enjoy the spectacle of *yangge* in Beijing's public spaces. What tales of the city would they tell one day when they return to their villages? How city dwellers in Beijing dance in the streets at night could occupy an important chapter in the stories they pass on to their kin.

Why the *yangge*?

Yangge is a dance that originated from peasants in northern China, traditionally performed on special celebrations on the agricultural calendar (Holm 1991). During Mao Zedong's Yan'an period, the traditional dance was appropriated and politicized by the Chinese Communist Party as a vehicle for communicating the party's message (Holm 1991, Hung 2005). *Yangge* was enthusiastically danced by young and old alike until the Cultural Revolution, when the dance, along with many other forms of art and expression, was banned. In the late 1980s under Deng Xiaoping's regime, control over daily life and leisure time was relaxed and *yangge* began to rise in popularity once again as aging Chinese, who had experienced the Cultural Revolution in their teens, searched for new activities in their new found leisure time, and to find ways to keep fit (Chen 2003, Farquhar and Zhang 2005, Gerdes 2008, Graezer 2004). The dance performed dual functions, reminding them of a time when they were "young and free" and offering them a social, low-impact aerobic routine they already knew by heart. Additionally, the *yangge* was a dance that reflected northern Chinese regional pride and identity, which was favored by Mao Zedong to communicate his political message early in the history of the People's Republic of China. In 2006, China designated the dance as a National Intangible Cultural Heritage (Chinanews.cn 2006).

Looking to the future, *yangge* dancers are encountering difficulties finding its cultural and spatial niche within modern Beijing. Many Chinese young adults whom we interviewed are not interested in learning *yangge*, regarding the dance as exclusively "for old people."[5] Newly designed spaces in the city are often not large enough to accommodate thirty to sixty dancing bodies – the size range of this collective dance. Both dancers and the Chinese government have attempted to direct the development of *yangge* in the city. From the grassroots, dancers have searched for opportunites to "loosen space" so they may continue their dance practice. From the top, the Chinese government has sponsored a new kind of dance, the *disantau yangge,* which involves more complicated body movements and uses recorded music instead of live drumming for accompaniment. Depending on the form of *yangge* – the old *yangge* (which I refer to as "big" *yangge*) or the state-sponsored *disantau yangge* (which I refer to as "new" *yangge*) – dancers face different constraints and considerations within the city.

Spatial typologies of *yangge*

All dancers we observed and interviewed between 2004 and 2006 participated in the "big" *yangge* with live drumming.[6] The experiences of "new" *yangge* dancers, whom we interviewed in 2007, will be examined elsewhere. Writing about the prevalence of urban *yangge* in the late 1990s, Florence Graezer described how the rural peasant dance to celebrate the harvest became an entirely different dance once it arrived in the city (Graezer 2004). The countryside dance was an elaborate celebratory affair that required extensive preparation and was closely bound to village identity and pride. The urban dance, in contrast, is an everyday routine akin to Americans going to the gym. Elderly dancers join to stay fit and to have an excuse to leave home to meet their friends. Although some dancers remember dancing *yangge* when they were young and had some nostalgic attachment to the dance, many others simply learned after seeing others dancing in the street, enjoying themselves.

Not all spaces are equal from the dancers' point of view, however. The ideal conditions for the "big" *yangge* are: (1) flat, paved areas; (2) overhead lighting for nighttime dancing; (3) overhead protection from undesirable "skin-browning" effects of the sun; (4) a large enough area to accommodate thirty to sixty dancing bodies; and (5) distance from residential areas or office buildings to ensure their dancing and live drumming will not disturb nearby non-dancers who dislike loud music (Figure 2.3).

"New" *yangge* was ostensibly created by the government "to regulate the dance form by simplifying the steps" (China Daily.com.cn 2004). However, the dancers in the streets and parks we interviewed explained that the new dance is actually more complicated, although many concede it is more appropriate for an international audience. In the words of one dancer, " 'New' *yangge*'s style is more formal. It fits showing the foreigner the individual's spiritual status; it is more vivid, younger, and more energetic." Another dancer told me that the dance is more difficult and requires precise body movements: " 'New' *yangge* is beautiful and graceful. When you dance it, in your heart, you can feel the beauty. It is fitting as a whole body exercise and it is also appropriate for the stage. It is fitting for the park and other places." The spatial requirements to dance the "new" *yangge* are nearly the same as for the "big" *yangge*, with some important differences. As noted above, instead of loud, live drumming, the new *yangge* music is melodic and *recorded*.[7]

Sonic woes

The dancers who perform the "big" *yangge* are encountering difficulties finding a place in what Michael Southworth calls the city's *sonic environment* (Southworth 1969). Many dancers have been forced to change their dancing space because nearby residents or office workers in high-rises complain about loud accompaniment. Two dynamics result: (1) *migration*, when dancers voluntarily leave in search of a new dancing space because their group size becomes too big for the present space or because a better space emerges, or (2) *dislocation*, when dancers are evicted, because of external factors. Causes of the latter include building construction, planting of grass and trees (urban greening), and residents' complaining about their noise.

Complaints from neighbors top the list for dancing *dislocation*, and the battle lines appear to be drawn along generational divides. We learned that many middle-aged residents with children often complain about retired "big" *yangge* dancers because they attract excited crowds to gather, as pedestrians and migrants stop to watch them dance. Parents complain that loud music accompanying *yangge* disrupts their children's concentration as they prepare for important college entrance

Figure 2.3 An ideal design for dancing: large, flat, open spaces with large shade trees. Tang Keming leading "new" *yangge* practice for the 2008 Beijing Olympics. Photograph by Caroline Chen.

examinations (Figure 2.4). Sometimes, the conflicts are resolved by compromise. One *yangge* group promised to abstain from dancing in the weeks leading up to the college entrance exams. However, other groups faced conflicts that were not so easily resolved. One dancer described to us a public confrontation:

> The residents in the neighborhood have come to complain about the noise many times. They even called the police. When the police arrived, we just said: "If you can find us a place for old people to dance and exercise, we'll move!" The police wanted nothing to do with that situation [and left].

We wondered why dancers weren't in the park. According to the superintendent of parks in Beijing, no one is targeted for exclusion from Beijing's parks as long as they can buy admission tickets. But, according to our interviews with "big" *yangge* dancers, they claim they are not allowed to buy tickets because their music disturbs others in the park. Some dancers are self-conscious about their effect on others: "Patients and elderly people go to the park to enjoy silence. Our dancing and music will disturb others and drumming is bad for people with heart problems." These "big" *yangge* dancers self-segregate and continue to search out spaces that may be "loosened" in the city where they may make noise, but not burden others.

Spatial difficulties

The sonic issue is not the only problem facing "big" *yangge* dancers, however. Both "big" and "new" *yangge* dancers feel require wide, flat spaces. Flat, paved spaces inside modern parks are often too small and changes in topography present obstacles for the dancing elderly. Parks designed for strolling cannot accommodate collective

Figure 2.4 Musicians playing drums, cymbals and *suona* at Minguang Qiao, drowning out the sound of traffic. Photograph by Caroline Chen.

Figure 2.5 From infrastructure to stage: Beijing's residents claim their right to the city by appropriating residual urban space for their own uses. Photograph by Caroline Chen.

dance. Winding pathways and wide expanses of lawn without overhead protection from sun are inadequate for dancing groups of thirty or more. Additionally, parks in Beijing often close in the evenings, and many "big" *yangge* groups prefer to dance after dinner, "to help digestion." They point out that the parks that do stay open at night are often unsafe. What dancers mean by this is they fear not criminals, but uneven pavements that may cause them to trip and fall. Still, when faced with no alternatives, dancers continue to dance, even in the dark.

Both "big" and "new" *yangge* dancers both the need for more danceable spaces within Beijing. They dream of spaces that are close to where they live. Apparently, this is a problem that proves difficult to resolve. Many dancers of the big *yangge* are retired women in their sixties and seventies, and they are often charged with taking care of their grandchildren, as well as cooking and cleaning for their now adult children who are working. They value "convenient" places, close to the home, where they can easily step out and dance with their friends for a couple of hours without a great deal of effort. Thus, their ideal danceable space is close to home, so they may quickly return to their chores. The problem is, if a space is highly convenient for them, it is also likely located near residential areas where families with school-age children live, where noise is not tolerated.

Dancing rights

Dancers we interviewed spoke about "dancing rights," how dance should be an activity open to all. Like the elderly female disco dancers of Shanghai that Susan Brownwell studied (1995), one Beijing *yangge* dancer pointed out that "good health and friends are the most important things in life," and that their group dancing is a basic "human right" that belongs to both natives and visitors of any age in Beijing. Various dancers point out, however, that the level of physical difficulty required by the "new" *yangge* tended to exclude those who were more frail. Many of the "big" *yangge* dancers reported that they could not remember the more complex steps of the new dance. Some also said they did not have the strength to raise their arms high above their heads, new movements in the new dance. We were surprised to learn that many dancers were using "big" *yangge* as therapy to rehabilitate themselves from illness: *yangge* was their form of self-help. We also learned that *yangge* musicians included many retirees who were permanently handicapped. Playing music was a way for them to continue participating in public life. By smashing cymbals or striking drums on the street they could overcome their physical limitations and still stay active. One musician told me he had few activities left to choose from:

> This activity suits me extremely well. I have diabetes, which makes my eyesight very poor and my body weak and thin. My weight has dropped from 78.5 kg to 54 kg. In 2003, I fell over and broke my leg. As a result, I was unable to participate in other activities any more except this one – sitting and playing *qia*.

We learned that dancers who do not transition to the "new" *yangge* consisted not only of those who loved loud, live drumming, but also of those who were experiencing memory problems or who were disabled. In other words, the "big" *yangge* population also includes those who are most vulnerable. Yet the "big" *yangge* dancers are the ones who must travel the farthest from their homes to find a dancing space, since they do not frequent neighborhood parks and cannot dance close to home without disturbing neighbors.

Form follows culture[8]

An experiment that has already started, Beijing provides the shifting, transforming ground that residents actively manipulate to continue an everyday practice they are unwilling to do without. They improvise in the city, creating for themselves what is missing (Figure 2.5). Resilient and adaptable, *yangge* continues to flourish in the urban environment. Unscripted and ubiquitous, grassroots dancing in the streets reveals the tensions between how the modern city is imagined and constructed, and how the real city is remade, fitted, and lived. Beijing residents are actively tailoring a city to fit the contours of their everyday lives, defining for themselves new spaces for the old and the young, the athletic and the disabled. But, for the city to fit, the urban fabric must be pliable enough for some play. Examining what is happening on the ground in "loosened" spaces reveals the hidden city local Chinese residents have crafted for themselves, as they unselfconsciously find ways to create continuity in their lives in the face of disruptive and massive social and urban change. Perhaps in an indirect way, improvising dancers are dancing a thinly veiled message to designers: *here are the kinds of physical space we dancers prefer, though the spaces we control at present may still be far from optimal!* Let's hope that planners and designers working in China will recognize the importance of learning from these spontaneous improvisations, cultural processes that are transforming the city from the bottom up.

Notes

1 Hanchao Lu (2004: 21) called for "a more detailed and nuanced picture of the life of the ordinary people before we can say that any theoretical construct has meaningfully framed the nature of Chinese history."
2 The author would like to express her gratitude to research assistants from Peking University who contributed their effort, energy and insight to this project: Xiang Yunke, Han Yanfei, Zhang Yuping, Zhu Min, Liu Haofei, Minyu Fang, Deng Tingting, Xu Jingsi, Hou Anyang, Xu Liyan, Peng Siyuan; and also part-time research assistants: Xu Zhiyi, Shen Fanbu, Zhao Zhigang, and Hu Jiawen, who helped with exploratory research in 2004–2006 and in the summer of 2007. Special thanks also to Dihua Li and Kongjian Yu, and to Carl Steinitz and Peter K. Bol, who made the initial introductions possible. The author would also like to further thank the US Fulbright Program, the Society of Women Geographers and the Beatrix Farrand Fund for funding this project, along with Laurie Olin, Ron Henderson, Betsy Damon, Randy Hester, Louise Mozingo, Galen Cranz, Karen A. Franck, John Radke, Mirka Benes, Jürgen Steyer, Dan Abramson, David Nasatir, Freda Murck, Masami Kobayashi, Jeff Hou (for organizing all of this and making this book possible!), mom and dad, and my wise advisor Michael Southworth, who provided confidence and support through the rough patches in Beijing, David Nasatir, who provided cheerful, daily encouragement both online and in Berkeley coffee shops, while firmly insisting on a sample size of over 400, and my adviser Michael Southworth for sharing with me the wisdom of musicians and the secret of the oak tree.
3 I have never observed a woman engaged in "bird walking."
4 We also found the "bird walkers" at Deshengmen and Yiheyuan. Galen Cranz also observed this activity in Hong Kong in 1977 and again in Nanjing in 2007.
5 However, in recent years, middle schools in China have begun teaching *yangge* – along with other kinds of dancing – to students again in an effort to control a new problem in China: childhood obesity. What this means for *yangge*'s popularity in the future remains to be seen.
6 My later research in 2007 widened to incorporate the perspectives and activities of "new" *yangge* in Beijing and examined the competition between "big" and "new" *yangge* groups for urban space.
7 However, although the "new" *yangge* adapts more readily to the sonic demands of new, denser urban environments, it faces new challenges that the old dance does not: lack of electrical outlets for their cassette players in public spaces.
8 This phrase emerged from a conversation with Timothy Duane, Berkeley, California, September 23, 2006.

Bibliography

Brownell, S. (1995) *Training the Body for China: Sports in the Moral Order of the People's Republic*, Chicago: University of Chicago Press.

de Certeau, M. (1984) *The Practice of Everyday Life*, Berkeley: University of California Press.

Chen, N. N. (2003) *Breathing Spaces: Qigong, Psychiatry, and Healing in China*, New York: Columbia University Press.

China Daily.com.cn (2004) 'It's Time to Bring Out the Dancing Shoes'. Online.

Available   HTTP: http://www.chinadaily.com.cn/english/doc/2004–08/03/content_357306.htm (accessed 15 March 2007).

Chinanews.cn (2006) 'Yangge Dance Chosen as Intangible Heritage'. Online. Available HTTP: http://www.ipr.gov.cn/ipr/en/info/Article.jsp?a_no=10428&col_no=99&dir=200608 (accessed 2 May 2007).

Cranz, G. (1979) 'The Useful and the Beautiful: Urban Parks in China', Landscape, 23 (2): 3–10.

—— (1982) The Politics of Park Design: A History of Urban Parks in America, Cambridge, MA: MIT Press.

Farquhar, J. and Zhang, Q. C. (2005) 'Biopolitical Beijing: Pleasure, Sovereignty, and Self-Cultivation in China's Capital', Cultural Anthropology, 20 (3): 303–327.

Franck, K. A. and Stevens, Q. (eds.) (2007) Loose Space: Possibility and Diversity in Urban Life, London: Routledge.

Gerdes, E. V. P. (2008) 'Contemporary Yangge: The Moving History of a Chinese Folk Dance Form', Asian Theatre Journal, 25 (1): 138–147.

Graezer, F. (2004) 'Breathing New Life into Beijing Culture: New "Traditional" Public Spaces and the Chaoyang Neighborhood Yangge Associations', in Feuchtwang, S. (ed.) Making Place: State Projects, Globalisation and Local Responses in China, London: Routledge Cavendish.

Holm, D. (1991) Art and Ideology in Revolutionary China, Oxford: Clarendon Press.

Hung, C. T. (2005) 'The Dance of Revolution: Yangge in Beijing in the Early 1950s', China Quarterly, 181: 82–99.

Lu, Hanchao (2004) Beyond the Neon Lights: Everyday Shanghai in the Early Twentieth Century, Berkeley: University of California Press.

Rivlin, L. G. (2006) 'Found Spaces: Freedom of Choice in Public Life', in Franck, K. A. and Stevens, Q. (eds.) Loose Space, London: Routledge.

Southworth, M. (1969) 'Sonic Environment of Cities', Environment and Behavior, 1: 49–70.

Stavrides, S. (2007) 'Heterotopias and the Experience of Porous Urban Space', in Franck, K. A. and Stevens, Q. (eds.) Loose Space: Possibility and Diversity in Urban Life, London: Routledge.

Zhang, Li, (2001) Strangers in the City: Reconfigurations of Space, Power, and Social Networks within China's Floating Population, Stanford, CA: Stanford University Press.

CHAPTER 3

Latino urbanism in Los Angeles

A model for urban improvisation and reinvention

James Rojas

Latino settlement patterns in Los Angeles (LA) are transforming inner-city neighborhoods and inner-ring suburbs into vibrant, reinvigorated places. This is achieved by Latinos retrofitting the auto-oriented built form to make it pedestrian friendly through their behavior patterns. Like many other immigrant groups, Latinos arrive to this country with few resources and settle into economically depressed, fragmented parts of the city that typically lack parks and adequate housing. However within these fragmented zones, Latinos often retrofit elements of the built form to satisfy their economic and social needs: outdated gas stations become *taquerías*, defunct rail yards become parks, large abandoned manufacturing plants become *mercados*, and front yards become courtyards. Latinos bring with them different uses of urban space to an already existing built environment (Rojas 1991).

Mobility and encounters

Through their everyday behavioral patterns, LA's growing Latino population offers a new, grassroots model for sustainable transportation. For economic reasons, Latinos walk, bike, and use public transit. These everyday activities bring people together and integrate human needs with mobility. Very few signs or landmarks will indicate Latino LA. One will know when one has arrived at a Latino neighborhood only because of the large numbers of people outdoors. In the typical LA neighborhood very few people can be seen on the streets and sidewalks. Streets are an integral part of the community fabric because they bring people together by allowing for mobility and social exchanges. Latinos become "Eyes on the street," as Jane Jacobs (1961) stated. Whether one is sitting on the front porch or fixing a car, eyes provide a sense of safety and promote walking as a viable transportation mode for neighborhoods. By marrying mobility and community needs, Latinos create a sustainable transportation system that is based not on fossil fuels but on the encounters of friends and neighbors.

Every morning many Latinas walk their children to school and are greeted by street vendors selling *champurado*, a rich, thick drink made from chocolate and corn. The numerous small, brightly painted mom and pop shops that line many streets in Latino communities indicate that most customers walk to these stores for their everyday items, such as tortillas and Pampers. Many supermarkets in Latino neighborhoods provide a free shuttle service for their customers because they realize many walk to buy groceries and it is cheaper than locating shopping carts in neighborhoods.

The high pedestrian volumes in Latino neighborhoods help support and facilitate transit usage, from biking and illegal shuttle services, to bus and rail services. Throughout the day Latino men can been seen biking to and from work on busy streets or placing their bikes on buses. Along streets such as downtown LA's Broadway, dozens of workers wait for illegal vans or *Pesetas* (the cost of a peso) to drive them home.

Latinos represent the highest percentage of ridership on the Los Angeles County Metro buses and rail system. This high transit usage has created a demand for the Metro to develop innovated systems to move people rapidly and inexpensively. The twenty-eight Rapid Red bus lines, with special bus stops, crisscross LA County to move people for miles to and from work.

Whereas most middle-class Angelinos cannot locate their local bus stops, Latinos' bus stops are major nodes of neighborhood activity for pedestrians, transit riders, and vendors. From selling mangos to *elote* (corn), vendors hang around bus stops greeting transit riders with quick purchases and inexpensive items that enhance the transit experience. Yet waiting for the bus in LA is not a pleasant experience because many bus stops lack amenities and are sometimes placed in front of gas stations.

Figure 3.1 The Cesar E. Chavez Memorial Plaza. Photograph by Antonio Castillo.

The César E. Chavez Memorial Plaza is one of the most celebrated transit stops in a low-income community and is a center of community pride for San Fernando's working-class residents. This project transformed a small vacant piece of land between a railroad track and major streets into a national showcase by integrating local art and community needs (Figure 3.1).

The Memorial consists of a fountain, a bronze sculpture of Chavez, a sculpture of ten farm workers, and a 100-foot mural placed in a 23,000 square-foot park-like setting. These elements as a whole create a space that educates and provides an opportunity for reflection on the significance of Chavez's life. The Memorial is the largest and most intricate monument in the nation that honors the great civil rights and labor leader, César E. Chavez. The effort serves as an example of the abilities of both the community and local government to create public space devoted to the interests of community members.

Latinos transform staid, auto-oriented urban neighborhoods and suburbs into hubs of lively pedestrian and commercial activity through their legal or illegal DIY urban design interventions to commercial and residential streets. Moveable objects (props) and graphics add a second layer of architecture to the Latino landscape that support human activity in public space. The props include objects to sit on, talk over, and play with. These props allow residents to use the outdoor space by giving them flexibility and freedom over their environment. From graffiti to store signs and murals, the use of paint helps Latinos to inexpensively claim ownership of space or express themselves. The use of graphics adds a strong visual element to the urban form. Buildings become kinetic because of the flamboyant words and graphics used. Many building areas are covered from top to bottom with graphics (Figure 3.2). These props, graphics, and murals scale down the auto-oriented landscape to a pedestrian scale.

Entrepreneurship

The streets of Los Angeles provide Latinos a space and opportunity for economic survival by allowing them to sell items and/or their labor. From men selling their labor to others selling clothing in front of one's home, Latinos blur the line between commercial and residential activities. Whereas most Angelinos use streets only for driving cars, Latino street vendors have ingeniously transformed auto-oriented streets to fit their economic needs by strategically mapping out intersections and temporarily transforming vacant lots, sidewalks, and curbs into pedestrian-oriented *mercados*. Vendors temporarily transform the urban landscape by adding a rhythmic activity to the street. When the highway engineers were planning LA's famous freeways they did not foresee people selling oranges from the on and off ramps, but Latinos do, and this expands the use of this infrastructure. Street vendors in Latino LA add an importance to the streets by bringing services to people. Their ephemeral nature bonds people and the place together. These uses enriched the urban landscape by adding more activity to the commercial corridors and residential streets.

Mariachi Plaza located at First and Boyle Streets mixes culture, music, and commerce. This informal location was the site of a donut shop where Mariachis

Figure 3.2 These props, graphics, and murals at a muffler shop create a sense of place in the neighborhood. Photograph by James Rojas.

waited for work, to sing at local parties and social occasions. The donut shop was replaced by a beautiful stone kiosk donated by the State of Jalisco, Mexico, and has become a landmark in the Boyle Heights community. The traditional Mariachi music is celebrated at the annual Mariachi Festival, which takes place at this site.

Throughout South Los Angeles, large abandoned manufacturing facilities have been retrofitted into community-serving *mercados*, which provide numerous services from shoe repair to printing Christmas cards. Old industrial, corrugated steel buildings are painted bright, lively colors with signage and murals. Inside these buildings, rows of small vendors sell everything from CDs to produce. Colorful piñatas, wedding dresses, and other objects contrast with the interior metallic ceilings. The produce selection is a cornucopia of beautiful colored fruits and vegetables from the US and Latin America. Outside areas are transformed into restaurants, children's play zones, and plazas. These plazas with their stages program everything from bands to church masses. Alameda Swap Meet, located along the Blue Line Light Rail, is a large facility that covers many city blocks (Figure 3.3). The Los Amigos Mall is painted lavender and is laid out like a small village complete with street names of famous places in Mexico.

Many outdated gas stations in East Los Angeles have been converted into taco restaurants by the use of tables and chairs and only minor changes to the structure. Instead of saying Shell or Arco the thirty foot signs now say King Taco or other names. Wrought iron sheds are sometimes added in an attempt to enclose some of the open parking space. Pumps are replaced by tables and chairs and arranged in very formal setting. People sit and eat here having direct visual access to the street, thus capturing and reinforcing street activity.

Figure 3.3 Alameda Swap Meet. Photograph by James Rojas.

Latino homes

Non-Latinos once built the homes in Latino neighborhoods, but these homes have evolved into a vernacular form as new residents make changes to suit their needs. Every change, no matter how small, has meaning and purpose. Bringing the sofa out to the front porch, stuccoing over the clapboard, painting the house vivid colors, or placing a statue of the Virgin of Guadalupe in the front yard, all reflect the struggles, triumphs, and everyday habits of working-class Latinos. A bastion of two architectural vocabularies, Latino homes create a new language that uses syntax from both Latin American and US forms.

The front porch becomes one of the main focal points of Latino homes. In most American homes today the use and importance of the front porch has declined for various reasons. However, in Latino homes the front porch has gained a new importance with residents enlarging and expanding them for their heavy use. Residents sit on the porch to escape summer heat or just be outside with family, friends, and neighbors. The driveway and front yard can serve as a party or work space.

Waist-high fences are ubiquitous throughout the residential landscape of Latino neighborhoods. The fences function as a place to keep things out or in, hang wet laundry, sell items, or just chat with a neighbor. Fences are a useful threshold between the household and the public domain. Boundaries bring people together, and the fences in Latino neighborhoods redefine boundaries between public and private space. Here the fences break down the social and physical barriers by creating a place where people can congregate. In contrast, the middle-class suburban neighborhood people rarely congregate in the front yard. This visible expanse of land in a typical American suburb acts as a psychological barrier that separates the private space of the home from the public space of the street. In LA's Latino neighborhoods, the enclosed front yards collectively create a different urban landscape and transform the neighborhood.

Nowhere else in the urban landscape of Latino Los Angeles is the use of space so illuminated and celebrated than in the front yard. A typical middle-class front yard is an impersonal space in which no one sits and no personal objects are left lying out, whereas the front yards in Latino homes are personal vignettes of the owner's life. Depending on the practical needs of the owners, the use and design of the front yard vary from elaborate courtyard gardens reminiscent of Latin America, a place for children, to working places. Middle-class Americans put their daily habits in the backyard. Latinos bring the party, workspace, and conversation to the front yard, creating activity in the public space. The Latino front yards reflect the Latino cultural values applied to the American suburb form.

The lack of housing and the high price of it in Los Angeles has led to increased density in both single- and multi-family neighborhoods. Thousands of low-income families share homes and apartments, and garages in many neighborhoods have been illegally converted into living quarters. Backyards have become small villages with numerous families living in illegal dwelling units and sharing facilities and creating social networks. However, because of their illegality, these conversions may not conform to building and safety codes. As a result, many of these housing units/ garage conversions can be unsafe places to live because they do not meet safety regulations. In addition to safety concerns, many of the families who occupy these units are constantly in a state of fear of being reported to officials by neighbors.

Unlike the typical middle-class suburban house that pulls itself away from the street, the Latino household extends graciously to the street. Each house communicates with the street and others through the use of fences and props. Enclosed front yards help transform the street into a plaza. This new plaza is not the typical plaza we see in Latin America or Europe with strong defining street walls but has an unconventional form. Nevertheless the streets in Latino neighborhoods have all the social activity of a plaza. Residents and pedestrians can participate in the social dialogue on the street from the comfort and security of their enclosed front yard.

Public and religious life

Latinos bring new innovative uses of the suburban built environment to meet their open space needs for socialization and celebration. The Latinos have a full social calendar of activities ranging from birthday parties to *quinceaneras*, celebration of a girl's fifteenth birthday, that are expressed publicly in parks, front yards, and driveways. The numerous small rental shops for tables and chairs cater to these activities that take place on weekends throughout many Latino neighborhoods.

Latinos are predominantly Roman Catholic. Their devotion is expressed publicly through the creation of sacred spaces in the urban landscape dedicated to the Lady of Guadalupe, who is the patron saint of Mexico. These sacred spaces vary in size and shape from a small nook on a front porch, a garden shrine, mural on a side of a building, to a corner public parking lot shrine. The streets serve as

Figure 3.4 Nacimiento.
Photograph by James
Rojas.

centers for collective celebrations especially during the Christmas season beginning on December 12 with the feast day of Our Lady of Guadalupe. During this feast day numerous Latino neighborhoods host small fiestas on their streets, where children dress in traditional garb, mingling with devoted parents and grandparents and street vendors. This event is followed by the *posadas*, which are evening processions that residents partake in.

The building of *Nacimientos*, or nativity scenes, is a tradition that many Latin Americans practice during the Christmas season that ends on January 6, the Epiphany, when the three kings arrive (Figure 3.4). Latinos spend countless hours with their families creating them in their front yards, on porches, on roofs, as well as in the home. Nacimientos range in size, complexity, and creativity, from a simple scene of Mary, Joseph, and Jesus to elaborate landscapes with tinsel waterfalls, sparkling lights, and hundreds of pieces. Each Nacimiento reflects the creator's devotion to Christmas and their neighborhood.

Recreational open space

Many Latinos live in dense, park-poor Los Angeles neighborhoods. The lack of recreational facilities in Latino neighborhoods causes children and teenagers to play on the streets or in vacant lots as well as look for other opportunity sites for exercise. The Evergreen Cemetery jogging path (Figure 3.5) is an innovative example of how Latino residents helped transform a crumbling sidewalk on the perimeter of a cemetery into a rubberized jogging path that promotes social interaction and neighborhood goodwill, and encourages good health through exercise. For at least fifty years, hundreds of community residents had been using the crumbling sidewalk as a de facto jogging path because the areas lack recreational facilities.

Figure 3.5 Evergreen Cemetery jogging path. Photograph by James Rojas.

The residents organized and the city installed the track. Over a thousand people use the jogging path daily, and it has become a linear plaza serving all members of the community. The elderly use the jogging path in the morning, younger folks use it in late afternoons, and mothers walk pushing baby strollers with their friends in the evening. Vendors strategically station themselves around the jogging path. This jogging path is a great source of community pride and serves as a multifunctional open recreational space, public right of way, and urban green space.

The lack of parks and open space for the Latino constituents has been an environmental justice issue in LA. The debate concerning the Cornfields Park (Los Angeles Historic State Park) testifies to such issue. The park was created out of an abandoned thirty-two-acre rail yard after a bitter fight between the city officials and community residents. This site is one of the last vast open tracts of vacant land in the heart of downtown Los Angeles, which the city officials once envisioned as a large industrial development. The surrounding communities, including some of the most culturally diverse yet underserved residents in the city of Los Angeles, formed the Chinatown Yard Alliance to stop the industrial development and advocate instead for parkland. Needless to say the community won out and the state of California purchased the land for a park.

Thousands of Latinos arrive yearly from the ranchos and pueblos of Latin America to Los Angeles for a better life. However, many Latinos have very little education and are unprepared for the challenges of living in urban LA, which provides very little space for these twenty-first-century farmers. Latinos are transforming their yards and vacant lots into food-producing gardens; however, this is not enough in the dense metropolis of apartments and concrete. Community gardens offer access to inexpensive fresh produce as well as offering drug-free, gang-free, and graffiti-free areas where residents can visit for peace of mind, and relax with family and friends.

Community gardens create strong social networks and reinforce family values by allowing multigenerational gardening between parents/grandparents and their children and grandchildren.

The fourteen-acre South Central Farm, which is now closed, was a model for the type of open green space that Los Angeles needs to meet the demands of LA's growing Latino population. Projecto Jardin is a medicine community garden located in a very urban neighborhood. The garden also serves as an open-air classroom for users and nearby residents.

Conclusion

The March 25, 2006, Gran Marcha immigrant rally in downtown Los Angeles drew more than half a million immigrants and their allies to protest against legislation that would have increased penalties for entering the US illegally and for assisting or hiring undocumented workers. Whereas for years people have lamented how LA lacks a center or public space, within a few hours public space was created out of asphalt streets of downtown Los Angeles. People and vendors were roaming freely in the streets. In a city that is increasingly dense and increasingly Latino, downtown remains the center for this community. The Gran Marcha illustrates how Latinos are retrofitting the urban/suburban form of LA on both a micro and macro level.

Los Angeles's growing Latino population is transforming the auto-oriented built form into pedestrian-oriented places. From walking, biking, riding transit, street vending, and hanging out in the streets, Latinos retrofit the built environment to promote these activities. Without the help of government or formal architectural interventions, the do-it-yourself urban designers construct front yard fences, paint murals, and add porches to homes. All these interventions turn streets into plazas rich in social neighborhood activity. Latino growth is occurring at a time when California is conflicted between two urban development models: developing compact cities and preserving undeveloped spaces, or increasing urban sprawl and slums. Latino urbanism offers a model for urban improvisation and reinvention that addresses the issues of sustainability, public life, social justice, and the economic needs of the diverse urban dwellers and embraces the everyday acts of individuals, families, and communities. It suggests innovative ways for sustainably retrofitting our cities and suburbs from the ground up.

Bibliography

Jacobs, J. (1961) *The Death and Life of Great American Cities*, New York: Random House.
Rojas, J. T. (1991) 'The Enacted Environment: The Creation of Place by Mexicans and Mexicans/Americans', unpublished master's thesis, Department of Architecture and Planning, MIT.

CHAPTER 4

Taking place

Rebar's absurd tactics in generous urbanism

Blaine Merker

On a sunny October day in 2005, Rebar, the San Francisco-based collective of artists, activists, and designers, paid a curbside parking meter in downtown San Francisco and built a temporary park within the white lines of the parking space – complete with lawn, a large shade tree, and a park bench (Figure 4.1). For the legal duration of our "lease," we reprogrammed the public right-of-way: no longer a space dedicated to the movement and storage of private automobiles, for two hours this seven by twenty-two feet of street became a place for rest, relaxation, and socializing in an area of downtown San Francisco previously underserved by public open space.[1] At first, passersby reacted with a mix of indifference and curiosity. Eventually several people ventured into the "park," found a place to sit and took advantage of the novelty of cool grass and shade. Some of the strangers enjoyed

Figure 4.1 This image of Rebar's first experiment in *Park(ing)* quickly circulated through the blogosphere and became a readily transmittable meme. Source: Rebar.

some unplanned social interaction by exchanging a few words with each other; others took the occasion to rest or read. After two hours and having generated 24,000 "square foot-minutes" of public open space, Rebar dismantled the park and returned the space to its normative function. All that remained of the incident were the photos and video footage shot. We posted these on our website as a record of the experiment.

Within several weeks a seminal photo had appeared in dozens of references on the Internet and news stories. Within six months Rebar had received hundreds of inquiries about the project, which we dubbed *Park(ing)*, from individuals and groups around the world. The combination of the iconic image of parking-space-as-park and its accompanying descriptive name created a "sticky" idea that transmitted readily across electronic media. Without much explanation, other groups disposed to guerrilla intervention quickly grasped the basic tactic. Still, the amount of interest Rebar received warranted some codification of the idea, so we posted a short "how-to" manual on our website to help others get started. The essence of the tactic was to legally claim a parking space using materials that were symbolically associated with parks: trees, lawn, and a bench. Rebar treated the idea itself as open source and applied a Creative Commons license: as long as it was not used for profit, we encouraged people to replicate and reinterpret it.[2]

The following year, Rebar organized a one-day, global event in which participants – mostly in San Francisco but now joined by groups in other cities around the United States and Europe – built temporary parks in parking spaces, in a coordinated effort to produce a greater critical mass and to demonstrate solidarity with the effort to reprogram urban parking spaces. In each of the forty-seven cities where *Park(ing) Day* took place in 2006, different legal codes had to be negotiated by the participants: the traffic codes in San Francisco were different from those in London, New York, or Eau Claire, Wisconsin. Nowhere, however, did participants meet with significant opposition to their installations, which ranged from a do-it-yourself lemonade stand through stormwater demonstration gardens to a seed giveaway (Figure 4.2).

The event effectively operated within an undervalued niche space and successfully exploited a legal loophole – a tactic at once radical but superficially unthreatening to the system of spatial commodification it critiqued.[3] Although the space we collectively allocate to parking – how much, where, for whom, and at what cost – is usually hotly contested, *Park(ing) Day* operated within a discrete unit of that contested terrain, neutralizing potential backlash with a sense of humor and the honest application of a simple and uncontested market rule: just as it is completely within the rights of individuals to buy up shares of a publicly traded company, *Park(ing) Day* participants paid meters and exercised their option to do something other than park cars in real estate that they, for the moment, owned.

In 2007, ongoing widespread interest in *Park(ing)*, concentrated in San Francisco but also now coming from Europe and other American cities, led us to organize an even larger scale event when people around the world would temporarily turn parking spaces into parks. With help from partner organizations such as The Trust for Public Land and Public Architecture, Rebar set a date for the event and facilitated the participation of hundreds of volunteers by holding community organizing

Figure 4.2 Early grassroots *Park(ing)* installations explored creative new uses of spaces previously given over to the doxa of automobile use. This *park* from 2006 offered lemon trees and presses for do-it-yourself lemonade. Source: Rebar.

sessions in San Francisco and distributing how-to information on the web. Rebar itself built the *Parkcycle* (Figure 4.3), a human-powered "park" that could deploy 250 square feet of green open space at the whim of its pilots, and we took the day to visit some of the fifty-eight parking space parks built around San Francisco.

In all, more than 200 parks were constructed on September 21, 2007 – entirely by volunteers – in over fifty cities worldwide. The installations ranged from dinner parties to croquet courses, dog parks to massage parlors, community health clinics to urban micro-farms. Some participants did insinuate advertising and business promotion into their installations (in Florida, for example, a Starbucks set up a park). But what most of the *Park(ing)* installations had in common was a sense of humor and the promotion of some kind of artistic, ecological, social, or cultural agenda (Figure 4.4). The playful yet passionate tone of the event first set in 2005 continues to resonate each year.

What, exactly, had taken place in these playful acts of transgression in the broader context and construction of urban landscape and the so-called public realm? How can we begin to articulate these actions and events as ways and maneuvers for repurposing the landscapes of our contemporary city? Can the tactical maneuver on the part of Rebar and the specific instances possibly becoming a turning point that could lead to larger changes in the way public spaces are used and perceived?

This chapter explores these questions by examining some core themes in Rebar's projects, including *Park(ing)* and other artistic work. Specifically, the chapter addresses these questions by relating the projects to the problems we have grappled with in our own understanding of public space and our agency within it.

Figure 4.3 The *Parkcycle* incorporated a water-storing skin and solar panels to power the brakes and lights, and used almost all recycled materials. Although pedal-powered, it used no bicycle parts. Source: Rebar.

Figure 4.4 This *park* built by volunteers/ participants in San Francisco in 2007 explored a theme common to many installations: an interactive element (in this case, a library) to encourage social exchange. Source: Rebar.

Niche spaces

The evolving *Park(ing)* project is typical of the medium in which Rebar works: "niche spaces" are undervalued, or valued inappropriately for the range of potential activities within them. We believe that such niches – once identified – can be opened up to revaluation through creative acts. *Park(ing)* identified the metered parking space as just such a niche within the urban landscape, and redefined it as a fertile terrain for creative social, political, and artistic experimentation. It was only through the replication of this tactic and its adoption by others that a new kind of urban space was measurably produced, as it was in the two years following Rebar's first *Park(ing)* experiment. With Rebar providing others with "permission" to act, new users rushed into this niche, challenging the existing value system encoded within this humble, everyday space. The parking space became a zone of potential, a surface onto which the intentions of any number of political, social or cultural agendas could be projected. By providing a new venue for *any* kind of unmet need, revalued parking spaces became instrumental in redefining "necessity." Thus the creative act literally "takes" place – that is, it claims a new physical and cultural territory for the social and artistic realm.

As artists, the *Park(ing)* phenomenon ignited our curiosity about the street. We saw that the street could be defined as a territory inscribed by a greater number of interests than the landscape has room to accommodate. It is only by the tacit *undervaluing* of certain activities (such as, say, play or eating or socializing) that other activities (such as parking and driving) can thrive. *Park(ing)* set up an operational precedent for intervening in such a contested, value-laden space and proposing a new system of valuation. Embedded within this approach are what have emerged as three core strands of our practice so far: tactics, generosity, and absurdity.

Tactical urbanism

Rebar defines tactical urbanism as the use of modest or temporary revisions to urban space to seed structural environmental change. Our use of tactics is based on a belief that deep organizing structures (social, cultural, economic, and other) have a two-way relationship with the physical environment: they both produce the environment and are *re*produced by it. Rebar has been consistently interested in the sociologist Pierre Bourdieu's notion of the *doxa* and *habitus* as ways of explaining how we perceive this highly coded landscape. According to Bourdieu, "every established order tends to produce (to very different degrees and with very different means) the naturalization of its own arbitrariness" (Bourdieu 1977: 164). These doxa are deep, self-evident beliefs that not only explain the way the world works but are reinforced by the physical environment and our ways of operating within it – that is, habitus. "The habitus is the universalizing mediation which causes an individual agent's practices, without either explicit reason or signifying intent, to be nonetheless 'sensible' and 'reasonable'" (Bourdieu 1977: 79). Doxa favor the power relationships of the status quo because it is those relationships that have produced the landscape itself. The landscape's apparent neutrality requires justification: the doxa. Thus, when Rebar considers a parking space, the allocation of space to sidewalk or utilities, an enclosed corporate atrium, or the vocabulary of materials and symbols in the city, we think of these things as engaging in a dialogue with the doxa. The environment and habitus are locked in a mutually reinforcing and self-referential cycle. This is the field in which tactical urbanism, as an interruption of habitus, operates.

There are also ways in which institutions and other actors, such as government and corporations, actively reinforce the doxa. Michel de Certeau contrasts two ways that power is exercised in space: *strategies* and *tactics*. Strategies "conceal beneath their objective calculations their connection with the power that sustains them from within the stronghold of its own 'proper' place or institution" (de Certeau 1984: xix). Artifacts of strategies, for example, are the painted markings in the roadway, the invisible boundaries of property, or the zoning laws that control whether a neighborhood is made up of houses, factories, or brothels. In other words, strategy is power working at a distance upon the landscape. This power in turn shapes the doxa and reinforces our perception of the "neutral landscape." Because it both projects power and obscures its source, strategy depends on contriving a convincingly self-evident environment.

In contrast, tactics "are isolated actions or events that take advantage of opportunities offered by the gaps within a given strategic system . . . Tactics cut across a strategic field, exploiting gaps in it to generate novel and inventive outcomes" (Wikipedia 2009b). A tactic (deployed, for instance, in an urban niche space) "insinuates itself into the [strategy's] place, fragmentarily, without taking it over in its entirety, without being able to keep it at a distance" (de Certeau 1984: xix). Deploying a tactic means one "must vigilantly make use of the cracks that . . . open in the surveillance of the proprietary powers. It poaches in them. It creates surprises in them" (de Certeau 1984: 37). In doing so, the tactic disrupts the doxa and temporarily projects a new set of values onto a space. Rebar's choice tactic has been to *remix* environmental signs and symbols, often within the official vocabulary that gives doxa its force and meaning.

Generous urbanism

Contemporary industrialized societies have generally accepted the banishment of unscripted, generous exchange in the public realm in favor of a hyper-commercial alternative. In this preferred mode of relationship-building between strangers in public space, generosity's converse is omnipresent in the signs and artifacts of economic transaction. When the transaction is complete, the voluntary bond between buyer and seller is severed; both go their separate ways without obligation. In the North American city, public behaviors unrelated to commercial exchange or economic production fall into two basic categories: loitering or other illegal and disruptive activity; and assembly, celebration, and cultural spectacle, which are heavily scripted and contained by permits and other official permissions. ("Leisure" pursuits are another possible exception, but do not necessarily involve relationship-building between strangers.) When an unregulated act of generosity is interjected into this environment of commercial consensus, the result is a cognitive disruption – a "blow against the empire" (Purves 2005: 22–44). Offering the public something without expectation of anything in return is at once subversive, suspicious – and potentially profound and transformative. Stripped of commercial adornment, the "generous" public act foregrounds its own assumptions: it says, *this is possible, and it need not be bought or sold.*

Rebar defines *generous urbanism* as the creation of public situations between strangers that produce new cultural value, without commercial transaction. This isn't to say that money doesn't play a role in the execution, since materials may still be bought, and grants or commissions distributed. However, the ultimate value is produced independently of commerce. It's possible to call this activity art production ("art" being a convenient category for cultural goods that are ends in themselves), but there are no absolute "consumers" or "producers" for this type of art, only participants with varying levels of responsibility for instigating the situation. This kind of cultural practice has an established pedigree in San Francisco, and includes activities of groups such as the Diggers, the Free Stores movement, and even the more recent free summer bluegrass festival in Golden Gate Park. A notable example of generous urbanism is Critical Mass, which began as a spontaneous group bike ride and has swelled, in the last fifteen years, to a monthly global event. There is always the danger among the more successful forms of generous situations that they will be absorbed by the dominant cultural milieu and, once absorbed, their critical dimension diminished as they join familiar, acceptable, and potentially commercial categories of festival and spectacle.

Rebar's second major urban project, *Commonspace*, employed a generous urbanism by crafting eight experimental interventions in San Francisco's privately owned public open spaces (or "POPOS"). With slight presumption, we guessed that a certain tolerance for generous urbanism was the acid test for true public space, and set forth to discover *just how public* POPOS were (Figure 4.5). The eighteen-month project began with a physical and social mapping of the spaces produced as a result of Section 138 of the San Francisco Planning Code. The code requires that new downtown developments make 2 percent of their area available "in order to meet the public need for open space and recreational uses" (San Francisco Municipal Code Sec. 138). The spaces take the form of rooftop terraces, corporate atriums, plazas and breezeways, and even some oddly shaped snippets connected to public streets where the "public" seems to be neither aware of POPOS nor in great need of them. We loosely positioned our approach within the Situationist tradition of *detournment*, the creative repurposing of familiar elements to produce new meaning (which is not that different from the remixing we'd been doing to date).

Working from our web-based survey of the physical and psychogeographic terrain of the spaces, we launched a series of events in them: public tours, rooftop kite flying, an interactive game of "Assassin," a "Nappening" for underslept office workers and other accidental participants (Figure 4.6), a game of "counterveillance" in response to security cameras, and a public workshop for teaching Balinese monkey chant, or Kecak (Figure 4.7). In each instance, public participation was encouraged through outreach before and during the event. We saw the events as opportunities to recast spaces that had often become, by virtue of their literal

Figure 4.5 This POPOS
in the headquarters
of the C-Net building
provides indoor seating
in a corporate lobby. The
privilege of public use
comes with a caveat,
though: Big Brother is
watching. Source: Rebar.

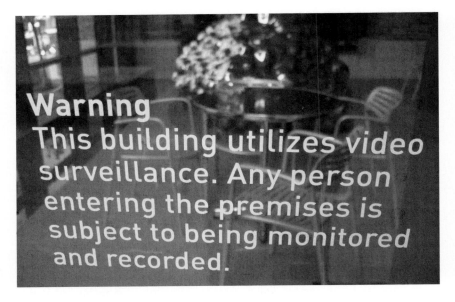

Figure 4.6 Rebar
advertised the
Nappening on the
street and by flyering
the offices of the law
firms above the POPOS.
The free event quickly
"sold out," and many
participants inquired if
it could be a permanent
service. Source: Rebar.

enclosure in corporate space, de facto private realms. By deploying generous acts that fulfilled various unmet needs we had identified in our mapping (such as the need for rest, play or community), we created a "rupture between the expected and the unexpected" where participants might experience "not just the subject of the dissent, but also the structure that supports the world and worldview that contains both the dissent and the status quo" (Purves 2005: 28).

This active, generous approach to urbanism contrasts with the paternalistic "generosity" implied in the wording of the plaque posted outside the POPOS at 235 Second Street:

Figure 4.7 Rebar held Kecak workshops in POPOS where the public had been discouraged from lingering by private security. Legal observers from the American Civil Liberties Union also watched the event. Source: Rebar.

The plaza and inside seating area of this building is provided and maintained for the enjoyment of the public. The interior seating area is open to the public Monday–Friday 8am–6pm. Warning. This building utilizes video surveillance. Any person entering the premises is subject to being monitored and recorded.

We discovered that some POPOS indeed warranted recent critiques of "institutionalized generosity on an unprecedented scale" that "reveal[s] that when the act of giving is not only enforced but completely rationalized, the result is nothing more than a representation of the public sphere." All are highly socially codified spaces, and many seemed steeped in doxic expectation that "nothing is supposed to happen, apart from perhaps pondering the philosophy of all the contortionist formats modern life makes us fit into" (Fowle and Larsen 2005: 23).

However, we eventually found the social dynamics of POPOS to be as complex and varied as the governance structures and publics that operated in each of them.[4] Most are overseen by private security employed by the building management, and it was with these actors that we most often came into contact when trying to reach out to the "public." We realized that they indeed *were* a part of the public we were trying to engage. Whereas some were suspicious of our activities and even unaware of their obligation to provide an open space to the public, others responded positively to the generous spirit of the activities we initiated. In fact, it seemed that framing our activities as a "free" gift was so unexpected that it gradually overcame the institutional resistance by the management overseers to non-commercial acts in commercial space.

Rebar has benefited from the level of authenticity and street cred that the framework of generous urbanism imparts on a creative act, but to be motivated by the knowledge that generosity is a powerful and transformative tactic is not to say that we use it cynically. Most of what Rebar does takes place outside galleries and outside traditional valuation systems for art, design, and urban infrastructure. We "give away" our work (that is, set up situations for people to use and enjoy, or to fulfill an unmet need) for anyone nearby enough to experience it because that is the only way we can do our work. The primary recipients are the inhabitants of the public realm, but there are many more who will experience this non-commercial transaction through images and descriptions of the work. This secondary, mediated experience is probably more important to the goals we are trying to achieve. Simply by communicating that such an exchange took place, the work influences people's notions of what is possible and acceptable in public space, far beyond what was communicated at the moment the work is made. If generosity is the medium of this kind of work, then the medium does become the message. Recently, other actors have taken up their own explorations of POPOS based on the groundwork laid by Rebar: the San Francisco Urban Research Association (SPUR) is engaged in an extensive evaluation of the spaces and is hosting public forums on their place in the downtown public space network, and several other individuals and groups have launched their own generous repurposing of POPOS, ranging from lunch-hour picnics to free figure-drawing classes.

Figure 4.8 Rebar's Matthew Passmore inspects the contents of the *Cabinet National Library*, which includes a guest book, snack bar, and all back issues of *Cabinet* magazine. Source: Rebar.

Absurd urbanism

Rebar holds that deep within every rational system holding societies together are assumptions that, if taken to their logical conclusion, tend toward absurdity. As such, they are highly fertile terrain for artistic exploration. Property ownership, arguably the mother of absurd ideas, served as the jumping-off point for Rebar's first project, the *Cabinet National Library*. For its Spring 2003 issue on "Property," *Cabinet* magazine, a non-profit art and culture quarterly, purchased a half-acre of land site unseen for $300 on eBay. The land was part of a failed 1960s residential development called the Sunshine Valley Ranchettes, now a desolate tract of desert scrubland outside Deming, New Mexico. *Cabinet* dubbed their new purchase Cabinetlandia and divided it into manageable sectors: Readerlandia, Editorlandia, Nepotismia, and so forth. Magazine-sized parcels were offered to readers for a penny for a 99-year lease.

Upon our reading the Cabinetlandia article, it occurred to us that Cabinetlandia would obviously require a *Cabinet National Library* (i.e., a library containing all and only back issues of *Cabinet*). What better way to establish a civilization than to create a repository for its organizing documents (Figure 4.8)? Fortunately, we were the first to propose the idea to the magazine. The editors published our library proposal and a sketch in Issue 12 (Winter 2003–2004). From the outset, it was paramount to us that the project be an actual, usable library, aside from (or in addition to) being an odd spectacle and a play on words. Moreover, it was crucial that the project express its library-ness down to the last minute detail; this idea guided the project at every stage of its development. The *Cabinet National Library* is built from a three-drawer file cabinet and is laid out thus:

- top drawer – the Card Catalog, Guestbook, and Guest Services.
- middle drawer – the Collection: back issues of *Cabinet*.
- bottom drawer – the Snack Bar.

Among the strands of Rebar's practice, absurdism often acts as the lightning rod; since its construction, the *Library* has attracted its share of pilgrims, detractors and even pillagers.[5]

In the summer of 2006 Rebar made its first foray onto the rarified world of the institutional art gallery with its *EnCanment* project. *EnCanment* was a performance installation included in the "Between the Walls" exhibition at San Francisco's Southern Exposure art gallery, a non-profit art space with a thirty-four-year history and reputation as a perennial mainstay on the cutting edge of the San Francisco art scene. "Between the Walls" was the final show in 2006 before the gallery closed for seismic retrofitting and, given this, the gallery administration put the entire interior structure of the gallery up for grabs: the walls, the floor, the very space itself was offered up as an artistic medium. Participating artists were encouraged to consider ideas of migration, transition, improvisation, and community.

In response to the concept of the exhibition, and in celebration of Southern Exposure's rich history in this space, Rebar created a temporary industrial canning operation that harvested, processed, and canned the gallery itself. Rebar systematically mapped and cored sections of the gallery wall and, utilizing traditional assembly-line technology, canned the cores in metal cans on site during the opening and closing night events. Cans were then labeled and sold to support SoEx and Rebar. (*EnCanment* is situated in the historical context of the gallery, which occupies a former industrial site that once housed the American Can Company. The earliest incarnation of SoEx called itself the "American Can Collective.")

In extending the commoditization of art objects to its logically absurd conclusion, Rebar sought to industrialize the production of gallery art, and simultaneously to invert the traditional commercial art-world exchange: in *EnCanment*, the cultural value embedded in the gallery itself was offered as a commercial art object, draped though it was in the banal trade dress of a mass-produced, canned good. And, standing in open revolt to a system that prizes mystique, unmoored valuation, and, above all, unrestrained consumption, *EnCanment* was designed to reduce the art gallery, *qua* institution, to a fungible unit of general commerce.

And here one may find traces of a nascent insurgency. *EnCanment* sought, playfully and absurdly, to insert a sliver of democracy into an otherwise deeply hegemonic system. Rebar harvested the gallery wall together with its associated cultural value (and the insular space it encloses), and distributed the wall to the public in an easily transportable, affordable package: the tin can. As one purchaser remarked, "I've always wanted a show at Southern Exposure. I'm hosting an open studio this weekend and one of my photographs will be hung on a piece of Southern Exposure procured from the *EnCanment* project. My first solo show in an art gallery!"

Conclusion

Although we've identified some of the key themes in our work to date here, this is done winkingly *ex post facto*. We can't pretend to have had any of this in mind during the work itself, except at the intuitive level fostered by the kind of late-night discussions that take place at Rebar's choice meeting spot, a pub in San Francisco's Mission District. Absurdity, generosity, and a tactical approach have been the hallmarks of our projects thus far but hardly the test of an idea's validity prior to its execution. In fact, what seems to have driven our thinking as much as anything else has been the sense of *niche*, *loophole*, and *opportunity*. These tantalizing gaps in the urban structure – these *necessary* pieces of the urban structure, as long as that structure is generated by strategic forces seated in power and authority – are what feed our practice. As long as we have the right eyes to see them, the cracks in the system will continue to elicit our curiosity. The landscape itself is a field for experimentation and play about space but also about structure, one where the final results of that experiment can lead to broader conclusions.

To conclude then, we come back to one of our early questions in this chapter: can the result of this play become a tactical turning point in the structure itself, more than a specific instance of absurdity in public space? We could judge this not by how many others engage in repeating a spatial meme, but by how possible it becomes for anyone to use the public landscape as a field of experimentation and play. The rules of that game are an open secret.

Notes

1 The San Francisco Planning Department's Downtown Plan, Recreation and Open Space, Map 3 – Major Open Spaces indicates which areas of the city are considered deficient in open space. Rebar chose one of these areas in a highly visible part of downtown as an ideal test site for its first *Park(ing)* intervention.

2 According to Wikipedia (2009a), "Creative Commons has been described as being at the forefront of the 'copyleft' movement, which seeks to support the building of a richer public domain . . . [some] have credited Creative Commons with generating interest in the issue of intellectual property and contributing to the re-thinking of the role of the 'commons' in the 'information age'. Beyond that Creative Commons has provided 'institutional, practical and legal support for individuals and groups wishing to experiment and communicate with culture more freely'. Creative Commons works to counter what the organization considers to be a dominant and increasingly restrictive permission culture. According to Lawrence Lessig, founder of Creative Commons, it is 'a culture in which creators get to create only with the permission of the powerful, or of creators from the past'. Lessig maintains that modern culture is dominated by traditional content distributors in order to maintain and strengthen their monopolies on cultural products such as popular music and popular cinema, and that Creative Commons can provide alternatives to these restrictions."

3 In this and many other endeavors, we have been inspired by other artists whose work engages interstitial urban space, in particular Gordon Matta-Clark's "Fake Estates" project.

4 In other words, each POPOS has its own unique governing ecology to be uncovered, unlike a "properly public" city park in which the rules are public, codified, and relatively consistent (see Amoss 2007).

5 In spring 2007, art students from a joint program of the University of New Mexico and the University of Texas launched an attack on the *Cabinet National Library* in order to erect their own archive atop the site. They were repelled by a sudden storm, common in the area at that time of year. See Taylor (2007). In July 2009 Rebar returned to Cabinetlandia to repair and expand the *Library*, which itself had suffered from storm damage, and added a drawer-sized white-wall art gallery (for itinerant exhibitions). Rebar's 2009 expedition to Cabinetlandia also included an experiment in projecting the dreamworld of the *Library* onto the upward-blown dust of the New Mexican desert at night: using a high-powered projector, fractured images of architectural speculation were cast onto/into a churning miasma of wind-borne sand, evoking the eerie specter of weightless and ephemeral libraries of fantasy.

Bibliography

Amoss, M. (2007) 'Challenging the Commons: A Yearlong Experiment Tests a New Breed of Urban Public Space in San Francisco', *The Next American City*, 16 (Fall): 11–12.

Bourdieu, P. (1977) *Outline of a Theory of Practice*, Nice, R. (trans.), Cambridge: Cambridge University Press.

de Certeau, M. (1984) *The Practice of Everyday Life*, Berkeley: University of California Press.

Fowle, K. and Larsen, L. B. (2005) 'Lunch Hour', in Purves, T. (ed.) *What We Want is Free*, Albany: State University of New York Press.

Kayden, J. (2000) *Privately Owned Public Space: The New York City Experience*, New York: New York City Department of City Planning.

Najafi, S. (ed.) (2005) *Odd Lots: Revisiting Gordon Matta-Clark's Fake Estates*, New York: Cabinet Books.

Purves, T. (ed.) (2005) 'Blows against the Empire', in Purves, T. (ed.) *What We Want is Free*, Albany: State University of New York Press.

Roach, C. (2008) 'Urban Guerillas: Streets and the Sociopolitical Architecture of the Public Realm', *On Site*, 19 (Spring/Summer): 27–33.

Sadler, S. (1999) *The Situationist City*, Cambridge, MA: The MIT Press.

San Francisco Planning and Urban Research Association. (2008) *Secrets of San Francisco: A Guide to Our City's Privately Owned Public Open Spaces*. Online. Available HTTP: http://spur.org/publications/library/report/secretsofsanfrancisco_010109 (accessed 15 September 2009).

Taylor, C. (2007) 'Projecting ARTLIES Into the Void,' *ART LIES: The Texas Contemporary Art Journal*, 53 (Spring).

Wikipedia. (2009a) 'Creative Commons'. Online. Available HTTP: http://en.wikipedia.org/wiki/Creative_Commons (accessed 20 July 2009).

—— (2009b) 'Tactic (Method)'. Online. Available HTTP: http://en.wikipedia.org/wiki/Tactic_(method) (accessed 1 December 2009).

PART TWO

RECLAIMING

eXperimentcity

Cultivating sustainable development in Berlin's *Freiräume*

Michael A. LaFond

eXperimentcity describes a critical, cultural approach to urban development, but perhaps more importantly practical strategies for supporting sustainability experiments that are especially taking hold in dynamic Berlin's *Freiräume* (free or open spaces; http://www.eXperimentcity.net). The non-profit id22: Institute for Creative Sustainability (http://www.id22.net) initiated eXperimentcity in 2003, recognizing that theoretical sustainable development discussions urgently need to be linked to on-the-ground demonstrations. eXperimentcity's communications platform emphasizes self-organized reuses of vacant land and buildings, such as ecological housing, alternative cultural centers, and community gardening projects. eXperimentcity brings attention to synergies found in combining "non-used" spaces with civil society resourcefulness, resulting in new methods for the production and management of urban space. In Berlin, such bottom-up efforts are increasing support for "informal planning" methods: innovative land recycling groups are being recognized as partners in the city's development.

Berlin: capital city of politics + possibilities

This post-war, post-Wall, post-industrial city's landscape is dotted with more than 5,000 idle spaces.[1] Although some are troubled with this, many see these *Freiräume* as opportunities, for example a growing population of "creatives" including hundreds of thousands of students and precariously employed artists and bohemians looking not just for ways to get by but beyond that to test their visions.[2]

Berlin is characterized not just by abandoned buildings but also by aging and diversifying populations as well as a stagnating economy and overwhelming financial debts. The city has won a reputation as being "poor but sexy," as Berlin's charming mayor, Klaus Wowereit, sums it up. This could simply be propaganda but perhaps there is something forward-thinking in the celebration of being quantitatively modest and qualitatively attractive?[3]

Berlin's built environment with its seemingly endless supply of vacant lots is largely a product of World War II and the following Cold War decades. More than 50 percent of the city's structures were destroyed in the World War, and the wall that was built in 1961 to surround West Berlin, an island created in the middle of East Germany, encouraged countless people and activities to abandon the city. Planners, in East as well as West Berlin, also did their part to create yet more vacant land, often unwittingly through urban renewal and *Autobahn* projects, especially during the 1970s and1980s. These years witnessed many demonstrations and initiatives against destructive and elite urban renewal projects, giving rise to a couple hundred building occupations in West Berlin. Berlin *Freiraum* activists have over the decades invested a great deal of energy in protest actions, for example in recent years in fighting to maintain public access and affordable use of the shores of the Spree River between the neighborhoods of Kreuzberg and Friedrichshain.[4]

The fall of the Berlin Wall in 1989 was followed in the early 1990s by another couple of hundred building and land occupations, this time in the East. The return of Germany's capital to Berlin in the 1990s finally fueled hopes of population and economic expansion. The city-state of Berlin as well as many thousands of investors speculated on dreams of growth: instead the remaining industry all but vanished, and people and jobs continued to leave the city, leading to more idle real estate, widespread financial disaster, and a bankrupt city.

Compounding Berlin's problems is its location in a region of *Shrinking Cities* with depressed economies and populations (http://www.shrinkingcities.com). But economic crisis is nothing new for this metropolis, and so Berlin is not really phased by the current global financial crisis. The city is happy not to be shrinking and at least to be stable and holding its own. Not able to develop much of its idle land and space in a traditional way, that is, through cooperations with international investors working on large-scale construction projects, the city planning establishment has been forced to reconsider the advantages of going in on new cooperations with civil society-based, smaller "developers" more interested in self-use than speculation. In addition the significance of a cultural economy and urban creative industries has been discovered in recent years. Berlin planners are hopefully studying relationships between cultural and urban development initiatives as they relate to the regional economy. Out of all this Berlin has witnessed a considerable movement since the late 1990s of informal, sometimes insurgent planning and space production, including a wide range of smaller-scale projects making use of *Freiräume*, often as *Zwischennutzungen* (temporary uses) but also as long-term reuses.

Berlin is emerging as a great laboratory for "cultures of sustainable development," meaning cooperative, participatory initiatives that serve to create and maintain urban spaces, further democratize planning and development, and increase local capacities.

In poor but sexy Berlin idle land and buildings are still to be found, even downtown, allowing not only for more shopping centers but also for countless smaller, temporary uses such as underground clubs, guerrilla gardening, and beach volleyball. More permanent fixtures, such as innovative housing, are also blossoming, where the trend is no longer pursuing happiness in a nuclear-family dream home with garage and lawn in the suburbs, but rather seeking identity in self-managed urban living.

In the city are more than 100,000 vacant apartments, many more thousands of idle offices and shops, and countless abandoned industrial buildings. Entire airports have been closed and are waiting for new uses. Berlin is not in any way under pressure to increase the quantities of square feet of usable real estate. New developments are, however, being sought, especially concerning housing projects, which have much more to do with the creation of new qualities. Housing is in demand that expresses new identities: ecological, self-designed and -managed, creative, sustainable. *Wohnkulturen* (residential forms) are called for that reflect changes in demographics, in lifestyle, in shifting cultural, social, ecological, and economic forces.

Berlin, traditionally a city of renters – less than 14 percent of the population owns its living accommodation – is diversifying to embrace everything from anarchist trailer communities to eco-coop-condominiums. In this post-ideological city of 3.5 million the search is not for any one perfect *Wohnkultur* but rather for an increasing variety of living arrangements.

id22 + eXperimentcity: communicative uses + idle spaces

id22 along with eXperimentcity finds its roots in the ufaFabrik, an insurgent, cultural and ecological urban village established in 1979 through an illegal but tolerated occupation of a collection of buildings and spaces used between the 1920s and 1970s by the Universum Film AG (UFA film studio; see LaFond 1999). After working out of the ufaFabrik between 1999 and 2007, id22 moved in 2008 into the MARIE Baugemeinschaft, a self-organized, ecological housing project realized on a lot that had been vacant for many decades.[5] An inspiration for this housing project is the expansive city park just next to it (*Ein Platz für die Marie*), which in the late 1990s was fought for and then designed by people living and working in the neighborhood after buildings were demolished on the site. This newly created public *Freiraum*, with its community garden, sports facilities, and adventure playground serves as a model of cooperative space production among citizens and local government.[6]

id22 cultural planners are mainly active in Berlin, but also engaged in other parts of the world, for example in Taipei, Taiwan, where id22 has in recent years worked with OURs (the Organisation of Urban Re's) on the Treasure Hill and Da-Li Street urban space redevelopment initiatives.[7]

Since 2004 eXperimentcity has been recognized as a model project for the implementation of the Agenda 21, which was finally adopted in 2006 as a guiding, sustainable vision for Berlin's future development.[8] In 2009 eXperimentcity was being publicized by the European Commission as a best practice in the "Year of Innovation and Creativity" (http://create2009.europa.eu/projects/participating_countries/deutschland_germany.html).

eXperimentcity is a call to action, learning from existing projects and helping to mobilize new generations of initiatives interested in sustainably reusing and redeveloping city spaces. eXperimentcity has been able to identify, review, and network hundreds of such projects and directly assist a good number of them in recent years. These projects are seen as small laboratories involved in an action research focused on progressive urban alternatives. A "creative sustainability" is understood here to mean developing places and communities in ways that do not lead to rapid gentrification. The question is asked how to do more with less, and to engage and empower civil society in the design and management of urban spaces, without completely excusing local government of its responsibilities to maintain certain qualities in the built environment. eXperimentcity works with an ongoing inner-city renaissance, meaning a rediscovery of quality of life in Berlin and other

European cities. Sustainability in this sense prioritizes qualitative developments over quantitative, for example in increased local identity and security, reduced air, water, and noise pollution, less time spent commuting, and opportunities for self-expression through shaping local living conditions. A communicative and cultural rather than a technological approach is emphasized as well as a process orientation.

Creative forces and actors, and not just artists and architects but the local populations in general, have special roles to play in these developments, for example in helping to recognize, shape, and communicate innovative and appropriate projects in their communities. To this end eXperimentcity works to network, support, and publicize a wide range of "space-recycling" projects and artistic interventions.

As an "open source platform," moving between theory and practice while stressing support for the realization of innovative urban space reclamations, eXperimentcity begins with the goal of supporting a "culture of sustainable urban development." This involves working with, studying, comparing, networking, and publicizing practical projects, and to this end Internet homepages have been created and maintained as forums for communicating and finding support for specific projects.

eXperimentcity also organizes events such as the yearly EXPERIMENTDAYS, to bring together a great variety of projects, generating publicity while mobilizing people and resources. The EXPERIMENTDAYS 09, for example, took place on an October weekend in 2009, in Berlin's Uferhallen, a conversion of former public transit maintenance buildings into a diversified cultural center (Figure 5.1). During these two days about 100 projects were presented and more than 2,000 participants and guests were involved. eXperimentcity activities are to an extent volunteer efforts, but funding does come from Berlin's local government, a range of progressive foundations and banks as well as project and participant fees and donations.

Figure 5.1
EXPERIMENTDAYS 08 in the Uferhallen, Berlin-Wedding. Photograph by Robert Knobloch.

Examples + experiments

To illustrate the kinds of initiatives eXperimentcity supports and publicizes, several housing and cultural projects are briefly described in the following.[9] To begin with,

significant influences for id22 as well as eXperimentcity are found in the ufaFabrik, one of Berlin's most fascinating examples of culturally based, sustainable urban reclamation.

The *ufaFabrik* is a creative, non-profit redevelopment of buildings and spaces that were for decades used by the UFA film studio, a German Dream Factory (http://www. ufafabrik.de). Where films such as Fritz Lang's *Metropolis* were processed, screened, and stored, since 1979 an alternative community has been living and working. One of West Berlin's most spectacular squats, the ufaFabrik took the radical position right from the beginning that the spaces were reclaimed not exclusively for their private pleasure but rather to be made available for public use. ufaFabrik activists have been working for three decades to test and demonstrate what is possible with local places and resources, culturally, socially, and ecologically speaking. And so for more than thirty years now people coming from the neighborhood as well as around the city and even around the globe have been able to use the ufaFabrik as a *Freiraum* where the public is invited to be active in producing and enjoying culture (Figure 5.2). Thanks to its many inspiring projects including the organic bakery, alternative "Free School," solar and co-generation energy systems, neighborhood center, international cultural center, and much more, the ufaFabrik has been recognized as a UN Habitat Best Practice for the improvement of the urban environment.[10]

The Berlin Wall finally fell in 1989, making the Iron Curtain border separating East from West available for more peaceful activity. In the following euphoric months many new uses emerged on this liberated Death Strip, for example a number of Caravan Communities, such as the group of artists with their mobile trailers and wagons that occupied a section of this former no-man's-land, settling on the East Berlin side of a canal separating the Districts of Treptow and Kreuzberg. The *Gesamtkunstwerk* (Total Art Work) *Lohmühle* is at the time of writing in 2009

Figure 5.2 Romy and Sebastian in the ufaFabrik, Berlin-Tempelhof. Photograph by Michael LaFond.

still tolerated by the local government and loved by the local community, known for providing a publicly accessible space for cultural and ecological experiments, as well as a place for a number of people to live (http://www.lohmuehle-berlin.de/). One of the independent souls that has been squatting for more than eighteen years here is the Lohmühle's own Mayor Zosch, who has been pursuing his dream of an experimental-artistic-ecological-cultural lifestyle since Berlin's reunification. After many years of illegality, Zosch and friends have been given official permission to stay here, at least until 2012. Artists and activists are welcome to visit, live, and work with the Lohmühle, known for summer jazz festivals and ecological experiments. In summer the collection of trailers resembles a large playground, but in winter be prepared to chop a lot of wood for the oven in your trailer (Figure 5.3).

Also in this former East Berlin District is the *Sonnenhaus* (Sun House), a self-help housing project, which, thanks to a great deal of sweat-equity and the support of a non-profit foundation, has been able to buy and renovate a run-down building in a struggling part of the city (http://www.sonnenhaus-berlin.de). The old structures have been removed from the speculative market and in the last few years ecologically renewed as an intergenerational apartment building including organic café and store with public meeting space at the ground level. An expressed objective is offering peaceful alternatives, and spaces, in a neighborhood with problems ranging from unemployment to neo-Nazi groups. In Figure 5.4 posters can be seen on the pole in the foreground, alternatively advertising for the far right NPD nationalist party and for the Greens.

Located in the poor West Berlin District of Wedding, and significant as another example of an opening up of formerly private spaces, is the *ExRotaprint* cooperative, a socio-cultural redevelopment of a former industrial complex of buildings (http://www.exrotaprint.de). After years of organizing, a small team of artists with the

Figure 5.3 Experimental accommodations at the Gesamtkunstwerk Lohmühle, Berlin-Treptow. Photograph by Michael LaFond.

Figure 5.4 Sonnenhaus and political party posters in Berlin-Treptow. Photograph by Michael LaFond.

Figure 5.5 Michael and Lena from id22 with Les and Daniela, ExRotaprint artists, entering a studio at the project. Photograph by Michael LaFond.

assistance from architects and a non-profit foundation was able to buy and permanently remove the historical buildings from the market. In a neighborhood characterized by immigrants and high unemployment, the ExRotaprint project is committed for the long term to providing space for a mix of art and small business as well as educational and cultural initiatives. ExRotaprint, in reclaiming and restoring the former *Rotaprint* printing machine buildings, combines the potentials of spectacular architecture with the local needs of a socially marginal area and connects aesthetic qualities with socio-political activities (Figure 5.5).

By far the greatest challenge – and opportunity – regarding a recycling of spaces that Berlin has been confronted – and blessed – with is the conversion of the *Flughafen* (Airport) *Tempelhof* (http://www.berlin.de/flughafen-tempelhof/). This inner-city airport is best known for the *Lutfbrücke* (airlift) during 1948–1949, organized by the USA and Great Britain to supply West Berlin with food and other resources while the city's land supply routes were blocked by the Soviet Union. The Tempelhof airport was closed to air traffic at the end of October 2008, positively interpreted by some as an "opening" of the airport's buildings and spaces. The building was the largest in the world at the time of construction in the 1930s, only to be surpassed by the Pentagon. It is hoped that the area, which for a century was used and controlled by a combination of military and civilian flight agencies, meaning very limited public access and high levels of security, can now be made accessible to civil society uses.

And so the airport is the subject of ongoing, intensive discussions as to who should be reclaiming the spaces as well as how the area should be reused. As large investors are not being found to privatize the airport *en masse*, the city is giving more attention to a process-oriented involvement of a great number of smaller actors. In addition to the usual backroom negotiations, ideas are being called for internationally and competitions organized to find new uses for the area.

id22 along with many others is engaged in "opening" the airport, working for example with students from the RaumStrategien (Space Strategies) Program of the Berlin-Weißensee School of Design,[11] the Beuth University of Applied Sciences summer academy,[12] and other partners. RaumStrategien is an interdisciplinary master's program combining architecture and planning with public art and other creative fields to explore culturally based urban reuse and redevelopment strategies, especially emphasizing the potentials for art and artists. The summer academy is a four-week intensive course bringing students together from Berlin, New York City, and other areas to study sustainable design and land reuse approaches.

Crisis + experimentation, cultural research + development

eXperimentcity has been studying and supporting urban redevelopments, especially in Berlin's *Freiräume*, for more than six years now: over this time the going has got tougher in the world and this has begun to call forth a new generation of experimental projects. The previously reviewed examples are only a small sampling of Berlin's innovative landscape, as many dozens of projects are currently being planned with new ones coming along every month.[13] Although this article has focused on the "positive" side of reclaiming urban spaces, it must be noted there is also a long tradition in Berlin of resistance, for example to city renewal and elite space production initiatives suspected of leading to gentrification and further privatization of the public sphere. Often it is the act of protest or fighting to save something that gives birth to the idea of taking the next step and organizing more desirable developments.

Still, real and pressing questions for shrinking, or just stagnating, cities in Europe as well as North America and elsewhere remain. Capitalistic strategies for developing cities are challenged as never before, including long-accepted approaches to valuing, using, and reusing land. But in the current crisis we see possibilities of finding alternative, more efficient, more just, and more attractive ways for organizing ourselves. Technological innovations are important, but more significant is making progress with communicative, cooperative processes of placemaking. Through this experimentation arise new opportunities for cultural, sustainable planning, for community-building approaches to space production and management that serve to overcome fears of violence and terrorism.

Stressed economies and diversifying populations are calling for space- and placemaking strategies that work to develop idle spaces even when our cities are no longer growing. A goal is to recognize and take advantage of opportunities in vacant land and buildings, helping to increase understanding and support for informal and democratic approaches.

Although cooperatively designing and managing our own parks or our own housing is not easy, it is doable, and it provides us with living research and development centers – building blocks in the larger project of the sustainable redesign of our cities. In the end, we have not just the ecological challenge of recycling paper and bottles, but more importantly the social opportunity of redesigning land and buildings, saving natural resources while encouraging more communication and public space, in the process expressing ourselves and together creating a culture of sustainability.

Notes

1 Berlin's Department for Urban Development together with the Berlin Districts publicize building lots in the city. The Building Lot Management service provides information about more than 1,000 building plots. See http://www.stadtentwicklung.berlin.de/bauen/baulueckenmanagement/.
2 One of many Internet pages for the cultural sector and the creative industries is called "Creative City Berlin" (http://www.creative-city-berlin.de/).
3 For another review of creative sustainability in Berlin by the present author, 'A Planet of Cities', see http://www.worldchanging.com/archives/006497.html.
4 *Mediaspree Versenken* is a citizens' initiative working to fight river shore development visions proposed by local government and investors (http://www.ms-versenken.org/).
5 For a short review of the MARIE Baugemeinschaft see the WOHNPORTAL page: http://www.wohnportal-berlin.de/marie-marienburger-strasse-40berlin-prenzlauer-bergluxus-des-weitblicks-wohneigentum-zum-selbstkostenpreis-im-vordergrund-steht-wohnen-fuer-die-familie-sowie-die-einrichtung-verschiedener-gemeins/.
6 For more information about the citizen-created city park *Ein Platz für die Marie* see http://www.stadtentwicklung.berlin.de/wohnen/freiraeume/de/buergerengagement/platz-marie1.shtml.
7 For a review of the cooperation between id22 and OURs in Taipei regarding the

Treasure Hill project, see LaFond (2008). See also the homepage of the OURs organization, based in Taipei, Taiwan (http://www.ours.org.tw/).

8 For an English summary of the Berlin Agenda 21 see http://www.stadtentwicklung. berlin.de/agenda21/en/service.shtml and for the complete governmental resolution see http://www.berlin21.net/fileadmin/pdf/d15-5221.pdf.

9 For another review of projects related to eXperimentcity in Berlin, see LaFond (2007).

10 For a UN Habitat Best Practices review of the ufaFabrik in Berlin see http://www. bestpractices.org/database/bp_display_best_practice.php?best_practice_id=1454.

11 See http://www.kh-berlin.de/index.php5?groupID=20&Action=showGroup&local e=en.

12 See http://www.summer-academy.architekten-tfh.de/.

13 For short reviews of innovative housing models (in German), see http://www. wohnportal-berlin.de. This Internet platform is a virtual communications center for about 500 users every day. Also see http://www.eXperimentcity.net for more information about the Berlin network of creative reuses of vacant land and buildings: self-organized housing, cultural centers, and community garden initiatives.

Bibliography

LaFond, M. (1999) 'From Century 21 to Local Agenda 21: Sustainable Development and Local Urban Communities in East and West Berlin (Germany), and Seattle (United States)', unpublished doctoral dissertation, University of Washington.

—— (2007) 'Experimental Homes', *EXBERLINER: The English-Language Paper for Berlin*, May: 14–16.

—— (2008) 'Berlin Taipei Round Trip: eXperimentcity Meets Treasure Hill', *Umelec*, 1: 51–53.

CHAPTER 6

Re-city, Tokyo

Putting "publicness" into the urban building stocks

Shin Aiba and Osamu Nishida

Since the late 1990s, the word "sustainability" has been used commonly as a keyword in Japanese urban planning. One of the ways of realizing urban sustainability is the "utilization of building stock" through conversion, reform, and renewal of existing building structures particularly in older districts of cities. At that time, during the economic slowdown in the 1990s and early 2000s, developers and citizens were hesitant to invest in new buildings. For the first time in a long period, "utilization of building stock" was discussed again in the market economy as a realistic, promising choice. In particular, the market has discovered some cases where the cost or risk of removing old buildings and constructing new ones was higher than that of utilizing the existing building stock. After numerous feasibility studies were conducted, several stock utilization projects were put into action.

However, around 2005, various efforts by the market sector and the relaxation of regulations by the government began to gradually take effect, and the development and construction market took an upturn. Subsequently, efforts to utilize existing building stock were put aside. The economy recovered first in the central, high-land-price areas in cities, and then in the surrounding areas. In addition to the high-profile redevelopments such as the Roppongi Hills and the Mitsui Building in Jinbocho, small developments were conducted in many places, and the efforts to utilize old building stocks became less active. So, is "utilization of building stocks" already a thing of the past? Is stock utilization just a "poor man's" choice in a bad economy?

It is not hard to explain why stock utilization is important, particularly in light of global environmental issues such as waste reduction as well as preservation of urban heritage. However, the prospects for expanding the reutilization of building stocks remain challenging. So far, the existing attempts have focused primarily on improving the "marketability" of the building stocks. In contrast, there have been few attempts to improve their "publicness," including historical values, urban environmental performance, and harmony of townscape. Although "marketability" and "publicness" do not conflict with each other in all cases, there has been almost no successful attempt to integrate these two approaches of reutilizing urban building stocks in Japan. We (a project team at the Tokyo Metropolitan University) conducted studies and experimental practices in stock reutilization in the urban core areas of Tokyo in a period from 2003 to 2007 to add "publicness" to the stock utilization. This chapter presents the outcomes of these four-year activities.

Target area: Kanda, Tokyo

To study the problems, we chose Kanda as a case-study area because it faces many problems and possibilities under the high development pressure in central Tokyo. Located in the center of Tokyo, the Kanda area was developed in the Edo era (1603–1867) for merchants and craftsmen. The area was divided into small lots to be used in the construction of small buildings. However, the entire Kanda area was burned down in the Great Kanto Earthquake (1923), and the subsequent land adjustment has brought about significant modernization through the completion of a gridded street pattern. In the eighty-odd years since then, this area has been growing as the central business district of Japan. Now the district is occupied by buildings of various ages and shapes that sit close to each other.

Taking a look at the Kanda area, one can say positively that the area has a rich collection of building stock in a variety of manners, but others may have the impression that the area is a mess. As high-density land use is required in Kanda, the shape of a building is determined by the configuration of the parcel and the building height. The complexity can be attributed to the land adjustment projects introduced after the earthquake to the area where rows of temporary sheds were densely built by the local residents. The land adjustment projects created roads everywhere inside the city blocks, which made the subsequent reconstruction of the city easier. On the other hand, because of the occupation of the temporary sheds, the unit of land management before the earthquake (i.e., the size of the land sections into which large lands were divided for lease) remained unchanged. This resulted in a high number of small parcels that were sold and bought individually. With this background, as well as the good road conditions, Kanda was developed into a high-density, high-rise district inside Tokyo, in which a variety of land sizes led to the construction of buildings with various shapes (Figure 6.1).

Methods of urban design in the age of stock activation

The purpose of stock utilization is to renew and reuse the existing buildings without reconstructing them (Aoki 2001, Matsumura *et al.* 2007, Kobayashi *et al.* 2008). What urban design methods do we need to manage and coordinate the reconstruction, activation, and renewal of building stocks that are often conducted individually and separately? It should be noted here that typically each architectural activity is conducted by a private corporation, a public entity, or an individual in Japan. The purpose of urban design is to inform and coordinate each architectural activity from a city-based viewpoint in order to induce high-quality architectural activity. But how is this realized? We consider this problem by dividing the process into the following four stages.

1: sharing information

First of all, one needs to start the planning by understanding the status of each building stock in an area, analyzing its function, which is expected to work in the framework of the overall city functions, and sharing the information with the residents.

Figure 6.1 Bird's-eye view of Kanda (drawn using 3D-GIS). Source: Shin Aiba and Osamu Nishida.

2: sharing images on the space and cost

Most building stocks are owned privately, and it requires much energy and time to raise the owner's awareness. Information sharing is not enough to induce the citizens' architectural activities. It needs the additional provision of a detailed vision to the citizens by sharing with them the images of the space and cost.

3: individual constructions

The third stage is when various architectural activities are induced as a result of the second stage. In some buildings, for example, the air conditioners will be renewed with the additional purpose of improving the surrounding urban environment, and in some buildings the intended use will be changed by taking into account the balance with the surrounding city areas. The urban designer has the role of giving advice on these architectural activities and making adjustments.

4: evaluation and feedback of the constructions

The fourth stage is the stage of evaluation and feedback whereby each architectural activity is re-evaluated from the perspective of the district to see how the performance of the entire city district has improved and how the next architectural activity should be conducted. The repetition of the second, third, and fourth stages will form more coordinated city spaces.

Experiments in the Kanda area

As the first step of the project, we surveyed the building stocks in the Kanda area to accurately understand their status, and collected the earthquake risk data for each building stock. We then held a workshop to share the information with the citizens. At the same time, we also showed the citizens how the utilization of the existing building stocks could create valuable spaces by conducting actual renovation of some building stocks and temporal projects in some urban spaces.[1]

Sharing information on seismic risk

We issued the following maps of the Kanda area: the ground map of the Kanda district based on the earthquake history, the ground's characteristic period, the expected seismic intensity on the occurrence of an earthquake, the distribution map of structures and construction building stocks, the building's characteristic period, the distribution map of exterior materials, and the simulation of road impassibility. We also issued a booklet to provide the information in an easy-to-follow format. A workshop was held to report it to the residents' association in the Kanda area (Figure 6.2). The area where we held the debriefing session happened to have relatively good ground, and many buildings were securely built. The residents who participated in the session seemed to be proud of their district and architecture.

Figure 6.2 Scene from a citizens' workshop in the neighborhood. Photograph by Shin Aiba.

Sharing images on the space and cost

After we collected and analyzed the information for each building stock and reported them to the residents, the next questions were "how does this change the city?" and "how does this lead to the reutilization of each building stock?" The information may be able to change the citizens' consciousness to a certain degree but it is necessary to raise awareness and activate practical activities toward actual, physical space utilization. In other words, we need to proceed from the stage of sharing information to the stage of sharing images on the space and cost.

In Kanda, most building stock is owned by individuals, and it hence requires tremendous energy to change the stock. We tried, from a slightly different viewpoint, to share the "image of the space created by the utilization of the city building stock" by conducting social experiments to slightly change the spaces that had an intermediate nature between private building stock and public spaces. For this purpose we held three student workshops:

1 *Re-Street.* We first held a workshop, called "Re-Street," to study an alley among the existing building stocks. After developing ideas and communicating with local residents, the students conducted a project to create a space by covering the alley with wooden boards, a workshop with children, and a cinema party in the alley (Figure 6.3). Many people had nostalgic feelings because of the slatted wooden boards on the alley. Making canvas cloth walls involved a large number of children who had not known the alley as a playground. The adults also enjoyed watching the children during their playtime. Many people realized that the large cloth was being used to close alleys for parties and events, and learned about the history of the district during the film event. This activity showed that a slight change of alleys could create wonderful urban spaces and provide spaces for attractive events.
2 *Kuuchi+.* Next, a workshop called "Kuuchi+" was held, focusing on empty *spaces (kuuchi) around the existing building stocks. The students communic*ated with the local residents and conducted three projects (Figure 6.4). These projects involved organizing activities as temporary events.

    The first project, "Signboards of the Signboard Architecture," was an exhibition about the old Kanda town using an alley-shaped empty space between high-rise buildings. "Signboard architecture" refers to architecture for commercial uses such as stores that were built after the Great Kanto Earthquake and constructed with plate decorations on façades for fireproofing. They seem like signboards. The scaled photographs of the buildings showing the town's history were installed in a public open space between two buildings. There are two meanings in this project. First, these signboards induce the rediscovery of and fascination with historical art in Kanda. Second, they try to illustrate the possibility of utilizing exterior building walls in one of the public open spaces in the area.

    The second project, "Batten School," utilized an empty pilot space in front of the gymnasium where there was a primary school about forty years ago. The goal of this project was to create an evening school. A total of nine lecturers taught three subjects, namely People, History, and Skills, as related to the

Figure 6.3 Re-street: turning alleyways and streets into active social spaces. Photographs by Osamu Nishida.

traditions of Kanda. In the district, there is still a warmth and deep sense of history that many contemporary people have forgotten. As a result, a part of Kanda was revealed when we introduced the Batten School.

The third project, "Footbath Café," was a footbath using an empty space in the front garden of a building. The place is called a café, but it is more like a food court. People can buy food and drinks from the surrounding fast-food restaurants, stalls, and newsstands. Then they can take off their footwear and dip their feet into the baths. The project was very successful and a number of people would come by every day during the operating hours.

3   *Machi-oku*. The last workshop, called "Machi-oku," took place on the rooftops of the existing buildings. The students conducted two projects (Figure 6.5). The roofs are the parts of the buildings farthest from the town streets and are often used only as storage. This workshop demonstrated their potential as a public open space. The first project was a "Cinema Party on the Roof." The project proposed a new way of enjoying rooftops, the Kanda area, and the cityscape by projecting lights and images on surrounding buildings, using them as alternative screens in a part of central Tokyo. Amazing views were produced on the rooftops, where children chased the images and neighbors held a feast. The second project was a fantastic installation called "Rooftop Laundry." The clothes poles are made of 15-mm diameter metal bars. They are bent, welded, and painted in order to be used for hanging T-shirts. A large number of hanging T-shirts constantly alter the appearance of the rooftop according to

the changing wind. They represent the breeze and offer a sight of the natural comfort that is difficult to see on the ground in the city center. A total of over 120 people visited the project during the week. The event provided them with an opportunity to experience the extraordinary space on the rooftop, different from the normal everyday life on the ground.

Figure 6.4 Kuuchi+: bringing attention to old building façades and turning street corners into active public space. Photographs by Osamu Nishida.

Let us consider the relationship between the three workshops. An alley is just a part of the city space where anyone can come and go at any time, whereas an empty space (*kuuchi*) that lies inside a building stock is often off-limits to the public. For example, one needs to go through a building to reach the roof. The series of the workshops were conducted first outside the building stocks, but later inside them. In other words, we approached gradually from the streetscape into the buildings to examine possibilities of reutilizing the individual buildings for public use.

Held on the rooftop of a twenty-year-old office building, the experiment of "Machi-oku" occurred not only through the workshops, but also through the activation and renewal of building stocks. At the beginning of this article, we suggest the significance of reutilizing the building stocks through "publicness." This project is one such solution. In this particular case, the building owner is also a resident of Kanda, where the workshop to share information of seismic risk was held. Some time after the workshop, he contacted us. He wanted to have a seismic diagnosis

Figure 6.5 Machi-oku. Photographs by Osamu Nishida.

of the building and renovate the building (which has been used for business) by opening it up to the residents in order to suit his future life.

With the seismic diagnosis of the building showing its sufficient anti-earthquake performance, the renovation work of the building began. Particularly, two areas inside the building needed to be renovated. One was the residence area of the owner, and the other was the staircase and rooftop. In addition, there were rental office spaces managed by the owner. He wanted to prevent vacancy by creating a staircase space attractive for the tenants, and to create a semi-public space on the roof open to the local community via the staircase.

We renovated the staircase and rooftop by changing the lighting and the material of the walls. We then invited an artist to display his drawings in the staircase and on the rooftop. Several events were held for the display of the work by the artist. In addition, his friends came to play music in the staircase and perform contemporary dance on the roof (Figure 6.6). The performances were conducted in various ways in relationship to the artwork or with it as the background. The artist's work accentuated the value of the staircase as a medium for people and performances. The project was completed during the workshop "Machi-oku" in which the artist and students discussed in a serious way how to use the owner's roof space. Many citizens have since visited the staircase and rooftop. This was merely a small project but one that is significant in considering ways of building stock utilization with a public nature. In urban stock reutilization, it is important that many citizens first sympathize with this kind of project, and then develop ways to utilize their own stock in a manner similar to this case.

Conclusion: activation and renewal of building stock

To create an urban space by reutilizing existing urban stock, attention should be paid not only to the "marketability" of the stock, but also to the methods that enhance its "publicness." In this four-year project, we first surveyed the existing building stock in Kanda, Tokyo, to understand the stock accurately. We then reported the information to the citizens to let them know the relative importance of each building stock in the district. We also held the social experimental workshops to show to the citizens that a small renovation could create a wonderful public urban space. The results from these experiments provided important opportunities for the citizens to discuss and envision how the improved publicness of the building stock can enhance the value of the district and the city. This project presents an initial step in ways that a richer variety of approaches can be made to reuse the existing building stock and enliven both the private and public realms of the city.

Figure 6.6 Renovated staircase and performance on rooftop. Photographs by Osamu Nishida.

Note

1   The project was carried out as a research project by the Department of Architecture
    and Building Engineering at the Tokyo Metropolitan University. The project was
    funded by a research grant from the central government, entitled "Targeted Support
    for Creating World-standard Research and Education Bases (Centers of Excellence,
    a.k.a. COE)" by the Ministry of Education, Culture, Sports, Science, and Technology
    (MEXT), and another part of the project was funded by Housing Research
    Foundation (HRF). The Department of Architecture and Building Engineering started
    the research project "Development of Technologies for Activation and Renewal of
    Building Stocks in Megalopolis" as a COE program from 2003 to 2007, and the
    Kanda area research was carried out as a part of the project. (See http://www.comp.
    tmu.ac.jp/4-met/il/ for more details.)

Bibliography

Aoki, S. (2001) *Refine Architecture: Shigeru Aoki Complete Works*, Tokyo: Kenchiku
    Shiryo Kenkyusya.
Kobayashi, K., Mitamura, T., Kitsutaka, Y., and Toriumi, M. (2008) *Architectural
    Conversions in the World*, Tokyo: Kajima Institute.
Matsumura, S., Shinbori, M., Seike, T., Satoh, K., Wakiyama, Y., and Tsunoda, M.
    (2007) *How to Lead Building Regeneration: Building Engineering Primer in Stock
    Age*, Tokyo: Ichigaya.

CHAPTER 7

Claiming residual spaces in the heterogeneous city

Erick Villagomez

How are we to approach the design of existing North American cities amidst increasing population pressures, the ever-increasing complexity and diversity of people and uses, and dwindling resources? This is the question that current and future generations are bound to face.

Residual space, as it exists today in the form of vast tracts of underused parking lots, derelict urban sites, obsolete industrial wastelands, and similar environments, is a relatively recent urban phenomenon. Alan Berger describes this fact in *Drosscapes: Wasting Land in Urban America* (Berger 2006), as he follows the creation of wasteland as a natural result of modern urbanization and the complex interaction of social, technological, and economic processes that drive contemporary urban growth.

Historically, land was too valuable a resource to be simply left unused and neglected. From the medieval fortified towns throughout Europe to the dense cities of Asia, urban life and intense land use were interdependent phenomena. This tendency continues today, within countries that lack the economic means to do otherwise. Only within the past century – a time of unprecedented material wealth and technological progress – and within developed countries has this legacy of spatial utilization been forgotten.

Past urban intensification through enhancing residual spaces was also closely tied to other factors, including the smaller size of settlements, local involvement, and the slower pace at which urban centers developed. Thus, the walkable scale of these cities and towns allowed for direct daily contact by those people (often local residents) who ultimately changed their built environment. Furthermore, it accounted for the beautiful craft and care with which they engaged their settlements – as is often the case when decision- makers live in the neighborhoods they transform. Lastly, the extended periods of time over which the evolution of cities took place allowed for longer, more thorough periods of observation as well as piecemeal implementation and adjustment; a fact clearly supported by Edmund Bacon's well-known analysis of the spatial development of European public spaces over the centuries. Referring to the evolution of Piazza San Marco between the ninth and twelfth centuries, he notes "the space design over this period was a self-conscious process and was the result of a long series of 'agonizing decisions' constantly aimed at perfecting the squares" (Bacon 1976: 105).

Despite the fact that these processes of intensifying residual spaces have created some of the most magnificent, interesting, and renowned spaces on the globe, current urban design and planning practices work against such undertakings. The creation of meaningless, residual spaces has reached an extreme in North America where early illusions of limitless material resources have translated into a value system that encourages – and legally mandates – low-intensity land use. Yet, despite policies and laws, there are various local examples of intense, creative spatial use. Such examples, however, are often limited to preserved historical urban neighborhoods – spatial remnants of the time when resource management was of the utmost importance – or lower-income areas in which residents must make the most of the space that surrounds them.

As a greater urban phenomenon, the large auto-oriented size of modern cities, rapid development practices, deindustrialization, and increasingly centralized political structure encourage the creation and maintenance of neglected space. This occurs as those in charge of urban development make decisions far from the neighborhoods that are affected, without the observation necessary to make meaningful decisions or the desire to do so. Technological and economic developments have simultaneously made expanding the city outward more profitable than focusing on enhancing and intensifying the existing urban fabric.

Times are changing, however. As resource scarcity, population pressures, and demands to create a better-quality living environment increase, we are being forced to re-evaluate the decisions and values of the recent past. The simplistic birds-eye view and "master planning" approach to the urbanism that has dominated the past century – and, in turn, created the majority of North American cities – has demonstrated itself to be unfit to supply meaningful solutions to the issues faced by contemporary urban development. This has been achieved through a deeper understanding of the complex social, economic, and environmental systems that govern the world in which we live. In response, the traditional top-down processes that supported typical city planning are starting to dissolve and opening up to more inclusive and democratic planning processes, in which the public is called upon to make important decisions that govern urbanization.

However, the traditional planning processes that outsource important local decisions to "specialists" who have minimal contact with neighborhoods they transform have left deeply embedded cultural myths and values that have led us to neglect the creativity and improvisation inherent to typical urban processes. In short, we, the public, have lost our critical sense of what constitutes good urbanism, and how and why to go about transforming the cities in which we live. This is detrimental to the evolution of robust cities and is largely due to our detachment from how people interact directly with the everyday built environment.

We must relearn how to look more carefully at the existing urban environment and understanding its potential and limitations. Within this context, the neglected and residual spaces left by the modernization process offer a great benefit to our ailing cities. For not only are they plentiful, but also, given their current derelict state, they often require minimum economic investment to see drastic improvements.

On the global scale, the intense use of residual spaces occurs throughout older settlements, developing countries, and high-density centers where Western patterns of settlement are not viable. With humble gratitude, we must turn to these places and seek lessons regarding how to create more humane urban landscapes.

Although the sizes, shapes, and activities within neglected urban spaces can – and do – vary dramatically, their reinterpretation provides us with a glimpse into how we can begin to address the issues around making our existing cityscapes more inclusive, and ultimately, more livable. Giovanni La Varra describes the importance and pervasiveness of these "Post-It" spaces:

> In the city center or on the edges, at the heart of the nineteenth century tissue or in the great external zones, they compose an infinite catalogue of informal spaces with innumerable articulations . . . literally occupying the urban public space whose meaning and value they transfigure.
>
> (La Varra 2001: 426)

One important step in this direction is to identify and articulate the types of residual spaces common to urban landscapes, learn how they are created, and understand their potential uses. Towards this end, residual spaces can be categorized into eight spatial types. In no particular order of importance, they are *Spaces Between*, *Spaces Around*, *Rooftops*, *Wedges*, *Redundant Infrastructure*, *Oversized Infrastructure*, *Void Spaces*, and *Spaces Below* (Figure 7.1). A short description of each, accompanied by illustrative examples – both local and abroad, as well as built and open space options – will serve to show how each spatial type carries a diversity of inherent opportunities.

Spaces between

This type of residual space often results from urban demolition, municipal bylaws (e.g., side setbacks), or the elimination of obsolete functions (e.g., service entrances). The proliferation of lot-centered single-family dwellings throughout North America and the side yard setbacks that enforce this settlement pattern have made this one of the most abundant types of residual space. The dimensions of *Spaces Between* vary dramatically in width and length, and thus offer some of the most abundant and interesting opportunities for appropriation.

In the residential context where they occur so frequently, one side is often used to circulate between the rear and front yards while the other is left neglected – used for the storage of rarely used objects such as rusty bikes, leftover construction material, and firewood. Although many reasons contribute to this condition the most detrimental is the minimal dimensions of the setback (typically 3–5 ft) – making it difficult to use for purposes other than storage – as well as the location in space within intimate view of the neighbors.

One of simplest solutions to this condition is offered by the unique settlement pattern of historic Charleston, South Carolina, where zero lot line setbacks create side yard outdoor 'rooms' integrated into the larger built fabric of the city. Renee Chow's in-depth study of Charleston and other dwelling patterns in *Suburban Space: The Fabric of Dwelling* (2002) thoroughly explains how this organization of detached homes creates an interdependent structure of alternating interior and exterior spaces, and ultimately, a robust urban fabric.

In the urban context, where building walls often enclose very narrow residual

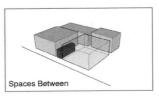

Spaces Between

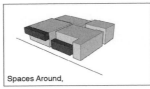

Spaces Around,

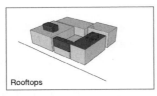

Rooftops

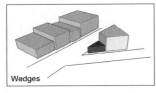

Wedges

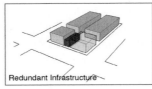

Redundant Infrastructure

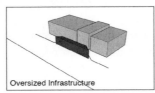

Oversized Infrastructure

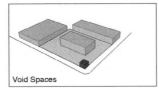

Void Spaces

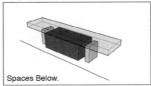

Spaces Below.

Figure 7.1 A typology of urban residual spaces. By Erick Villagomez.

spaces, more extreme solutions result. These include appropriation for mutually supportive commercial purposes (e.g., cigar and music shops, where products can be hung from walls and a linear circulation pattern is desired) and/or the creation of very thin buildings. The renowned 10-ft wide spite house in the North End of Boston, Massachusetts, is a great example (Figure 7.2). Not only is minimal space put to good use – offering occupants unique forms of dwelling – but also, its small size offers entrepreneurs and homebuyers an affordable alternative to expensive city costs.

As open-air spaces, *Spaces Between* offer great environmental attributes. In the past such spaces allowed for light and air flow within buildings. Asian urban courtyard buildings (variations of which are found throughout the world) are

Figure 7.2 Skinny house (Boston, MA, USA). Source: Wikipedia.

excellent examples. On each urban lot, this building type often incorporated a central courtyard with narrow breezeways connecting to surrounding streets. In tandem, these shafts of light and air maximized natural ventilation throughout the building, and gave inhabitants a rich palette of open spaces in which to dwell. These few examples give us a glimpse of the potential richness and diversity of cityscapes once human creativity is allowed to engage this type of residual space.

Spaces around

Within the past century, the rules and values governing how buildings interact with the public realm have changed radically. In general, these changes led to standards that pushed new buildings further from the street, creating an intermediary zone between the public street and the private interior space of the building. In historic city centers, this transformation happened in piecemeal fashion, breaking up street walls and creating odd pockets of neglected gaps around buildings.

The contemporary re-evaluation of modern planning practices and its ideas about the division between public and private space has opened up new potential as to what can occur to the residual spaces around buildings. One interesting contemporary urban phenomenon, which harkens back to the arcades of the ancient world, is the creation of "elevated office spaces" above existing sidewalks that create a layered and complex edge along construction sites. Although these are temporary in nature, one can't help but wonder about the opportunities of such constructs: where would this type of architecture be suitable? Bordering the edges of fragile ecological zones? What activities can be accommodated?

More typically, the spaces around buildings have been "thickened" in order to take advantage of street activity. This is seen most often along residential streets that have transformed into intense commercial corridors. Some of the most interesting examples exist in Montreal, Canada, where street level spaces of old residential buildings have been appropriated for commercial activities and extended to engage the street. The rooftops of these commercial extensions, in turn, have become transitional residential platforms – accessed via stairs that run along one side of the store – for the dwellings above (Figure 7.3).

Interesting solutions as to what can be done with *Spaces Around* buildings can also be found in older suburbs, as well. Such is the case in the Grandview-Woodland neighborhood of Vancouver, Canada, where one encounters a small corner store barnacled to the front of a typical single-family detached home (see Figure 7.4). One can easily see how such an example offers important potential options for suburban area transitioning into denser and more intensive residential neighborhoods.

Conversely, when this type of space is left unbuilt, another set of opportunities arise: informal squares, sidewalk cafes, spaces for the display of food and products are but a few ways that it can be – and has been – used. Although overlaying an ecological structure within such open spaces has great opportunities relevant to the concerns of our time, currently such potentials remain unexplored.

Figure 7.3 Rue St. Laurent (Montreal, Quebec, Canada). Photograph by Erick Villagomez.

Rooftops

Rooftops offer the most abundant and least recognized form of residual space. They are phenomena that appear in various forms throughout high- and low-density urban landscapes. Yet, despite this, there are rarely any meaningful discussions on the potential uses and the multiple forms that rooftop development can take.

The easiest and most popular form of rooftop use is for plants and vegetation. Green roofs have remained popular for centuries throughout the world, and continue to be built. In North America, urban heat, island concerns, and densification have revitalized an interest in rooftop gardens and the technologies required to construct them. Unfortunately, many green roofs remain inaccessible to the public, owing to bylaws and regulations regarding egress and fire safety.

One must look abroad to see other potential opportunities offered by rooftops.
Two Tokyo projects will serve to demonstrate how roofs are used in ways that layer
different and potentially conflicting activities. The Fuji Kindergarten designed by
Tezuka Architects uses the roof as an extension of the central courtyard playground
located at ground level (Figure 7.5). Although there is no typical play equipment on
the roof, small design elements encourage the children to interact with it directly,
such as rope ladders that allow the kids to climb onto the skylights and the slide
that connects the roof to the lower playground. The Hanamidori Cultural Center by
Toyo Ito and Atelier Bow-Wow is a larger-scale example where a public roof garden
is located on top of a cultural facility.

The latter examples serve to show the diversity of uses that rooftops offer urban
civilization. Dismissing such projects as irrelevant to contemporary North American
cities would be detrimental to future possibilities for urban development. The
increasing pressure to densify implies packing an increasing number of activities
and people in less space – and thus layering functions creatively. Using rooftops in
diverse ways offers us a solution to increasing the quality and quantity of space,
simultaneously.

Figure 7.5 Fuji Kindergarten (Tachikawa, Japan). Photograph by Jeffrey Hou.

Wedges

The urban environment consists of a layering of several different physical, social, and natural patterns. Wedges often occur as a result of the intersection of these different urban phenomena (e.g., conflicting grids systems) and/or infrastructural elements (e.g., railroad tracks) that leave irregularly shaped urban conditions.

Because these sites are irregular, small wedge spaces are often undeveloped and left simply as neglected spaces. These spaces offer a great opportunity to contribute to and enrich the public realm by being appropriated for undervalued functions. Such was the case when Vancouver officials allowed the transformation of a neglected wedge space below the Georgia Street Viaduct into an urban skate park.

Written about in various magazines and publications, this controversial decision has given skateboarding youth a place to practice their sport and has added to Vancouver's palette of public spaces.

Aside from the creation of public open spaces, small neglected wedge spaces can be sites for unique architecture. At the large scale, people are familiar with wedge-shaped buildings such as New York City's Flat Iron. However, buildings need not always be so extravagant, as small irregularly shaped lots can support buildings of various sizes and functions. The Kadokko restaurant in Setagaya-ku Tokyo and several others described in Atelier Bow-Wow's *Pet Architecture Guide Book* (Kajima and Tsukamoto 2002: 105) demonstrate how extremely small buildings can be creatively accommodated within irregular spaces. Not only do such installations create interesting architectural highlights, but also they serve to intensify the urban experience in a delightful way.

Redundant infrastructure

This type of residual space primarily exists in the form of redundant laneway systems and/or urban infrastructure that has fallen out of use (e.g., dead-end streets). Given this, they are usually found in older parts of the city that have a street-alley urban pattern and/or whose structure has undergone radical transformation. Although

Figure 7.6 Alma Laneway (Vancouver, BC, Canada). Photograph by Erick Villagomez.

rarely found in the contemporary city, the appropriation of this type of space offers the potential creation of wonderful, well-defined open spaces. Two Vancouver examples of different scales serve to show the range of opportunities offered by these residual spaces.

Completed in 2002, the Napier Greenway was a community project done in collaboration with the City of Vancouver, neighborhood residents and artists, and the Faculty of Landscape Architecture at the University of British Columbia. Through the process of holding workshops and on-site information sessions, it saw the transformation of a dead-end street into a new public plaza/community gathering and garden space that links one of Vancouver's busiest commercial streets to the local community center, elementary school, and secondary school.

On the other side of the city lies a similar solution at a much smaller scale. Adjacent to a high-traffic road and between a couple of one-story buildings, the 12 ft. space of a redundant laneway system was transformed into a charming, intimate public space through the addition of two benches, permeable paving, a garbage can, and potted plants (Figure 7.6). As is the case with all neglected spaces, small simple solutions have a large impact.

Given the importance and popularity of open spaces within existing neighborhoods, the above projects demonstrate how neglected spaces can be easily transformed into meaningful public places. Beyond that, however, they also

Figure 7.7 CD shop on wheels (Toronto, Ontario, Canada). Photograph by Erick Villagomez.

show how an ecological infrastructure (through the inclusion of permeable paving, gardens, etc.) can be integrated into the existing city. With the help of certain high-profile design projects – such as the preservation and redesign of New York's High Line – the importance of these types of transformations is slowly being recognized and implemented.

Oversized infrastructure

It is well known that engineering practices of the past century – anticipating future growth – have favored going beyond the calculated requirements for urban infrastructure. In many cases, however, the projected rates fail to materialize, leaving oversized land ripe for appropriation. Given this, this type of residual space results primarily from municipal traffic engineering practices that oversize roads, arterials, and rights-of-way in anticipation of overestimated automobile traffic.

The vast linear spaces lining everyday highways have a lot of potential in this respect. The large, treeless widths of the rights-of-way provide access to natural light and, thus, make them ideal locations for gardens, parks, and similar uses that need an abundance of direct daylight without any stringent acoustic requirements. Such practices also can easily overlap with the need to filter the pollutants emitted by adjacent cars. With the current focus on moving the public away from automobile use, the oversized rights-of-way of our highways are ripe for reinterpretation. If we look at these spaces closely, we can see that many innovative practices are already under way in many locations across North America.

Oversized infrastructure also exists in more urban environments. This CD shop on wheels along Toronto's heavily used Queen Street West (Figure 7.7) temporarily transforms the parking lane into a store – creating a double-loaded pedestrian sidewalk. Similar, less elegant solutions occur along commercial streets, where people park their automobiles in the under-used parking lanes and sell goods to passers-by.

This mobile "auto commerce" adds an interesting layer of temporary uses to the parking lanes that exist throughout North American commercial streets and is an affordable alternative to conventional land-based properties. Furthermore, these activities enliven the public realm through intensifying activities along sidewalk edges.

Void spaces

Owing to the proliferation of the suburbs, this is arguably the most common type of residual space that exists in North America. *Void Spaces* are described here as large, underutilized spaces surrounding buildings. Although intrinsically related to spaces around, their large scale holds many different opportunities and, thus, demands a separate category. Void spaces are directly related to areas of lower densities and/or land values, and often currently exist in the form of large parking lots. Given the scale of the space available, this type offers the most options and solutions can be implemented incrementally.

With so much space allocated to parking, shopping malls have been among the first locations where void spaces have been dealt with. Various projects – built and

unbuilt – engage the issue, attempting to transform underused parking spaces into usable, profit-generating commercial space. The addition to Park Royal Shopping Center in North Vancouver, Canada, is a case in point, where its original oversized parking lot was transformed into a new "lifestyle" mall. Another example is the Fruitvale Village in Oakland, California, which transforms a BART parking lot into a mixed-use commercial and office complex.

Figure 7.8 Parking lot kiosks (Portland, Oregon, US). Photograph by Erick Villagomez.

At a more modest scale, there are many North American examples of small-scale commercial activities appropriating neglected void spaces. This condition is evident throughout downtown Portland, where semi-permanent, small kiosks – some including covered seating areas – occupy parking spaces and create a thin commercial crust along the lot's edges (Figure 7.8). These minute urban additions extend pedestrian activity along an otherwise lifeless street edge and are also home to some of the best eateries in town.

Spaces below

These neglected spaces vary in shape and size, and are directly related to large infrastructural elements, such as highway overpasses and elevated rail lines. On account of conservative regulations regarding maintenance, these spaces are often left open and neglected, being used primarily for activities such as parking. At best, they are appropriated by local residents and transformed into community gardens.

This need not be so, however. *Spaces Below* have the potential to enrich the surrounding communities through the creation of diverse built environments. Figure 7.9 shows how the space underneath the Keio Rail Line has been used for housing. A gap is left between housing units, built within the bridge structure, and the bridge above in order to accommodate regular maintenance.

Figure 7.9 Keio Rail
Line Housing (Tokyo,
Japan). Photograph by
Jeffrey Hou.

Closer to home, an initiative looking at highway underpasses in Chicago
developed design alternatives demonstrating how these neglected spaces can be
transformed into meaningful, useful public spaces (see Berman 2005). In particular,
three possibilities were explored in detail: transforming space between structural
bays into small businesses; an open art gallery; and transportation storage. These
examples give one an idea of the diversity of uses that can inhabit these common
residual spaces. Other examples include Portland's well-known Saturday Market
under the Burnside Bridge and the new Colonnade Park in Seattle under the I-5
Highway.

Reinvigorating the urban environment through claiming residual space

Claiming residual spaces lies in opposition to current city planning practices and engages the city at the intimate scale of the person, focusing on the potential of ordinary spaces within our built environment. As demonstrated through showcasing a few of the rich precedents worldwide, exploiting and transforming neglected spaces that exist throughout our cities is one of the most direct ways to create a more equitable and dynamic urban environment. Moreover, the transformation of these everyday spaces can have large social, economic, and ecological impacts on the livability and quality of our cities. Given that such spaces are often in disrepair, small interventions need not require large capital investment, particularly through the engagement of local communities and individuals.

What is needed, however, is the will to look beyond typical regulatory practices and keep one's eyes and mind open for opportunities. Historically, this was intricately related to the strong relationship between decision-makers and the neighborhoods they transformed – a relationship that has long since been disrupted.

In light of the vast changes that have occurred in our understanding of the complex forces that shape urban development, this now places much of the onus on local residents, their keen awareness of the urban environment around them, and their ability to influence absentee decision-makers. Fortuitously, the latter coincides with the recent rise of democratic, community-informed planning processes.

Cities have been – and always will be – dynamic entities. They are constantly being transformed unpredictably in accordance with the various forces exerted upon them. As a strategy, reclaiming residual spaces provides a venue for testing innovative, unconventional urban ideas through rethinking the overlooked potential of undervalued sites. Creativity and improvisation are inherent to this process. Only through taking responsibility for the creation and evolution of the environments in which we live can we truly point ourselves in the direction of a better future.

Bibliography

Bacon, E. (1976) *Design of Cities*, New York: Penguin.

Berger, A. (2006) *Drosscape: Wasting Land in Urban America*, New York: Princeton Architectural Press.

Berman, C. (2005) 'Bringing Life to Underpasses'. Online. Available HTTP: http://www.gapersblock.com/detour/bringing_life_to_the_underpasses/ (accessed 29 August 2005).

Chow, R. (2002) *Suburban Space: The Fabric of Dwelling*, Berkeley: University of California.

Kaijima, M. and Tsukamoto, Y. (2002) *Pet Architecture Guide Book: Living Spheres*, Volume 2, Tokyo: World Photo Press.

La Varra, G. (2001) 'Post-It City: The Other European Public Space', *Mutations*. New York: Actar.

PART THREE

PLURALIZING

CHAPTER 8

Claiming Latino space

Cultural insurgency in the public realm[1]

Michael Rios

Latinos are the largest minority group in the United States, with over 40 million members, or 14 percent of the population, and are projected to reach 24.4 percent of the population by the year 2050 (Suro 2005).[2] In California, the most populous state in the country, Latinos now comprise over a third of the state's population and are projected to triple to over 31 million, or 52 percent, by 2050 (State of California 2007). As this growth continues throughout this century, it is likely to affect the racial, cultural, social, and even spatial character of regions and cities. Further, unlike other waves of immigrants in US history, the association and/or proximity of many Latinos to their places of origin has produced a transnational identity and behavior that has implications ranging from institutions as large as the World Bank (in terms of remittances back to originating countries) to phenomena as personal as the choice to assimilate and language use.

Taken together, these issues will lead to conflicts and contests over space and values in the United States, as well as tremendous social and cultural potential. However, little is understood about Latinos as this group includes people of different races, ethnicities, and religions that identify, through birth, ancestry, or social imagination, with Latin American countries of origin. Latino identity is also a cultural association as this group includes people with different social and political histories. Dominant discourses in the media depict Latinos as low-wage laboring immigrants who reside in the barrios of major metropolitan areas and/or rural border towns along the US/ Mexico border. Although these places comprise a portion of the geography where Latinos live, there is far greater variety in where this growing population calls home. For example, in predominantly Latino neighborhoods, there is a shift toward greater diversity than often perceived. These neighborhoods are home to both immigrant and native born, Spanish and English speakers, the middle class and the poor.

In considering the prospects for Latino urbanism, this chapter describes ways public space is claimed by Latino immigrant communities in the United States. Others have discussed the topic of Latino urbanism in terms of urban politics (Dávila 2004, Diaz 2005) and its relation to contemporary paradigms such as New Urbanism (Mendez 2003). However, absent in this discourse is the expression and instrumentality of culture in the public realm. In the following discussion, culture is inclusive of institutions, customs, interventions, and knowledge. From this perspective, culture serves as a creative force to instigate a shift in the use, identity, and meanings of public space. Conceptualizing culture vis-à-vis spatial production provides affordances for social imagination that can lead toward self-awareness, empowerment, and, ultimately, political efficacy.[3]

As a heuristic to analyze culture in spatial production, the following describes three types of spaces – *adaptive*, *assertive*, and *negotiative* – along a continuum to discuss different ways Latinos make group claims in the city. The first category, adaptive spaces, consists of those environments that are appropriated for everyday use including vacant properties, streets, and parking lots. The second type emerges when space is politicized to challenge dominant symbols and codes. Assertive spaces express an insurgent identity, especially when minority group claims are not represented. Last, negotiative spaces represent the leading edge of cultural interchange in the public realm. These spaces move beyond symbolic representation of a particular group toward the formation of polyvalent communities and the recognition of plural understandings. Collectively, these three types of spaces have implications for the planning and design of urban space and how spatial production can contribute to a process of affirming cultural identity and raising group consciousness.

Before presenting the different types of space mentioned, a brief discussion of public space is warranted. There is extensive literature on the topic whether presented as a domain, realm, or sphere that includes, among others, the effects of global capitalism and the privatization, consumption, cultural identity, and environmental behavior (Harvey 1989, Low 2000, Sennett 2000, Sorkin 1992, Whyte 1980, Zukin 1995). The use of, access to, and control of public space is increasingly a political issue. In a post-9/11 era, struggles over public space have become a battleground for issues related to terrorism, anti-immigration, and xenophobia, among other conflicts. With respect to the planning of urban space, manifestations of these antagonisms include regulatory mechanisms such as zoning ordinances and land use laws that can have the effect of limiting or barring access to basic social goods such as affordable housing, public transit, parks, and open space. In the United States, some examples include gang injunctions, curfew laws, the criminalization of undocumented renters, and government-designated "free speech" zones. Related, there has been a focus on the topic of citizenship (Barnett and Low 2004, Isin 2002, Low and Smith 2006, Wastl-Walter *et al.* 2005). Much of this work aims to reframe the issues of rights from those of individual citizens toward the idea that all citizens have rights to the spaces of the city. If the city is, as was the polis in ancient Greece, the territorially bounded space for a political community, then the argument goes that all urban inhabitants should (in theory) have access to the full range of benefits that the city provides. This includes not only positive but also negative rights: against displacement, discrimination in zoning, spatial segregation, etc.

Many of these theoretical developments draw from Henri Lefebvre's seminal work on "the right to the city" (1991, 1996) to argue for new citizenship claims at the scale of the city and beyond (Brenner 2000, McCann 2002, 2005, Mitchell 2003, Purcell 2003). New conceptions of citizenship and the city as a space for group claims draw attention to possibilities for public space praxis as a vehicle to encourage, facilitate, and organize groups toward common understandings and collective action. This allows new uses, identities, and meanings to emerge as an outcome of public space production. Adopting this perspective necessitates a reflexive stance in order to consider how the transformation of public space can serve to build the cultural capacity of different social groups. Given this, the built environment is a manifestation of evolving social relations in space and time that can be measured through cultural identity formation and dialogue between different social groups and institutions.

Latino urbanism: space, agency, and cultural insurgency

A growing number of cities in the United States and elsewhere are now home to transnational populations whose cultural practices differ not only from the majority, but also from prior generations of immigrants. Adding to this complexity are regional differences with respect to origin and destination, race, socio-economic status, gender, and age – distinctions that are not exclusive to Latinos. However, what makes public space distinctly Latino are the social and cultural norms that manifest in patterns of use, spatial practice, and material characteristics that derive from a particular history, time, and place. In the following, I describe three types of spaces along a continuum – from spaces of appropriation and adaptation to spaces that are brokered between different social groups – to demonstrate how culture operates in and through spatial production. The purpose is to offer contrasting examples that identify public space as a vital resource for cultural survival and resiliency. Relatedly, I argue that creative agents and the material spaces they create are vital to the formation of cross-cultural alliances between social groups.

Adaptive spaces of everyday urbanism

Much has been written about "everyday urbanism" drawing on the work of Michel de Certeau (1984) and others to valorize human participation in urban spaces that either negate or transgress the dominant logic of capitalism and how related processes of globalization strip the city of meaning (Jameson 1991). The everyday landscapes and enacted environments of local communities and identities are emphasized as opposed to the official public realm produced by the professional disciplines (Chase et al. 1999). Critics of everyday urbanism argue that it is overly populist and romantic (Kelbaugh 2001, Speaks 2005). Still, the strength of discourses of everyday urbanism is that they stress temporal processes over urban form, and use value over exchange value in the experience, perception, and meaning of public space. As a material expression of everyday urbanism, adaptive spaces are unclaimed environments that are appropriated for economic and social uses. This includes vacant properties, streets, parking lots, and other "terrain vague." Such indeterminate zones in the landscape are often perceived as indicators of decay and abandonment. However, these sites are also appropriated for spontaneous, improvisational, and creative uses. Some examples include sites where day laborers congregate (Figure 8.1) or parking lots that transform into informal swap meets and vending sites (Easton 2007, Valenzuela et al. 2006).

There are also "in-between" spaces that delineate a threshold between the public and the private realms of individual households and residential streets, restaurants,

Figure 8.1 Day laborers pass time playing dominoes in suburban Atlanta while waiting for work. Photograph by Terry Easton, August 2003.

Figure 8.2 Casitas in New York City provide a social space for Puerto Rican diaspora communities. Photograph by Daniel Winterbottom.

and sidewalks (Arreola 1988, Rojas 1993). Other instances of adaptive spaces include vernacular landscapes and the use of streets, open spaces, and buildings for social purposes such as plazas, markets, and community gardens (Apontes-Pares 2000, Arreola 1992, Forsyth et al. 2001, Sciorra 1996). One example is the Puerto Rican vernacular house, or "casita," which serves as a social hub in many New York City neighborhoods (Aponte-Pares 1997, 1998, Sciorra and Cooper 1990). Here, vacant lots are converted into culturally specific community gardens as the setting for playing dominos, pig roasts, and salsa, among other activities (Figure 8.2). The casita provides a space to share a "common sense" of territorial identity with a homeland other than the one that is currently being inhabited. The social processes that drive the use and making of these spaces are many, and emerge out of the particular histories of (im)migrant and diaspora groups. Paradoxically, the diaspora experience for many groups is essentially about settling down, but having a home, real or imagined, elsewhere.

Assertive spaces of insurgent citizenship

Among planning scholars, some have theorized the possibilities for "insurgent citizenship" and the promotion of "insurgent practice" that aim to support new citizenship claims (Douglass and Friedmann 1998, Friedmann 2002, Holston 2008, Holston and Appadurai 1999). What can be drawn from this work is that rights and claims are a defining characteristic of citizenship. However, there is a tendency to conflate the possibilities of insurgency with the pedestrian practices of immigrant, ethnic, and indigenous communities when empirical evidence on political efficacy is lacking.[4] Moreover, while speculating about the institutional basis for citizenship claims, theorists of insurgent citizenship say little about how the spaces of the city provide the material basis for group claims. From a cultural perspective, I would like to argue that insurgent citizenship might also be understood in the public realm as assertive space that anchors group solidarity in the urban landscape. These are spaces that express an explicit cultural identity. Common examples include public festivals and rituals such as Día de los Muertos in parts of northern and southern California or the Puerto Rican Day parade in New York City (Brandes 1998, Duany 2003). Assertive spaces also challenge existing codes and symbols, resulting in changing meanings of public space such as Los Angeles's Old Plaza and Olvera Street or Paseo Boriqua in Chicago's Humboldt Park neighborhood (Estrada 1999, Flores-Gonzales 2001, Ramos-Zayas 2007) (Figure 8.3).

An example of a more politicized space is Chicano Park in the neighborhood of Barrio Logan in San Diego, California (Ford and Griffin 1981). Chicano Park emerged out of protest when California Department of Transportation (Caltrans) planners decided to build the Coronado Bridge through the heart of the community, but failed to provide a park promised to the community. Residents occupied the construction site under the bridge, chaining themselves to bulldozers, with the result that the city provided a park. Inspired by these protest activities and the growing Chicano movement, community artists painted murals as a way to claim the space as theirs. In 1980, Chicano Park was officially designated a San Diego historical site (Figure 8.4).

Figure 8.3 Paseo
Boriqua marks the
territory along Division
Street in the heart of
Chicago's Puerto Rican
diaspora community.
Photograph by Angel
Nieves.

Figure 8.3 Paseo Boriqua marks the territory along Division Street in the heart of Chicago's Puerto Rican diaspora community. Photograph by Angel Nieves.

Negotiative spaces of transcultural polities

Given the increasing diversity of groups that live in US metropolitan regions, plural forms of cultural affiliation are also emerging. The changing migration patterns that result in transnational forms of urbanism are a notable example (Smith 2001). In contrast to the model of previous generations in which immigrants came to the United States and built their lives here, severing ties with their countries of origin after a generation or so, today's immigrants are likely to shuttle back and forth to their home countries. Remittances to Mexico alone now total $25 million, accounting for 2.6 percent of the total gross domestic product according to the World Bank (Ratha and Xu 2006). This example is one of many that problematize historical definitions of citizenship when groups occupy political and cultural spaces within, between, and/or outside local, regional, and national territories. As citizenship is inextricably linked to membership in a political community (Marshall 1977), this raises the issue of how citizen participation is constituted in the political organization of a group, also known as the polity.

One type of political community is what I refer to as "transcultural polities," defined by the participation of different social groups, but with a shared commitment toward a collective project or action. They are also polyvalent, producing common sites that have multiple identities and meanings. The term "transcultural" suggests that cultures are assemblages of imaginings and meanings and are constructed to communicate and create community (Lewis 2002).[5] The related term "polity," referencing the political, does not imply the exercise of power or authority over social relations, but rather focuses attention on an ensemble of individuals, groups, and institutions that seek to organize and order their coexistence despite the mixed motives of diverse actors. As one aim of transcultural polities is to forge alliances across cultural differences, these polities create the potential for transformative relationships (Guss 2000). The outcome of such processes is made manifest in the urban landscape as negotiative spaces characterized by transcultural iconographies, hybrid aesthetics, and recombinant cultural forms. One example is the borderlands between Mexico and the United States, viewed as a dynamic landscape of "cultural mixing and global bending" (Herzog 1999). Within cities this includes multiethnic neighborhoods where Latinos are one of many different groups living side by side (Maly 2005).

The Mission District in San Francisco is one case of a predominantly Latino neighborhood that also includes a growing number of other ethnic groups. During the mid-1990s much of the Mission's distinct cultural identity was being transformed as a wave of non-Mexican immigrants, Latino and others, as well as young urban professionals were moving into the neighborhood. These groups represented a changing resident population that stood in stark contrast to the predominantly Latino population that had dominated neighborhood politics since the 1950s. A site of growing tensions was a transit plaza at 16th and Mission Streets, which became a highly contested space given the numerous arguments made for its future use and

Figure 8.4 Chicano Park in San Diego played an important role in the early history and art of the Chicano movement. Photograph by Michael Rios.

Figure 8.5 Plaza del Colibrí in the Mission District of San Francisco serves a variety of social groups and uses. Photograph by Michael Rios.

identity. Beginning in 1996, a series of community dialogues were held to address community-wide concern about the transit plaza, leading to its renovation in 2005. Renamed "Plaza del Colibrí," the once sterile, institutional plaza was transformed into a heterogeneous space that validated the claims and aspirations of individuals, organizations, and agencies alike (Figure 8.5). Artists helped to reimagine the space and used hummingbirds, or colibrís, which migrate among Mexico, the United States, and Canada, as a transcultural symbol throughout the plaza. Colibrís also symbolize migrant workers, which spoke to the history of the Mission District as the home to many Irish, Latino, and, more recently, Asian immigrants (Martí 2003). To emphasize the multipurpose and temporal qualities of the plaza, sitting steps serve as a platform for public "speak outs" and spaces were also created for a rotating art exhibit and vendor kiosks. This prompted further discussions between the transit agency and local arts organizations, resulting in the formation of Plaza 16, a staffed project that coordinates rotating art exhibits and works with transit agencies, local galleries, and arts organizations to promote events and vending on the plaza. Plaza del Colibrí is a result of new channels of communication and dialogue not only at the scale of the local community, but also among policy, planning, and urban design interests at the regional level. Changes to transportation policy and institutional capacity building concerning station area planning and design were some of the outcomes (Rios 2008).

Implications for public space praxis

A growing number of regions and cities in the United States are now home to Latinos whose cultural practices differ not only from the white majority of the population, but also from prior generations of immigrants. A changing public sphere suggests a critical examination of what constitutes citizenship in light of these demographic trends. As operative sites, public spaces such as the ones described are culturally affirming and can serve as a basis for the formation of polities. In describing the prospects for Latino urbanism, my aim is to put forth a dynamic, not essentialist, conception of culture vis-à-vis the production of the public sphere. Latinos provide one case of historically specific, culturally constituted, social relations defined by racial, regional, class, gender, and generational differences. It is important to resist the tendency to identify universal categorizations, especially as the Latino population grows over time. To do so would run the risk of oversimplifying the range of spatial practices and expressions within this pan-ethnic group. A related concern is the aesthetization of Latinos as "Other." This includes the thematization and commodification of Latino spaces whether romanticizing a neo-traditional social imaginary of the past, promoting a pastiche postmodern aesthetic, or glorifying the ever-present post-colonial condition. This poses a further, even paradoxical, challenge to urban planners and designers who work with Latino communities: as instruments of market forces or as advocates of economically marginalized groups, enforcers of aesthetic standardization, or facilitators of cross-cultural exchange.

Beyond this reflexive stance, a culturally informed praxis illustrates multiple ways that capacity building is made possible through spatial production. Each of the three types of space described – adaptive, assertive, and negotiative – involves and enables a variety of actors with or without professional involvement (or interference). Key to this understanding is the equal treatment of indigenous and non-indigenous, expert and non-expert forms of knowledge. Regardless of position or status, a central focus is the engagement in dialogical processes that bridge understandings across group differences resulting in new alliances and an empowered citizenry. In addition, a culturally informed praxis also reveals syncretic and creative dimensions of cultural production that can be translated into material space. Adaptive, assertive, and negotiative spaces combine and recombine cultural forms and practices with the territorial specificity of inhabitation. Creative possibilities abound and can be drawn from a multiplicity of sources that circulate between and among local, regional, national, and transnational spaces.

Notes

1 This research is supported by the USDA Cooperative State Research, Education and Extension Service, Hatch project # CA-D*-END-7717-H. I would like to thank Naomi Adiv, who provided invaluable research assistance, as well as Mark Francis, who shared his comments on an earlier draft of the manuscript.
2 For the purposes of this paper, I use the term "Latino" to describe a pan-ethnic group that identifies with Latin American countries. This also includes regional

differences with respect to origin and destination, race, socio-economic status, gender, and age. The predominance of the term "Latina/o" does not suggest universal acceptance or explicate the limits to the term (for example, see Gimenez 1999).

3 For an expanded discussion of the role of culture in political efficacy, see Rios (2009).
4 For example, see Crawford (1995).
5 Transculturalism is consistent with polyculturalism, the interchange of cultural forms (for example, see Prashad 2001).

Bibliography

Aponte-Pares, L. (1997) 'Casitas, Place and Culture: Appropriating Place in Puerto Rican Barrios', *Places*, 11 (1): 54–61.

—— (1998) 'What's Yellow and White and Has Land All Around It? Appropriating Place in Puerto Rican Barrios', in Darder, A. and Torres, R. D. (eds.) *The Latino Studies Reader: Culture, Economy and Society,* Malden, MA: Blackwell.

—— (2000) 'Appropriating Place in Puerto Rican Barrios, Preserving Contemporary Urban Landscapes', in Alanen, A. R. and Melnick, R. (eds.) *Preserving Cultural Landscapes in America*, Baltimore: Johns Hopkins University Press.

Arreola, D. D. (1988) 'Mexican American Housescapes', *Geographical Review*, 78 (17): 299–315.

—— (1992) 'Plaza Towns of South Texas', *Geographical Review*, 82 (1): 56–73.

Barnett, C. and Low, M. (2004) *Spaces of Democracy: Geographical Perspectives on Citizenship, Participation, and Representation*, London: Sage Publications.

Brandes, S. (1998) 'The Day of the Dead, Halloween, and the Quest for Mexican National Identity', *Journal of American Folklore*, 111 (442): 359–380.

Brenner, N. (2000) 'The Urban Question as a Scale Question: Reflections on Henri Lefebvre, Urban Theory and the Politics of Scale', *International Journal of Urban and Regional Research*, 24 (2): 361–378.

de Certeau, M. (1984) *The Practice of Everyday Life*, Berkeley: University of California Press.

Chase, J., Crawford, M., and Kaliski, J. (eds.) (1999) *Everyday Urbanism*, New York: Monacelli Press.

Crawford, M. (1995) 'Contesting the Public Realm: Struggles over Public Space in Los Angeles', *Journal of Architectural Education*, 49 (1): 4–9.

Dávila, A. (2004) *Barrio Dreams: Puerto Ricans, Latinos, and the Neoliberal City*, Berkeley: University of California Press.

Diaz, D. (2005) *Barrio Urbanism: Chicanos, Planning, and American Cities*, New York: Routledge.

Douglass, M. and Friedmann, J. (eds.) (1998) *Cities for Citizens: Planning and the Rise of Civil Society in a Global Age*, Chichester, UK: J. Wiley.

Duany, J. (2003) 'Nation, Migration, Identity: The Case of Puerto Ricans', *Latino Studies*, 1 (3): 424–444.

Easton, T. (2007) 'Geographies of Hope and Despair: Atlanta's African American, Latino, and White Day Laborers', *Southern Spaces*. Online. Available HTTP: http://www.southernspaces.org/contents/2007/easton/1a.htm (accessed 11 February 2008).

Estrada, W. D. (1999) 'Los Angeles' Old Plaza and Olvera Street: Imagined and Contested Space', *Western Folklore*, 58 (2):107–129.

Flores-Gonzales, N. (2001) 'Paseo Boricua: Claiming a Puerto Rican Space in Chicago', *Centro Journal*, 13 (2): 6–23.

Ford, L. R. and Griffin, E. (1981) 'Chicano Park: Personalizing an Institutional Landscape', *Landscape*, 25 (2): 42–48.

Forsyth, A., Lu, H., and McGirr, P. (2001) 'Plazas, Streets, and Markets: What Puerto Ricans Bring to Urban Spaces in Northern Climates', *Landscape Journal*, 20 (1): 62–76.

Friedmann, J. (2002) *The Prospect of Cities*, Minneapolis: University of Minneapolis Press.

Gimenez, M. E. (1999) 'Latino Politics – Class Struggles: Reflections on the Future of Latino Politics', in Torres, R. D. and Katsiaficas, G. (eds.) *Latino Social Movements: Historical and Theoretical Perspectives*, New York: Routledge.

Guss, D. M. (2000) *The Festive State: Race, Ethnicity, and Nationalism as Cultural Performance*, Berkeley: University of California Press.

Harvey, D. (1989) *The Condition of Postmodernity*, London: Basil Blackwell.

Herzog, L. A. (1999) *From Aztec to High Tech: Architecture and Landscape across the Mexico–United States Border*, Baltimore: Johns Hopkins University Press.

Holston, J. (2008) *Insurgent Citizenship: Disjunctions of Democracy and Modernity in Brazil*, Princeton, NJ: Princeton University Press.

Holston, J. and Appadurai, A. (1999) 'Cities and Citizenship', in Holston, J. (ed.) *Cities and Citizenship*, Durham, NC: Duke University Press.

Isin, E. F. (2002) *Being Political: Genealogies of Citizenship*, Minneapolis: University of Minnesota Press.

Jameson, F. (1991) *Postmodernism or, the Cultural Logic of Late Capitalism*, Durham, NC: Duke University Press.

Kelbaugh, D. (2001) 'Three Urbanisms and the Public Realm', paper presented at the 3rd International Space Syntax Symposium, Atlanta, GA.

Lefebvre, H. (1991) *The Production of Space*, Cambridge, MA: Blackwell.

—— (1996) *Writings on Cities*, Oxford: Blackwell.

Lewis, J. (2002) 'From Culturalism to Transculturalism', *Iowa Journal of Cultural Studies*, 1. Online. Available HTTP: http://www.uiowa.edu/~ijcs/issueone/lewis. htm (accessed 12 February 2008).

Low, S. (2000) *On the Plaza: The Politics of Public Space and Culture*, Austin: University of Texas Press.

Low, S. and Smith, N. (eds.) (2006) *The Politics of Public Space*, New York: Routledge.

Marshall, T. H. (1977) *Class, Citizenship and Social Development*, Chicago: Chicago University Press.

Martí, F. (2003) *16th Street BART Plaza Dedication & Community Celebration*, San Francisco: Urban Ecology.

Maly, M. (2005) *Beyond Segregation: Multiracial and Multiethnic Neighborhoods in the United States*, Philadelphia: Temple University Press.

McCann, E. J. (2002) 'Space, Citizenship, and the Right to the City: A Brief Overview', *GeoJournal*, 58 (2–3): 77–79.

—— (2005) 'Urban Citizenship, Public Participation, and a Critical Geography of Architecture', in Wastl-Walter, D., Staeheli, L. A., and Dowler, L. (eds.) *Rights to the City*, Rome: Societa Geografica Italiana.

Mendez, M. A. (2003) 'Latino Lifestyle and the New Urbanism: Synergy against Sprawl', unpublished MCP thesis, Massachusetts Institute of Technology.

Mitchell, D. (2003) *The Right to the City: Social Justice and the Fight for Public Space*, New York: Guilford Press.

Prashad, V. (2001) *Everybody was Kung Fu Fighting: Afro-Asian Connections and the Myth of Cultural Purity*, Boston: Beacon Press.

Purcell, M. (2003) 'Citizenship and the Right to the Global City: Reimagining the Capitalist World Order', *International Journal of Urban and Regional Research*, 27 (3): 564–590.

Ramos-Zayas (2007) 'Becoming American, Becoming Black? Urban Comptetency,

Racialized Spaces, and the Politics of Citizenship Among Brazilian and Puerto Rican Youth in Newark', *Identities*, 14 (1–2): 24.

Ratha, D. and Xu, Z. (2006) *Global Economic Prospects 2006: Economic Implications of Remittances and Migration*, Washington, DC: World Bank.

Rios, M. (2008) 'Envisioning Citizenship: Toward a Polity Approach in Urban Design', *Journal of Urban Design*, 13 (2): 213–229.

—— (2009) 'Public Space Praxis: Cultural Capacity and Political Efficacy in Latina/o Placemaking', *Berkeley Planning Journal*, 22: 92–111.

Rojas, J. T. (1993) 'The Enacted Environment of East Los Angeles', *Places*, 8 (3): 42–53.

Sciorra, J. (1996) 'Return to the Future: Puerto Rican Vernacular Architecture in New York City', in King, A. (ed.) *Representing the City: Ethnicity, Capital and Culture in the 21st Century Metropolis*, London: Macmillan Press.

Sciorra, J. and Cooper, M. (1990) ' "I Feel Like I'm in My Country": Puerto Rican Casitas in New York City', *Drama Review*, 34 (4): 156–168.

Sennett, R. (2000) 'Reflections on the Public Realm', in Bridge, G. and Watson, S. (eds.) *A Companion to the City*, Oxford: Blackwell.

Smith, M. P. (2001) *Transnational Urbanism: Locating Globalization*, Malden, MA: Blackwell.

Sorkin, M. (ed.) (1992) *Variations on a Theme Park: The New American City and the End of Public Space*, New York: Hill and Wang.

Speaks, M. (2005) 'Everyday is Not Enough', in Mehrota, R. (ed.) *Everyday Urbanism: Michigan Debates on Urbanism*: Volume I, Ann Arbor: University of Michigan.

State of California, Department of Finance. (2007) *Population Projections for California and Its Counties 2000–2050, by Age, Gender and Race/Ethnicity*, Sacramento, California.

Suro, R. (2005) *Hispanics: A People in Motion*, Washington, DC: Pew Research Center.

Valenzuela, A., Theodore, N., Meléndez, E., and Gonzalez, A. L. (2006) *On the Corner: Day Labor in the United States*, Los Angeles: Center for the Study of Urban Poverty, UCLA.

Wastl-Walter, D., Staeheli, L. A., and Dowler, L. (eds.) (2005) *Rights to the City*, Rome: Societa Geografica Italiana.

Whyte, W. H. (1980) *The Social Life of Small Urban Spaces*, New York: Project for Public Spaces.

Zukin, S. (1995) *The Cultures of Cities*, Oxford: Blackwell.

CHAPTER 9

"Night market" in Seattle

Community eventscape and the reconstruction of public space

Jeffrey Hou

From selling street food and counterfeit goods to performances and entertainment, night markets have been a critical ingredient of the bustling urban life in cities such as Taipei, Hong Kong, Bangkok, Mumbai, and Seoul.[1] In Taipei's notoriously crowded Shilin Night Market, for example, street vendors turn a once residential street into the center of a sprawling outdoor bazaar with a bewildering variety of local snacks, international foods, clothing, toys, gadgets, and accessories, taking over every square centimeter of the dense streetscape. This historic neighborhood is transformed every night by thousands of visitors, shoppers, tourists, and vendors, arriving by subway, in cars, on motorbikes, and on foot. Smells of pork buns and grilled sausages are mixed with dance music and shouting of vendors from the loudspeakers. Families, teens, college students, international tourists, and migrant workers literally rub elbows with each other in order to move from one stall to the next.

With inexpensive food and merchandise, night markets traditionally provide a refuge for the working class and particularly migrant workers seeking to make ends meet in the big cities (Yu 2004). Like other forms of street market, night markets can provide an important source of income for small businesses and are a critical part of the local economy.[2] By operating in the evenings, night markets such as the Shilin Market in Taipei extend the social and commercial life of a city beyond the "normal" business hours. By occupying places intended for other uses, they create "loose spaces" in an otherwise regimented city (Franck and Stevens 2007). As events and activities, night markets are manifestations of "temporary urbanism" that challenge the conventional thinking in urban planning (Temel 2006).

Because of their transient nature, night markets have long been a murky, if not problematic, form of public space. Although night markets have been an important part of the local popular culture, their existence is traditionally marginalized (Yu 2004). Vendors in night markets are often accused of creating traffic congestion, excessive noise, and sanitation problems, and privatizing the public space. With the appearance of chaos, market vendors are frequently purged by local authorities. The market's status as an informal sector and temporary event complicates the enforcement of regulations and the notion of public space. Its temporality defies the conception of public space in terms of the permanency often associated with it. At the Shilin Night Market, the hundreds of street vendors occupying the narrow residential streets can magically disappear in a matter of seconds when the cops show up to write tickets. The drama unfolds several times in a night and has become part of the spectacle and experience of the market.

Despite the institutional marginalization, night markets are wildly popular in Asia. In Taipei, while traditional markets have been losing out to air-conditioned malls, supermarkets, and convenience stores, night markets have continued to thrive. Whereas most food stalls continue to sell traditional local delicacies, they are now joined by multinationals such as McDonalds and KFC. Because of their popularity and distinct cultural flavor, night markets are being marketed as international tourist attractions. But, regardless of its status, a night market is still best characterized as an in-between, crossover space between the public and private, temporary and permanent, formal and informal. The flow and accretion of activities defies any established boundaries of time and space. They are by nature a contested landscape that requires a constant negotiation of power, space, activities, and meanings. They offer the possibility of insurgency, with the power of individuals to change the way public space is traditionally conceptualized, produced, and utilized.

Night market in America?

In recent years, night markets have also emerged in several West Coast cities in North America, reflecting the growing Asian populations and their influences in the new continent. Here, however, the night markets have served not only as a popular form of leisure and commercial activity as found in Asia but also as a vehicle for community building and revitalization. In San Francisco, the Chinatown Night Market Fair was conceived to revitalize the community after an earthquake in 1989 that destroyed the Embarcadero Freeway and resulted in the loss of visitors and business. Located in Chinatown's Portsmouth Square, the market transforms the park in the summer and autumn evenings into a marketplace for bargain shopping and family entertainment. In the historic Vancouver Chinatown, a night market takes place on Keefer Street on every Friday, Saturday, and Sunday evening in the summer. Billed as a shopping extravaganza featuring Asian traditional handicrafts, fashionable gifts, and ethnic snacks, it was developed as one of a long list of festivals and events including a New Year Parade and Dragon Boat Festival to revitalize the area, whose customers and visitors have been drawn away by new ethnic malls in the suburbs.

Mirroring the pattern of population migration, the largest night market in North America can now be found in suburbia – more specifically the City of Richmond, British Columbia, where over half of its residents are of Asian descent on account of the influx of immigrants from Hong Kong just before 1997. During the summer months, thousands of visitors and vendors flood the market located on an industrial waterfront site. Much like going to a mall, visitors come to the Richmond Night Market for food, shopping, and entertainment, except here they can find the broadest array of ethnic food and merchandise possible on an outdoor industrial site. The market attracts not only the Asian immigrant populations but also the white Canadians. The City of Richmond even has an information booth on site. With vendors and visitors of diverse ethnic backgrounds, the popular Richmond

Night Market embodies the demographic shift and the growing multiculturalism of Canadian cities.

From San Francisco to Vancouver and even Richmond, night markets as ethnic events have transformed the way public space is traditionally used and created in American cities. In San Francisco, the market transforms a public park into a temporary market place, defying the way American parks have historically been conceived and institutionalized.[3] In Vancouver, the market helped extend the commercial life of the district into the streets, reversing the trend of internalizing and controlling the commercial activities in the urban setting. In Richmond, the market transforms an industrial waterfront site into a post-industrial, multicultural eventscape.

Night market in Seattle

In many ways, the night market in Seattle's Chinatown/International District is similar to its counterparts in San Francisco and Vancouver. In Seattle, the idea of creating a night market as a way to revitalize the neighborhood has been floating for some time; activists and community organizers often point to the night markets in nearby Vancouver and Richmond as successful examples of marketing and community economic development. In 2006, a night market finally materialized in the Hing Hay Park located in the heart of Chinatown. But the immediate driving force was not economic interest but rather an effort to activate the neighborhood's parks and open space, besieged by real and perceived crime and safety issues like many other downtown parks in Seattle (see Bedard 2007). In fall 2005, an intergenerational design workshop that involved youths and elderly residents in the International District was organized by the Community Design Studio at University of Washington (UW) in collaboration with Wilderness Inner-city Leadership Development (WILD), a youth leadership program based in the district.[4] The purpose of the workshop was to envision improvement of open space in the neighborhood to encourage more active use by the neighborhood's residents. To attract people back to the park, one of the youth groups came up with the idea of bringing in food vendors. Following the workshop, a group of WILD youths took up the project to create a pilot night market in the district (Figure 9.1).

The project began with soliciting feedbacks from the community and local businesses using questionnaires. The youths also made a trip to the Richmond Night Market to observe a real night market in action and to learn from its success. Those who spent their childhood in Asia were also informed by their memories of night markets from their home countries. In planning for the pilot night market, they studied and compared the different locations in the neighborhood. Located in the center of the neighborhood, the Hing Hay Park was selected eventually in consultation with other neighborhood organizations as the site for the pilot night market.[5]

The pilot night market took place in August 2006 as part of the community's National Night Out event.[6] Drawing hundreds of residents and visitors to the park for an evening of performances, games, shopping, and eating, the success of the event generated much excitement within the community. It also encouraged the

Figure 9.1 Immigrant youths developed ideas to improve local parks in a design workshop in Seattle's Chinatown/ International District. Photograph by Jeffrey Hou.

organizers to begin planning for a regular night market event in the following year. With a grant from the city's Office for Economic Development to support the development of a business plan, a steering committee was formed that included representatives from key organizations in the community. Following months of preparation and collaboration among several community-based organizations, two night markets events were held in the following year.

The night market in Seattle is an interesting case to examine because it builds on the patterns of other night markets in West Coast cities that transform the functions and meanings of public space in a North American city. More than an exotic event or a festival market place found in typical downtown redevelopment, the night market in Seattle involves a grassroots, community-building process. It creates a social, political, and transcultural space that engages a multitude of individuals and group across the established spatial and institutional boundaries. The following examines how such processes have occurred and the implications of their initial outcomes.

Night market as a social space

Historically, neighborhood parks in North America have operated under a paradigm that ironically discourages large social gatherings. Neighborhood parks were designed for active individual recreation for health, physical, and even moral development (Loukaitou-Sideris 1995, Cranz 1982). On the other hand, commercial activities and social gathering were discouraged and even suppressed. The provision of parks was once meant explicitly to move children and adults off the streets from such types of activities (Cranz 1982). It was not until recently that, in an attempt to bring people back to the deserted urban parks, programming of events was introduced.

From the outset, the night market event in Seattle was an attempt to create opportunities for residents to socialize. Besides business improvement and public safety, community building through social interactions was identified as one of the primary goals for the event. To make the night market a social event, a series of fun activities were purposely organized by the WILD youths to engage visitors and residents of different ages and ethnicities. The activities included mahjong, fortune telling, fishing, ring toss, chess, go, Chinese calligraphy, martial art, and even cooking demonstrations. There was also an inflatable jump toy for the younger kids to play. The program culminated in an outdoor karaoke contest for all ages (Figure 9.2). With these activities, the residents and visitors had a chance to interact with each other across the cultural and social boundaries, besides eating and bargain hunting in a typical night market.

At the night market event, kids can be seen playing mahjong in the park with the elders. Adults of different ethnic backgrounds challenged each other to a game of chess or go. Immigrant parents got to teach kids the games they used to play when they were kids themselves (Figure 9.3). Outside visitors inquired of the locals about the specific games and foods. Aspiring singers from both the community and outside the neighborhood competed against each other on the karaoke stage. In such a way, the event activities have transformed how the park has typically been used (or disused) and how people in the neighborhood have traditionally interacted with each other. They helped activate not only the space but also social relationships among people. The social aspect of the night market in Seattle perhaps best distinguishes it from others in West Coast cities, as well as those in Asia.

Night market as a political space

As in many long-established communities, local politics plays an important role in defining the relationships and boundaries in Seattle's Chinatown/International District. The district's hybrid name itself suggests two visions and political affinities within the community – one in favor of pan-ethnic collectivity and historic inclusiveness (International District) and the other in favor of specific ethnic identity (Chinatown). The two forces are further intertwined with different views of economic development and social priorities, with social service organizations typically in favor of protecting the area's low-income residents, and the traditional family associations and business organizations in favor of market-rate development (Hou and Tanner 2002, Abramson et al. 2006).

A key aspect in the success of the night market in Seattle has been its ability to bring together a coalition of individuals and organizations despite their political and ideological differences. On one hand, the potential of the night market to address a multitude of issues including economic development, public safety, community

Figure 9.2 The pavilion in Hing Hay Park was transformed into a stage for a karaoke contest during the night market. Photograph by Jeffrey Hou.

building, and recreation has made it possible to attract the diverse organizations. On the other hand, the youths of the WILD program as the initiator of the project also played a critical role. Besides the WILD program, the different organizations included non-profit social service organizations and business associations, as well as city agencies including the Seattle Police Department, Department of Parks and Recreation, and Department of Neighborhoods. Sponsors of the event also included a local grocery market and even a major developer.

Each of the organizations played a different but equally instrumental role in the planning and implementation of the event. After conducting the initial business survey and getting support from other partners, the WILD youths took the lead in developing the program for the night market. The Chinese Chamber of Commerce helped communicate and mobilize the support from the local Chinese business owners. The Community Action Program helped develop the public safety aspect of the event. The Chinatown/International District Business Improvement Area (CIDBIA), the organizer of the regular summer festival, helped coordinate the event logistics. Prior to the event, the WILD youths set up booths for fundraising and disseminating public safety information at other community gatherings. They also went door to door to invite businesses to participate.

The collaboration of the different organizations and individuals was critical to the event's success and the continued support. Besides bringing together unique resources and expertise, the collaboration ensured that all the major stakeholders in the neighborhood took ownership and pride of the event. The success of the event for two consecutive years has set a foundation for continued collaboration among these organizations. Albeit short of transforming the politics within the community, the night market did create a new "public realm" in which productive dialogue, collaboration, and negotiation were possible. Through the making of such public

Figure 9.3 Elders and youths played mahjong together in Hing Hay Park as part of the night market activities. Photograph by Jeffrey Hou.

realm, the night market can potentially strengthen the political capacity of the community to address the many challenges that it faces.

Night market as a transcultural space

With colorful signs, pagoda-style roofs, and Chinese gates, ethnic enclaves such as Chinatowns have long been the sites of cultural imaginations and stereotypes. The visual artifacts reduce cultural diversity and complexity into easily recognized iconography and sometimes caricature. The recent redevelopment of the many Chinatowns in North America including those in Washington, DC, Portland, OR, and Calgary, which rely heavily on these typical imageries, has reinforced the

Figure 9.4 Night
market installations
designed and built
by WILD youths and
landscape architecture
students from
the University of
Washington, Seattle.
Photograph by Jeffrey
Hou.

stereotypical cultural imagination. With the Chinese Lion Dance and kung fu demonstrations as well as ethnic food and shopping, the Seattle night market as a cultural spectacle is not unlike the stereotypical motif commonly associated with Chinatowns or other ethnic enclaves. However, as an event that engages individuals in close encounters, it has the potential for transcending stereotypes and provides opportunities for interactions, border crossing, and a more nuanced understanding of cultural diversity and complexity.

Realizing the potential of night markets for cross-cultural understanding was on the agenda of a design studio at the University of Washington that followed the pilot night market in 2006. In collaboration with the WILD program, the UW students worked with the WILD youths to explore the design and construction of

Figure 9.5 Undersides of the parasols depict folk stories representing the diverse cultures of Seattle's International District. Photograph by Jeffrey Hou.

installations that would provide cultural expressions and support the functional needs of the market.[7] Through weekly work sessions, the student teams designed and constructed six installations, ranging from seating and lighting elements to a game booth (Figure 9.4). To facilitate cross-cultural understanding, each installation also incorporates a narrative element that represents an aspect of the social life or history of the immigrant community.

For the students, the design process itself was an exercise in cross-cultural learning. Students worked through cultural stereotypes and barriers to arrive at designs that function as a medium for interpreting the neighborhood's rich cultural heritage and everyday nuances, as well as a critique of myths and stereotypes. For example, one project, called the Giant Lantern, features an eight-foot-tall lantern with a video installation inside that depicts one day in the life of the neighborhood. The lantern as a cultural icon in this case represents the stereotypical image of the neighborhood as often perceived from the outside. Created by the youths, the video installation inside the lantern represents the everyday reality of the neighborhood. The interplay of lantern/video, outside/inside enables visitors to reflect on their perspective on and understanding of the neighborhood. Another installation, the Parasol Project, also uses a similar technique by featuring a series of parasols hung above rounded benches that serve as the base for the supporting structure. The undersides of the individual parasols feature paintings done by the youth participants and depict folklore from the diverse cultures in the community (Figure 9.5). By sitting under the parasols, one enters the realm of stories hidden under the iconic parasols.

These outdoor installations were designed to adapt to different locations throughout the district where night markets could be held. As functional objects, they also support the activities of the market through seating, signage, lighting, etc. In an event that attracts outside visitors as well as different cultural groups within the district, the installations provide a window for interpreting and understanding the unique cultural heritage and the everyday life of the neighborhood. Furthermore, through familiar, iconographic elements, they function as a critical reflection on the stereotypical image of an ethnic enclave. Finally, as creative and interpretative elements, they go beyond the commercial nature of most night markets. Combining both functional and interpretative elements, they draw users to ponder the layers of meanings behind the night market as a cultural event. The installations expand the possibilities of the public open space for dialogues and interpretations.

Reconstructing public space

Compared with its counterparts in Taipei, Bangkok, and Seoul, the night market in Seattle is easily dwarfed in terms of size and intensity. However, the importance of the Seattle event lies not in the size and scale, but in the way it provides a means for the local community to reshape a public space and the public realm within the community. With the multiple goals of community building, economic revitalization, and public safety, the night market brought together a coalition of organizations and individuals. Initiated by a youth program and supported by other community stakeholders, the planning and organization of the event involved interactions and collaboration across a host of barriers within the community. Specifically, it has created opportunities for intergenerational interactions and collaboration despite political and ideological differences. The design/build installations have created opportunities for cross-cultural reflections and interpretations. The night market event allows the community to take back a neighborhood park besieged by crimes and disuse. The transformation of the park into a night market also addresses a critical deficiency of the current park design and programming that fail to meet the cultural needs of the community.

More than a cultural import or spectacle, the outcomes of the night market in Seattle suggest specific ways through which the public space in North American cities can be reclaimed, reconceptualized, and reconstructed. Through planning of events and activities and possible reprogramming, neighborhoods have the ability to transform the way open space is currently used. The activities and events can be designed to challenge the existing boundaries within the community and to expand the notion of publicness in the community. Through partnership and collaboration, neighborhood organizations and individuals can pool together resources to transform the existing public space. The partnership and collaboration in turn can help strengthen another dimension of public realm in the community: the network and reciprocity among individuals and groups within the community. The positive experience of working together can empower them to take on further challenges in the future. The event provides means for cultural expressions, representation, and reflections. Through specific design interventions and displays, the culture and everyday life of the community can be brought into the greater public realm of the city against isolation and misconception.

In the case of Seattle, whereas the night market itself can be temporary or even ephemeral, the processes and the outcomes can have a lasting impact on reshaping the public space and social relationships in the community. Like their counterparts in Asia, night markets in America test the preconceived boundaries and relationships in the urban setting. In expanding the notion and design of public space, the night market, like the people who created it, acquires a new life in the new continent.

Notes

1 Dating back to the late Tang Dynasty in China during the eighth and ninth centuries, night markets are particularly popular in countries with high concentrations of ethnic Chinese including Singapore, Indonesia, Thailand, and Malaysia (Yu 2004). They also exist in Mexico, Turkey, and even France (Jordan *et al.* 2004). Compared with other forms of markets, night markets tend to be leisure and tourist oriented (Wu 2005).
2 See Brown (2006). Street and public space are important to the livelihood of millions of people especially in the developing countries.
3 In the tradition of American urban parks, there has been a strong opposition against the inclusion of non-park-related facilities (Cranz 1982).
4 The WILD program is a youth leadership development and mentoring program based in the International District. The program focuses on community-building projects carried out by mostly high-school age students that address environmental justice issues.
5 Other sites that were considered included a bus terminal plaza and a parking lot under the Interstate Freeway 5. The Hing Hay Park site was chosen partly because of its prime location at the heart of the district.
6 National Night Out is a crime/drug-prevention program that encourages neighborhoods around North America to organize against crimes. See http://www.natw.org/nno/about.html (accessed 21 June 2009).
7 The studio was taught by the present author and funded through the Mini-grant for Internationalizing UW's Undergraduate Education by UW's Undergraduate Academic Affairs, Curriculum Transformation Project, and the International Program and Exchange. More information is available at http://courses.washington.edu/nightmkt/.

Bibliography

Abramson, D., Manzo, L., and Hou, J. (2006) 'From Ethnic Enclave to Multi-ethnic Translocal Community: Constructed Identities and Community Planning in

Seattle's Chinatown-International District', *Journal of Architecture and Planning Research*, 23 (4): 341–359.

Bedard, L. (2007) 'Few Resist Park Plan, but Questions Remain', *Northwest Asian Weekly*, 26 (15): 1 and 11.

Brown, A. (ed.) (2006) *Contested Space: Street Trading, Public Space, and Livelihoods in Developing Cities*, London: ITDG Publishing.

Cranz, G. (1982) *The Politics of Park Design*, Cambridge, MA: MIT Press.

Franck, K. A. and Stevens, Q. (2007) 'Tying Down Loose Space', in Franck, K. A. and Stevens, Q. (eds.) *Loose Space: Possibility and Diversity in Urban Life*, London: Routledge.

Hou, J. and Tanner, A. (2002) 'Constructed Identities and Contested Space in Seattle's Chinatown-International District', in Deming, M. E. (ed.) *Groundwork: CELA 2002 Conference Proceedings*, Council of Educators in Landscape Architecture Conference, SUNY, Syracuse, New York, September 25–27.

Jordan, D. K., Morris, A. D., and Moskowitz, M. L. (eds.) (2004) *The Minor Arts of Daily Life: Popular Culture in Taiwan*, Honolulu: University of Hawai'i Press.

Loukaitou-Sideris, A. (1995) 'Urban Form and Social Context: Cultural Differentiation in the Uses of Urban Parks', *Journal of Planning Education and Research*, 14: 89–102.

Temel, R. (2006) 'The Temporary in the City', in Haydn, F. and Temel, R (eds.) *Temporary Urban Spaces: Concepts for the Use of City Space*, Basel: Birkauser.

Wu, P. C.-C. (2005) 'Daily Consumption in a Globalizing City: Food Markets at the Crossroads', in Kwok, R. Y.-W. (ed.) *Globalizing Taipei: The Political Economy of Spatial Development*, New York: Routledge.

Yu, S.-D. (2004) 'Hot and Noisy: Taiwan's Night Market Culture', in Jordan, D. K., Morris, A. D., and Moskowitz, M. L. (eds.) *The Minor Arts of Daily Life: Popular Culture in Taiwan*, Honolulu: University of Hawai'i Press.

CHAPTER 10

Making places of fusion and resistance

The experiences of immigrant women in Taiwanese townships

Hung-Ying Chen and Jia-He Lin

In small towns in Taiwan, traditional public spaces have been tightly connected with everyday life and social relations within the community, as well as gender politics in the society. For example, the temple plaza, which has always been the space where most public affairs and activities took place, has been a typical gathering place for men. Men typically occupy the physical heart of a small settlement. On the other hand, the everyday life of women usually takes place in the markets or on the farms. They rarely claim legitimate occupation of these important public spaces despite being a major labor force in the local economy. As the social life in the community goes on, the symbolic meanings of those spaces remain, along with the power relation that lies beneath those spaces.

In recent years, a new group of people has emerged that has challenged the stability of those relationships and hierarchy. They are marriage migrants from Indonesia, Vietnam, Thailand, Cambodia, the Philippines, and mainland China who are married to Taiwanese men. Unfortunately, these transnational marriages have been stigmatized as "bride trades" or "commercialized" marriages, which leads to various discriminations and unequal treatments in these women's daily life. Discriminations remain embedded in the daily life of these immigrant women within social and public institutions. For example, in many instances, these immigrant women cannot access the typical social services provided for ordinary citizens and are often excluded from the public sphere. The condition of the immigrant women reflects a real disjuncture between the multicultural claims of the mainstream society and assimilative institutional and social practice.

In Meinung, a southern township known for its tobacco production, it is common to see women washing clothes alongside small irrigation channels. The area along the channels has become an alternative public space for them to escape from the control and surveillance of their patriarchal families. But even within such marginalized space the immigrant women are often excluded (Wu 2007). In Nanfang-ao, a fishing port on the east coast, some immigrant women were banned from accessing the local community center even though they have resided there for thirteen years or longer. In the following, using Meinung and Nanfang-ao as case study sites, we examine how the immigrant women engage in the making of insurgent public spaces as they struggle for their individual freedom and collective identity. Specifically, we will look at how some creative projects aiming to "make the invisible visible" have been developed owing to the need for solidarity and collective empowerment (Sandercock 1998). We also look at how public spaces come as a field for negotiation and contestation and how different citizenships contributed to the transnationality of public sphere (Low and Smith 2006)

Meinung: the tobacco barn as a new space for immigrant women

Located in southern Taiwan, Meinung is a small township with about 40,000 residents known for its strong Hakka culture and tradition.[1] After 1905, under the period of Japanese colonization, the small rural town became a center of tobacco production in Taiwan and was dubbed "the Tobacco Empire." The significant number of tobacco curing towers that still exist today testifies to the prosperous period of economic development in Meinung. In the 1990s, the industry faced a downturn, as it was not able to compete with cheaper imports and as the government considered phasing out subsidized purchasing (Hsia 1997). As the local community faced the economic crisis, a proposed major dam to supply water to the region's growing heavy industries galvanized a strong local resistance and social movement resulting in an active network of community activists and organizations. These included the Meinung People's Association, founded in 1994 to fight the proposed Meinung Dam and currently focusing on rural community development, and more recently TransAsia Sisters Association, Taiwan (TASAT), an advocacy group for the foreign spouses in Taiwan.

From domestic space to public space

Since 1995, TASAT has offered Mandarin language classes for the Southeast Asian spouses in Meinung. Lacking a permanent space, the location of the classes has shifted constantly for ten years. Frustrated with the frequent relocation, members of TASAT planned to have a gathering place of their own. A senior volunteer, Gui-Yin, suggested that they could use the old tobacco barn owned by her brother for the class. The tobacco barn is surrounded by farmland and a narrow road, with a runlet behind the property and a garden in the backyard. The idea was enthusiastically accepted in the class. The TASAT staff then started to look for suitable designers and builders who could coordinate with them and were willing to teach them the necessary building skills and techniques. Finally, they recruited two new members, an artist/eco-builder and a graduate student skilled in plumbing and electrical systems. The women from the Mandarin class also participated in the actual renovation and construction process, during which they still had to take care of their children.

To have the new space reflect the background of the immigrant women, TASAT approached the planning of the space through a life-story oral history course that took place over six months. The final plan made use of four existing components of the site: a traditional Hakka living room, a courtyard for drying grain, a vacant backyard, and a vacant pig barn (see Figure 10.1). They decided to change the arrangement of rooms and passageways so that there would be a room for children to play in and a room for TASAT to use as their office. As for the courtyard and pig barn, they adapted them into a tool shed and a bathroom. "We designed to conserve the tobacco barn, but we designed the interior spaces into a Cambodian-style meeting room, Thai kitchen, Indonesian and Vietnam bedchamber, and Meinung Hakka-style office," said a Vietnamese participant. Besides the rebuilding work of the pig barn (Figure 10.2), the toughest work was to replace the entire decaying wooden floor of the second story of the tobacco barn and convert the floor into livable spaces for visiting groups that reflect the different cultures in the community (Figure 10.3).

Construction and "labor exchange"

There were two other aspects of the constructing process that made the project different from other similar undertakings. One was the use of recycled materials for construction. At the eco-builder A-Shan's insistence, every single brick from the early demolition was salvaged, cleaned, and reused. Driftwood was collected and transported to the site. Rooftops were made from couch grass and tied down during the hot summer. After the summer a sister from Thailand said, "Even though my father and brother both worked in the architecture and construction trade, this is my first time mixing cement for a real house by myself!" The other unique aspect was the adaptation of the traditional labor exchange practice in Meinung.[2]

Because of the need for intensive manual labor during the tobacco-harvesting season, the people of Meinung have developed a method of shared labor in which families would help each other out to harvest the tobacco leaves. However, as the tobacco industry dies out, such exchange practice is also in decline. The TASAT Sisterhood decided to utilize and adapt this collective practice for the project. The labor exchange activities involving the local residents, the immigrant women, and the TASAT organizers created new opportunities for them to interact with each other.

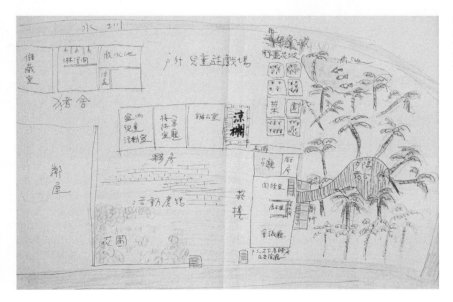

Figure 10.1 Hand-drawn site plan of the tobacco barn by immigrant sisters of TASAT. Source: TASAT.

Beyond construction work

Although the activities looked like nothing more than a collaborative repairing and
building project, they were challenging for the women who were mothers and
housewives at the same time. Some even had other part-time jobs to support their
families. They had to learn welding, brickwork, and carpentry while sacrificing their
leisure time. The intense workload challenged everyone's time and energy. Their

Figure 10.3 Immigrant sisters of TASAT working on the outdoor wooden platform. Source: TASAT.

participation in the project showed a strong determination to own a "public place" of their own. After nearly half a year's effort, including a community fundraising event, their hard work earned the praise from their families and other local residents. In Meinung, the self-help rebuilding experience successfully challenges two kinds of stereotype. First, it reverses the traditional role of women and questions the notion that construction work is a man's job. Second, it challenges the role of professionals in a design project, as the immigrant women in this case took charge of the design of the space.

For TASAT, the tobacco barn rebuilding experiment was an attempt to blend the local Hakka cultural traditions, preservation of the tobacco cultural landscape, and the empowerment of immigrant women in Meinung. The new building serves as an expression of the hybridity of the women's life experiences: their ethnic cultural background and the culture of their new home in Taiwan. Through a tenacious and unyielding claiming of a collective space by a marginalized women's community, the experiment provides an opportunity to advance issues of gender and community empowerment in Meinung. As bell hooks said:

> In fact I was saying just the opposite, that it is also the site of radical possibility, a space of resistance. It was this marginality that I was naming as a central location for the production of a counter-hegemonic discourse that is not just found in words but in habits of being and the way one lives.

Moreover:

> spaces can be real and imagined. Spaces can tell stories and unfold histories. Spaces can be interrupted, appropriated, and transformed through artistic and literary practice.
>
> (hooks 1990: 149–152)

The practice of transcultural interaction is an attempt to blur the boundaries between public and private, immigrants and local residents, and to find an alternative place for women in the community. Aiming at creating a radical "public place" that embraces diverse minority groups in Taiwan, it was clearly declared in the announcement by TASAT in a fundraising event (Figure 10.4) that their choice of a tobacco barn as the site of their project is meant to (1) let all the sisters from Southeast Asia make the place their second home in Taiwan, and have a space for relaxation, extend their social network, and acquire new knowledge; (2) provide a meeting space for local community organizations and other NGOs specializing in immigrant and gender issues; and (3) afford opportunities of understanding cultural multiplicity and diversity in Taiwan.

Nanfang-ao: creating the Lan-Shin community service center

Figure 10.4 Community fundraising night at the tobacco barn. Source: TASAT.

Located on the northeastern coast, Nanfang-ao is one of the largest fishing ports in Taiwan. Initially founded by Japanese in the late colonial period, Nanfang-ao

soon became a wealthy seaport that attracted domestic migration as the fishery industry grew rapidly after World War II. However, the industrialization in the 1960s soon changed the local economy with an abundance of manufacturing and service industry jobs. Coupled with the risky working environment that drove young people away from the fishing industry, this sent the once prosperous wealthy port into a decline (Chiu 1999).

Nevertheless, even with the decline of the local economy, the population of Nanfang-ao continues to diversify. Young people who stay locally are stereotypically considered as less capable of career achievements and often have difficulties finding marriage partners. As a result, transnational marriage arranged by private brokers became an acceptable and affordable solution (Lee 2006). Today, Nanfang-ao is known for having a high proportion of immigrant women. This phenomenon brought many concerns about possible social changes and subsequently resources through the social work system to deal with those changes. Through collaboration between the education institutions and the welfare system, various services focusing on family development have been provided.

Creating a bottom-up community service center

Lan-Shin Women and Children Service Center is a non-profit social work institution serving the Nanfang-ao area. Even though its main office is located in another township, Lan-Shin has been serving local families in Nanfang-ao for several years. During that time, they have developed strong social networks and committed more resources to the transnational marriage families than any other local organizations. Benefiting from strong partnership with the local government agency, Lan-Shin applied for official funding[3] to set up a branch office that would function as a community service center for the immigrant women in 2006. At the same time, we, a team of planning students from National Taiwan University, were seeking to initiate a community project in Nanfang-ao.[4] We found ourselves interested in the everyday life of the local immigrant women and decided to ask Lan-Shin for collaboration. Soon, Lan-Shin and we had come into an agreement to collaborate on the community service center. Through this collaboration, we expected to turn the top-down official welfare program into a bottom-up community development project.

An alternative process?

Originally, Lan-Shin thought about simply renting a space in the office building of the local fishermen's association. But we suggested looking for a more suitable location within the neighborhood. Soon, we found an old, two-story house with a good location and affordable rent. At the same time, Lan-Shin also agreed to proceed with a participatory planning and even self-help building process with the involvement of the local immigrant women. To start the process, we participated in the annual community fair and had home visits throughout the neighborhoods. *"Shin" home is your new home!* – with this double-meaning and memorable slogan, the message quickly spread (Figure 10.5).[5]

The immigrant women in Nanfang-ao were ethnically diverse, with Indonesian, Vietnamese, and mainland Chinese women each having their own social territories. Besides, their daily life tends to revolve only around their immediate families. The social life they enjoy outside the family happens mostly only in the alleyways in front of their houses. At the beginning of the participatory planning process, the only idea that came up in communication with the immigrant mothers was conversion of traditional "Banlou"[6] in the building into a kids' play space; another idea that most mothers wanted, a karaoke room, was adopted yet largely restricted in opening hours owing to concern about the neighbors. Beside these, we failed to move any further on more details.

To overcome this predicament, we decided to turn to the children through a series of weekend workshops. Surprisingly, the process turned out to be successful. It not only eased the mothers' pressure for daycare, but also excited dozens of kids to visit their "secret base" every weekend. They joined to clean up the house and painted the doors, windows, and walls (Figure 10.6). More importantly, as long as the kids came, the mothers had a good reason to come and linger at this place. Ultimately, two of the mothers stayed involved and contributed some decorative work. Through such an approach, the participatory process seemed to have produced an acceptable result.

Figure 10.5 Introducing the project of "Shin Home" at the community fair. Photograph by Jia-He Lin.

The unsolved puzzles

Despite the small breakthrough we had made during the initial period, a long-term result in terms of a collective sense of attachment to the place was still not

guaranteed. In the end, the community service center was opened officially in October 2006. But to this day, for lack of human resource, Lan-Shin can only afford to meet the minimal requirements by staying open for two days a week. Lately, despite some improvement, the center is still more like a service-oriented office of Lan-Shin, rather than a gathering place that the immigrant women can call "home" in Nanfang-ao. Outside the scheduled opening hours, collective social life seldom happens there.

Figure 10.6 Kids joining in the weekend "secret base" workshop. Photograph by Jia-He Lin.

The main obstacles in this project, it seems, are institutional challenges in social work practice. On the one hand, social workers are trained to treat people they serve as "clients" owing to their professional ethics. They give help to the clients mostly on very private situations; but the workers are strictly restricted from getting involved at a personal level. This paradox of distinction leads to an unavoidable consequence of "othering": the differentiation of social workers and the clients they serve. On the other hand, the traditional mission of the social workers has been to promote stability in the society through the advocacy of family harmony and happiness. As a result, this often leads to an "ideology of accommodation" that ultimately promotes assimilation and draws the immigrant women back to their spouses' families (Hsia 2005).

Conclusion: hidden community and "home" as public space

Both the cases of Meinung and Nanfang-ao focus on the process of placemaking, with the goal of establishing a place for gathering and solidarity among the local immigrant women. In the two cases, we could see that the practices of citizenship, in different settings of nationality, kinship, and gender, are deeply aligned with the relationships between places and people's lives. Aside from the process of border crossing, for most of the immigrants, public space in the host country becomes a critical element of different notions of citizenship operating in an everyday geography (Dickinson et al. 2008). The everyday geography of immigrant women, however, is mostly home based and limited to the marital home. In that sense, to extend their life to the seemingly untouchable public space and to create gathering places with the expectation of "a space of radical openness" (hooks 1990) becomes a critical issue.

Unlike the stereotypical urban public spaces, such as plazas, halls, or grand avenues, the gathering places of immigrant women in these two cases no longer subscribe to the traditional categories. Rather than serving the generic public, these places are important bridges that could enhance the visibility of these invisible women within the Taiwanese society. As a result, the strategic representation of visibility becomes important in both cases. It has to reveal the exclusion from traditional public space in the community. Furthermore, both the Meinung and Nanfang-ao cases challenged the boundaries between "public" and "private." A shared metaphor of gathering places for the immigrant women in Meinung and Nanfang-ao has been the "natal home." It is a strategic term with different contesting meanings. The positive usage is during the developing stage of internal solidarity. The metaphor of "natal home" made it easier for the immigrant women to understand and imagine how the spaces function. Once the "home" image of transnational sisterhood is shaped, the desire for a gathering place is invoked by those who were involved. In this sense, an intimate and private metaphor of "natal home" enables the migrant women to expand their social network beyond the household and ethnic boundaries.

Besides engaging themselves in the building process, the notion of home is also a powerful tool for the immigrant women to overcome barriers in the existing patriarchal system in the local families.[7] Lacking a sense of security, many local husbands often set restrictions on the activities of their wives. With the gathering place's function as an extension of one's "home," it provides an important assurance for immigrant women's spouses and families. In many ways, it was easier to explain to the local communities how these immigrant spouses need a "home" as opposed to a "gathering place." In contrast, as discussed in the case of Nanfang-ao, the traditional patriarchal structure might be reinforced if the gathering place still operates in a mode of cultural assimilation and firmly in pursuit of family harmony and social stability. As such, the cases of Meinung and Nanfang-ao suggest that public space for marginal groups is not only produced through public discourse and a product of the tangled relationship between social actions and physical space (Torre 1996). It is also a contested field on the meanings of "home" and a frontier place that breeds openness, solidarity, and actions.

Notes

1 The Hakka are an ethnic group of Chinese people, literally "guest people" or "strangers." The Hakka now mainly reside in southeast China, Taiwan, and some regions of Southeast Asia (Constable 2005).
2 "Labor exchange" is a literal translation of *jiao-gong* in Mandarin.
3 This project belongs to a ten-year, 3-billion NTD foreign spouse accommodation foundation program organized by the Taiwanese government in 2005.
4 This is a required studio of the master degree program of the Graduate Institute of Building and Planning at the National Taiwan University. The Institute is well known for participatory design and planning. In the required studio, students team up and are asked to initiate and accomplish a "real" design or planning project at the scale of community development.
5 In Mandarin, the pronunciation "shin" applies to two characters meaning "new" (新) and "fragrance." (馨). The latter suggests the name of Lan-Shin.
6 "Banlou" (半樓) is a mezzanine space common in traditional shop-houses in Taiwan.
7 Furthermore, how to bridge these immigrant women's public and private lives is another critical issue in the two cases. Community participation is important for empowering the immigrant women. In practice, however, this can never be achieved if the needs of their families are neglected. In the tobacco barn project, TASAT took the opportunity of a government's employment program to enable the female immigrants to join the activities and earn incomes for their families at the same time. This has proven critical to the success of the project. The project in Nanfang-ao found opportunities to improve participation through weekend workshops for the children that functioned as a daycare service for the local women.

Bibliography

Chiu, K. L. (1999) *The Rise and Fall of the Nanfang-ao Opera House*, Taipei: The Journalist Publication.
Constable, N. (2005) *Guest People: Hakka Identity in China and Abroad*, Seattle: University of Washington Press.
Dickinson, J., Andrucki, M. J., Rawlins, E., Hale, D., and Cook, V. (2008) 'Introduction: Geographies of Everyday Citizenship', *ACME: An International E-Journal for Critical Geographies*, 7: 100–112.
hooks, b. (1990) *Yearning: Race, Gender, and Cultural Politics*, Boston, MA: South End Press.
Hsia, H. C. (1997) 'Selfing and Othering in the "Foreign Bride" Phenomenon – A Study of Class, Gender and Ethnicity in the Transnational Marriages between

Taiwanese Men and Indonesian Women', unpublished PhD dissertation, Department of Sociology, University of Florida.

—— (2005) 'Empowering "Foreign Spouses" and Community through Praxis-Oriented Research', paper presented at the 9th International Interdisciplinary Congress on Women, Seoul, Korea.

Lee, C. Y. (2006) 'Sense of Place' and It's Many Manifestations on the Interior and Exterior of Local Museum – Case Study of Nanfang Ao Fishing Village, Hsin-Chu: Graduate Institute for Research and Culture Studies, National Chiao-Tung University.

Low, S. and Smith, N. (eds.) (2006) The Politics of Public Space, New York: Routledge.

Sandercock, L. (1998) 'Introduction: Framing Insurgent Historiographies for Planning', in Sandercock, L. (ed.) Making the Invisible Visible, Los Angeles: University of California Press.

Torre, S. (1996) 'Claiming the Public Space: The Mothers of Plaza de Mayo', in Agrest, D. (ed.) The Sex of Architecture, New York: Harry N. Abrams.

Wu, S. (2007) 'Difference and Identity: Immigrant Movement in Hakka Community', paper presented at the Conference of Liu-tui Hakka History, Culture and Future, National Ping-Tung University of Science and Technology, Taiwan (in Chinese).

CHAPTER 11

How outsiders find home in the city

ChungShan in Taipei

Pina Wu

Gypsies, Jews, Chinese coolies . . . throughout history, wandering outsiders have been a source of mystery, speculation, and fear to city dwellers. Their presence often evokes danger and suspicion for the mainstream society. The social exclusion as well as internal need within the communities have created cities within cities. In Europe, new immigrants have created diaspora communities at the fringe of cities. In North America, there are ethnic enclaves that function as centers of social and economic life for the ethnic communities.[1] In Taipei, the overseas Filipino guest workers have created ChungShan.

To many residents of Taipei, ChungShan is a corner of the city that is little understood. But to the overseas Filipino workers this place is full of life. Every Sunday, thousands of Filipinos come to Sunday mass at St Christopher's Church on Chung Shan North Road in Taipei (hence the name ChungShan).[2] From here they embark on their day off. They go grocery shopping, meet friends, go dancing and singing, and get their hair done. This area is no larger than a quarter square mile. It is like a traveling caravan that exists only on Sundays. Every Filipino in Taipei knows about ChungShan.

Jun M. Sanchez, a Filipino poet, has described ChungShan this way (2003):[3]

Every Sundays or either Holidays
To Filipinos, rain or shine, these are good days
Along the ChungShan North Road that day
You can see them finding their own ways.
You can hear someone; they'll go to the Disco
To enjoy life and do what they want to
Meet some friends and have a date to
Eat some native foods and drink beer too.

Sidewalk vendors filled the pathways
Selling different things along the hallway
Lower prices is the inducement they say
For the Filipinos who are shopping on the way.

Sunday should be worker's free day
Going to St. Christopher's Church to pray

Attending the Holy Mass on that day
But others at the movie theaters, they say.
At weekends, native dialects is not astray
Tagalog language is also spoken at bay
Watching Filipinos relaxing in this highway
At KTV, they sing their favorite songs in gay.

Some Filipinos are having their busy time
Enriching their ability with their precious time
At S.T.I. Inc. they spent there their borrowed time
Studying computer as backdrop at the end of migration time.

The following chapter tells the story of ChungShan: how it got started in the 1990s, what this place meant for the overseas Filipino guest workers in Taipei, how ChungShan as an outsider's space created tension and provoked changes in the city in the 2000s. This case study was conducted through year-long participatory observation in ChungShan. Much of the data was collected in 2002–2003, when I volunteered at the House of Migrant Workers' Empowerment (HOME) in Taipei.[4]

The seeding of ChungShan

There are close to 8.9 million overseas Filipino workers (OFWs) working in more than 150 countries worldwide (Philippine Overseas Employment Administration 2007). After 1992, an increasing number of Filipinos began to come to Taiwan.[5] They are here alone as "guest workers" and separated from their families in the Philippines for a period of up to nine years. Among the 20,000 workers in the Taipei area, a large majority (90 percent) work as domestic helpers, doing chores, looking after children, and taking care of the elderly. They spend most of their time in private homes, with long and boring work hours.

Other Filipino workers work in factories. The factory life is segregated and far away from the city. The workers are not allowed to search for jobs or change employers freely. Their activities are confined and monitored with strict employment regulations. And the police are entitled to stop any overseas Filipinos on the street to check their IDs (Kong 2002, Wong 2003). The press tends to paint a negative picture of their presence in the city (Yeh 1995, Chen 1999, Lu 1999, Yo 1999, Liu 2000). Having no home of their own, no citizenship, and no social support, overseas Filipinos are truly outsiders to the city.

In this hostile atmosphere, ChungShan was founded little by little. It started out from St. Christopher's Church. This classically designed church was built in 1957 on Chung Shan North Road, one of the main tree-lined boulevards in Taipei (Figures 11.1 and 11.2). It provided mass in English to the American soldiers till the 1970s. After the soldiers left, the church quieted down. Since the 1990s, when the overseas Filipino workers started to arrive in Taipei, St. Christopher's Church became the focal point for receiving thousands of Filipino attendees for its Sunday masses.

Why did they come to St. Christopher's Church? It is true that many Filipinos are Catholics back home. But coming to church is also essential for overseas Filipino

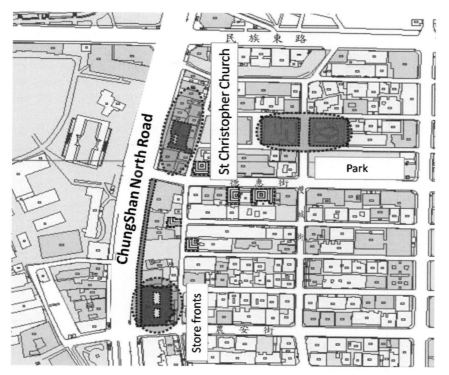

Figure 11.1 Area map of ChungShan. Map by Pina Wu.

民 族 東 路

St Christopher Church

ChungShan North Road

Park

德 惠 街

Store fronts

農 安 街

🔲 Eateries, cafes

Figure 11.2 Sidewalk space in front of St. Christopher's Church. Photograph by Pina Wu.

workers for other reasons. As Father Edwin Corr, a longtime priest at the church, said to the crowd, "Many of you have to work from eight to five every day in the factory with extra hours. For those of you who work in the household, the hours are even longer, you have to stand by twenty-four hours. One day after another, you feel every day is a repetition. And your family and friends are so far away. But everyone needs to learn new things, everyone needs to be comforted, you wonder where you can turn to."

Compared with the alienating environment outside, the church provides overseas Filipino workers with a place for healing and learning, where people can pause, reflect, and connect with friends and themselves. So that is why there are more than 6,000 Filipinos coming to the church every Sunday (Wang 1998, Hsu 2000, Hsu 2002, Yiu 2004).

Starting from 7 a.m., there are five mass sessions a day: two in English and three in Tagalog, the Filipino native language. Each session serves about 800–900 people. The church responds to many needs of the Filipino workers. It provides social support programs (Migrant Concern Desk), a translation service, and recreational activities. The workers' needs that are otherwise not met are now fulfilled by the community as a collective.

Starting from the church, small commercial businesses began to grow. St. Christopher's Church is located in a mixed-use area with storefronts and office buildings on the main boulevard, four-story residential apartments in the alleys, and neighborhood parks and markets nearby. Street vendors quickly took advantage of the crowd at the church. They occupied the sidewalks along the boulevard selling T-shirts, toys, jewelry, accessories, and electronics at low prices. Most of the vendors were Taiwanese initially, but then Filipino immigrants in Taiwan started to rent prominent storefronts and run Filipino specialty shops such as Bingo and Cosmos. They sell Filipino-brand snacks, cans, spices, soaps, cosmetics, and beverages, as well as newspapers, books, tapes, videos, and CDs (Figure 11.3).

More and more services continued to move in: remittance, mail, insurance, real estate, and human recruitment. One of the companies – EEC, branded for its "New York–London–Rome–Barcelona–Singapore–Hong Kong–Taipei" international networks – provides a "door to door" mailing service much more cheaply than the Taiwanese post office. There are also remittances agencies that provide Sunday services to the workers, as Taiwanese banks are not open on Sundays.

For many OFWs, gift packages are the only ways for their family back home to receive their love. So, very often the workers will select household appliances from a catalog in Taipei, and then an item such as a TV will be shipped to their villages in the Philippines. Or a mom will say "I want to send a Barbie to my daughter for her birthday. I am sorry I am not there for her." Many transnational family ties are maintained through these special services. Besides the specialized agencies and shops, there are also many eateries, cafes, KTVs, and discos, stretching several blocks beyond the church area. A Taiwanese Filipino has even rented a famous jazz bar in the alleyway on Sundays, open especially for the workers. There are computer classes being offered in the vacant office buildings. Finally, many Filipinos also go picnicking and play games or music in the nearby parks.

For many newly arrived workers, ChungShan is the starting point for entering

Figure 11.3 Filipino specialty shops and vendors. Photograph by Yu-Chun Lin.

the local Filipino community in Taipei (Chen *et al*. 2002). With so many activities happening, it is always easy to meet someone and start a conversation. For example, Rowena, a young Filipina being interviewed, had worked in isolation in a household without knowing anyone in the city. When she finally got her first day off (which was after one year), she came to ChungShan for the mass and some shopping, and got to know some people.

Many of the Filipinos put on their best outfits when they come to ChungShan. One Filipina said "On weekdays I am a maid, on weekends why can't I be myself?" Filipina often consciously dress poorly when working and living in the household (Lan 2002). To them, ChungShan is an energizing place, a place to show and express who they really are, in full color.

Many Filipinos cannot find home otherwise at their workplace, or in other public spaces in Taipei city. It is only in ChungShan that many Filipinos can feel truly at home. This is a place where Tagalog and English are spoken. There are food and goods to their liking, and social activities in which they can participate.

The poet Blessie L. De Borja Landingin (2002) has described her feelings about Taiwan this way:

> When a foreigner comes to your land,
> As if an intruder facing a hostile jury
> I have no intention to do wrongness,
> But an outsider seems to carry an original sin,
> I am a prisoner behind iron bars,
>
> Confused and helpless,
> Still standing straight as much as I can.

Tensions in the city

The growth of ChungShan does create some tensions with the rest of Taipei (Hsu 2000). The Filipinos have appropriated this district and made it their own on Sundays. They shop at the vendors on the sidewalks, chat in the parks, and gather at the squares. Residents in Taipei have mixed views towards the presence of thousands of Filipinos in the area. In interviews, some Taiwanese residents feel threatened: "The Filipinos are taking over our space!" But others have empathized: "The Filipinos are hard-working, and they should enjoy a good Sunday in the city." Some complain about the renting of storefronts to Filipino specialty shops. Others commented that ChungShan has brought a good business opportunity to the district, utilizing the commercial spaces that would otherwise be vacant on Sundays.

A majority of local residents in the district are not happy with their parks and alleys being overtaken by thousands of Filipinos on weekends (Hsu 2000). In interviews, they complained that the buses are always crowded, the garbage bins overflowing, the sidewalks full of vendors, and the kids having no space to play in the park. Indeed, some of the workers who come to enjoy a good Sunday in ChungShan have shown little consideration for the neighborhood environment. Their traveling Sunday carnival overloads the neighborhood. The city government has done little to mitigate the impact, for example by providing additional public facilities (such as toilets, benches, and garbage bins) and providing cleaning and maintenance. The head of the district complained to the church but this resulted in little improvement. The Filipino migrant workers themselves were not organized enough to assemble a clean-up team. When the communication failed, the head of the district called police to evict the vendors on the sidewalks, and to keep the Filipinos from lingering in the parks.

The tensions also occur at a deeper level. The district where ChungShan is located was once a shopping and entertainment district for American soldiers in the 1950s. It was a prestigious commercial and residential district, famous for its high-end imported clothing, jewelry, and household appliances since the 1970s. Even though the business was down since the 1980s, the shop owners and residents are concerned that their district is now associated with overseas Filipino workers. They do not consider the bustling commercial activities on Sundays as part of the local business. Instead, they would like the district to be redeveloped as a modern, upper-class commercial district in the future. This conflicts with the current image of ChungShan with its unregulated vendors and mini trucks selling cheap T-shirts and jewelry. The nearby residents accuse ChungShan's presence of lowering their property values.

But most importantly, the locals feel threatened that their space is being overtaken by outsiders. Even though there are thousands of Filipino overseas workers in Taipei, and many of them live intimately with Taiwanese families as domestic helpers, they have not been accepted in the public realm of the city. To some residents, this public space belongs to the Taiwanese. They believe that the Filipino workers as outsiders have no right to the city. On the sidewalk outside the storefronts in ChungShan, there was once an English sign saying, "This is a place you don't belong. So you are not welcome to enter this place." Many Filipinos would just leave when they saw the sign (Chen 1997).

Transforming Taipei

In response, ChungShan has been evolving, and there have been more interactions between ChungShan and the rest of the city in recent years. Particularly, local civic groups such as HOME began to provide services to the workers. HOME was first established in one of the back alleys in ChungShan in 2002 by the Taiwan International Workers' Association (TIWA). It provides language exchange programs, computer classes, legal consulting services, and recreational activities. It has become a place for Filipinos to form a number of social clubs. For example, SMI (Samahang Makata International – Taiwan), an international poetry club, had its annual meetings here. There were also basketball teams, dance groups, music bands, and cooking groups that found their homes here (Figure 11.4).

In 2001, the Taipei city government held its first migrant workers' poetry competition, attracting more than 700 submissions (Huang 2001). All poems were translated into Chinese. The winning poems were advertised on buses, subways, and train station, made into books, and broadcast on the radio, providing the Taipei residents with an opportunity to listen to the overseas workers' inner voice, which was often missing in mainstream media.[6] With support from St. Christopher's Church, TIWA, and Taipei city government, several traditional Filipino cultural events have been held in Taipei during the 2000s. In January, the Ati-Atihan Festival is a huge parade throughout ChungShan. The Ati-Atihan dance originated in the Philippines in the thirteenth century as a diplomatic dance between two tribes showing signs of friendliness. Now the dance is enacted on the streets in ChungShan, inviting the

Figure 11.4 Dancing group at HOME. Photograph by Pina Wu.

local residents to see the Filipinos perform. The Santa Cruzan Festival in May brings the Filipinos marching in front of Taipei Railway Station (Figure 11.5). This is the first time that the overseas Filipino workers' culture has been presented in the city center. Filipinos also participated in the Centennial Celebration of Chung Shan North Road in 2002, weaving their part of its history into the city.

Some of these events were planned consciously to overturn the Taiwanese people's notion of public space. Lorna Kong, a longtime advocate for workers' rights at TIWA, and later the head of Taipei City Foreign Workers Consultation Service Center from 1999 to 2003, had improvised a series of "cultural strategies." She believes that, whereas individual Filipinos in Taiwan may be powerless outsiders, given proper interfacing they can demonstrate their culture powerfully to the Taiwanese citizens. In the lively Ati-Atihan Festival in ChungShan, Filipinos dressed in costumes would reach out and give out flowers to the local Taiwanese residents standing watching. Some Taiwanese were shy; some were surprised to receive anything from the Filipinos. An invisible social boundary was crossed between individuals through this small gesture. The Filipino music band from HOME would also go to perform at the Eslite Book Store, a well-known upscale bookstore in Taipei, challenging the spatial notion of what is an "appropriate" place for the Filipinos workers to be in the city by "Inserting Filipino presence into the middle class public space" (Kong 2002).

In addition to challenging the notion of public space, ChungShan has also become the place where the new public action is generated (Kong 2002). As more and more labor disputes and cases of abuse against foreign domestic helpers arose in 2003, at St. Christopher's Church thousands of overseas Filipino workers have petitioned

Figure 11.5 Santa Cruzan Festival in Taipei. Photograph by Pina Wu.

the Taiwanese government to pass the "Household Worker Protection Law," urging the government to regulate and safeguard the workers' safety and welfare when working in private households. However, up to the time of writing, the law had not been passed by the legislature at the national level. To meet the demand, there are a growing number of social groups working on overseas workers' issues in Taipei and throughout Taiwan, advocating for more inclusive urban policies, thoughtful social programs, and better legal protection.[7] The former Mayor of Taipei, Ma Ying-Jeou, in several events in ChungShan had also stated "The guest workers are also residents in Taipei," urging the city to accept their presence and honor their culture (Huang 1999, Lin 2004).

Conclusion

With more than 340,000 overseas workers in various cities throughout Taiwan, places such as ChungShan provide welcoming, friendly, and comfortable spaces for them. These places can cause conflicts with the local residents. However, they also have the potential to engender new public views toward the overseas workers. Throughout Taiwan, there are more and more of such cases being documented (see Jin 2006 and Chen 2009).

Who has the right to the city? Is the right based on nationalities and ethnicities? Or is it based on a more fluid concept of citizenship? As Stuart Hall (1995) has proposed, diaspora and migration have seriously challenged the notion that the public spaces can be defined and owned by a single nationality. Places such as ChungShan therefore can steer changes in the nationalistic cities.

There are more than 82 million international migrant workers in Asia, Europe, North America, the Middle East, and other parts of the world (UN Population Division 2004, 2006). Although many countries have provided minimum legal protection as well as supporting services and spaces for these workers, abuses, labor disputes, and social isolation are common (Kofman 1998, Gurowitz 2000). In such cases, overseas workers have to rely on themselves. Whether it is in Hong Kong (Constable 1997), in Rome (Parrenas 2001), or in Dubai (Esim and Smith 2004), there are many stories like ChungShan where outsiders are striving to make a temporary home in a city that is hostile to them.

Changes can occur. The International Labour Organization has pioneered international conventions to guide migration policy and protection of migrant workers. Cities such as New York have started to view the migrants' neighborhood commercial activities as unique assets for the city, and even provided economic and social programs to support them. Best practice policies concerning overseas workers are also being developed and discussed throughout the world.[8] In an increasingly globalized world with greater movement of people and goods, we can look forward to seeing more places like ChungShan whose existence challenges and transforms the notion and practice of public space in the cities where they reside.

Notes

1 Cases include the Chinese in North American cities (Anderson 1991), Mexicans in California (Mitchell 1996), Pakistanis in London (Werbner 1996), Brazilians in New

York (Margolis 1998), West Indians in New York (Foner 2001), and Guatemalans and Salvadorians in Los Angeles (Nora and Norma 2001).

2   For the Filipino workers, ChungShan has become a new word with meanings and an identity distinct from the Chinese name of the street.

3   The poem is titled "ChungShan: A Little Divisoria." Divisoria is a spot near Manila famous for its cafés, restaurants, and shops that attract many crowds.

4   The research was carried out for a master's thesis at the Graduate Institute of Building and Planning, National Taiwan University.

5   In 2007, there were close to 80,000 overseas Filipinos workers living and working in Taiwan (Council of Labor Affairs 2007). The length of their stay ranges from two to nine years under the regulations.

6   A Taiwanese reader shared her feedback in an editorial section of a newspaper: "When I read the poem on the subway, I began to empathize with the overseas workers. I remembered how I felt when I first came to Taipei as an outsider from the countryside. Please treat the overseas workers with humanity" (Kong 2002: 260). The annual poetry competition, in its eighth year at the time of writing, has become a public way for the Filipinos to speak to the Taipei city residents.

7   Other organizations include the Alliance for Human Rights Legislation for Immigrants and Migrants (AHRLIM) and the Catholic Migrant Advocates of Taiwan.

8   Examples include *Best Practices Concerning Migrant Workers and Their Families International Workshop* (International Labour Organization 2000); *Empowering Women Migrant Workers: Examples of Good Practice* (United Nations Development Fund for Women 2005); 'Best Practices to Protect Migrants and Manage Migration' for the National Conference on Labor Migration in Thailand (Martin 2009).

Bibliography

Anderson, K. J. (1991) *Vancouver's Chinatown: Racial discourse in Canada: 1875–1980*, Montreal: McGill–Queen's University Press.

Chen, C. F. (1999) 'Kaohsiung Police Stopped Migrant Workers from Partying Hard', *Central News Agency*, 17 January (in Chinese).

Chen, H. Y. (2009) 'Urban Governmentality in an Indonesian Ethnic Gathering Place in Taipei', unpublished master's thesis, Graduate Institute of Building and Planning, National Taiwan University (in Chinese).

Chen, S. C. (1997) 'Masses at Church Alleviated Homesickness for Migrant Workers', *China Times*, 15 September (in Chinese).

Chen, Y. L. and the Migrant Worker Issues Survey Team (2002) *Study on Migrant Workers' Recreation and Consumption Style in Taipei*. Report to Taipei Labor Bureau (in Chinese).

Constable, N. (1997) *Maid to Order in Hong Kong*, Ithaca, NY: Cornell University Press.

Council of Labor Affairs. (2007) *Annual Statistics of Foreign Workers 2007*, Taipei: Bureau of Employment and Vocational Training.

Esim, S. and Smith, M. (2004) *Gender and Migration in Arab States: The Case of Domestic Workers*, Geneva: International Labour Organization.

Foner, N. (2001) *Islands in the City: West Indian Migration to New York*, Berkeley: University of California Press.

Gurowitz, A. (2000) 'Migrant Rights and Activism in Malaysia: Opportunities and Constraints', *Journal of Asian Studies*, 59: 863–888.

Hall, S. (1995) 'New Cultures for Old', in Massey, D. and Jess, P. (eds.) *A Place in the World? Places, Cultures and Globalization*, New York: Oxford University Press.

Hsu, H. Y. (2000) 'Study on the Impact of Filipino Migrant Workers' Presence in St. Christopher's Church Area on Chung-Shan North Road in Taipei', unpublished master's thesis, Department of Architecture, Tamkang University (in Chinese).

Hsu, L. C. (2002) 'St. Christopher's Church, Home away from Home for the Migrant Workers', *United Daily News*, 16 October (in Chinese).

Huang, H. W. (1999) 'Taipei Holds Migrant Workers Cultural Exchange Activities, Mayor Ma Expects to Change Residents' View against Migrant Workers', *Central News Agency*, 23 June (in Chinese).

Huang, S. F. (2001) 'Taipei Migrant Workers' Poem Competition Touches the Residents' Heart', *Central News Agency*, 26 August (in Chinese).

International Labour Organization. (2000) *Best Practices Concerning Migrant Workers and Their Families International Workshop*. Workshop material prepared by International Organization of Migration in Santiago de Chile, 19–20 June.

Jin, T. L. (2006) 'The Making of Filipino Community in Taiwan', unpublished master's thesis, Institute of Sociology, Tsing-Hua University (in Chinese).

Kofman, E. (1998) 'Whose City? Gender, Class, and Immigrants in Globalizing European Cities', in Jacobs, J. M. and Fincher, R. (eds.), *Cities of Differences*, New York: Guilford Press.

Kong, Y. C. (2002) 'An Exploration and Experiment in Changing the Migrant Workers' Policy', *Taiwan Social Review*, 48: 235–285 (in Chinese).

Lan, P. C. (2002) 'A Transnational Topography for the Migration and Identification of Filipina Migrant Domestic Workers', *Taiwan: A Radical Quarterly in Social Studies*, 48: 11–59 (in Chinese).

Landingin, B. L. De B. (2002) 'OFW's (The Plight of the Unsung Heroes)', in Kong, L. (ed.) *Taipei, Please Listen to Me: Selected Poem Collection of The Migrant Workers*, Taipei: Taipei Department of Labor.

Lin, M. Z. (2004) 'Ma Ying-Jeou: Great Cultures Make Great Cities', *Global View Magazine*, 217, July (in Chinese).

Liu, S. Z. (2000) 'Migrant Workers Gather at the Train Station, 90% of the Residents Have Negative Views toward their Presence', *United Daily News*, 27 April (in Chinese).

Lu, K. Z. (1999) 'Residents Intend to Defend against Migrant Workers', *United Daily News*, 9 November (in Chinese).

Margolis, M. L. (1998) *An Invisible Minority: Brazilians in New York City*, Boston: Allyn and Bacon.

Martin, P. (2009) 'Best Practices to Protect Migrants and Manage Migration', paper for the National Conference on Labour Migration on "Effective Labour Migration Management in Thailand: Maximizing Benefits while Upholding the Rights of Migrants and Learning from Good Practices", jointly organized by the International Organization for Migration, Ministry of Labour, and the National Human Rights Commission of Thailand, 17 June, Bangkok.

Mitchell, D. (1996) *The Lie of the Land: Migrant Workers and the California Landscape*, Minneapolis: University of Minnesota Press.

Nora, H. and Norma, S. C. (2001) *Seeking Community in a Global City: Guatemalans and Salvadorans in Los Angeles*, Philadelphia: Temple University Press.

Parrenas, R. S. (2001) *Servants of Globalization*, Stanford, CA: Stanford University Press.

Philippine Overseas Employment Administration. (2007) *2007 Overseas Employment Statistics*, Mandaluyong City: Department of Labor and Employment, Republic of the Philippines.

Sanchez, J. M. (2003) 'ChungShan: A Little Divisoria', in Sanchez, J. M. (ed.) *Poem Collection*, Taipei: Samahang Makata International.

United Nations Development Fund for Women. (2005) *Empowering Women Migrant Workers: Examples of Good Practice*. United Nations Development Fund for Women, 10 July.

United Nations Population Division. (2004) *World Population Prospects: The 2004 Revision (2005)*, New York: United Nations, Department of Economic and Social Affairs.

—— (2006) *Demographic Yearbook No. 37*, New York: United Nations, Department of Economic and Social Affairs.

Wang, C. C. (1998) 'St. Christopher's Church, Home to the Overseas Filipino Workers', *China Times*, 3 February (in Chinese).

Werbner, P. (1996) 'The Fusion of Identities: Political Passion and the Poetics of Performance among British Pakistanis', in Caplan, L., Parkin, D., and Fisher, H. (eds.) *The Politics of Cultural Performance*, New York: Berghahn Publishers.

Wong, Y. D. (2003) 'The Life Experience and Living Strategies of Filipino Household Workers in Taipei', unpublished master's thesis, Department of Anthropology, National Taiwan University (in Chinese).

Yeh, L. J. (1995) 'Chang-hua County Has More Than 15,000 Migrant Workers Causing Big Problems', *Central News Agency*, 5 August (in Chinese).

Yiu, C. (2004) 'Foreign Workers Living in Taiwan', *Taipei Times*, 25 January.

Yo, W. B. (1999) 'Prohibiting the Migrant Workers from Entering the Campus Causes Controversy', *United Daily News*, 23 October (in Chinese).

PART FOUR

TRANSGRESSING

CHAPTER 12

Machizukuri house and its expanding network

Making a new public realm in private homes

Yasuyoshi Hayashi

In Japan, community-based non-profit organizations called "Machizukuri houses" have developed their work and networks through activities focusing on small participatory projects. The phenomenon is a result of the Machizukuri movement that began in the radicalism and citizen activism of the 1960s and 1970s. Many of these organizations have emerged since the early 2000s. There are also more established organizations that have been around longer. The proliferation of the activities of Machizukuri houses has coincided with the emerging concept of the "new public" in Japan and contributed to increased social capital in local communities.

In this chapter, I would like to focus on the Setagaya Ward, an established residential area in western Tokyo, and discuss the significance of Machizukuri at the neighborhood level. Specifically, this chapter focuses on the activities of community-based non-profit organizations after the 1990s and how they have transformed the notion and expressions of the public realm in the community. The discussion will begin with an account of the current state of the Machizukuri movement in Japan after the 1990s, followed by a discussion on the development and significance of Machizukuri in the Setagaya Ward after the 1990s, including selected cases of Machizukuri activities.

Machizukuri in Japan: expansion and transformation after the 1990s

"Machizukuri" (town-making) has been a common word in Japan used by groups of citizens to describe their effort to rebuild and improve neighborhoods. In the 1960s, the concept was used by citizen activists to mobilize opposition against development projects promoted by governments and private companies. In the 1970s, it was used by progressive professionals and innovative local governments to engage citizens in participatory local planning, for example the Mano and Maruyama areas in Kobe and the Sakae-Higashi area in Nagoya. These cases in Kobe and Nagoya are among the first where citizens put together and proposed their own programs for improving the areas they lived in. The local authorities have gradually accepted and put into practice these proposals through citizen participation.

The 1980s saw a proliferation of Machizukuri activities throughout Japan.

Machizukuri professionals came into existence, and the experiments using various methods, including workshops for citizen participation, were popularized and practiced in many areas. The method of the "Machizukuri workshop" contains in its mechanism possibilities of converting Japanese traditional "vertical" human relationships into "horizontal" ones (or a dialogic relationship). The method has since been accepted widely by Japanese society and contributed to the spread of Machizukuri activities nationwide.

At the national level, the Japanese government introduced the Detailed Plan System (a system of small-area regulation through a combination of detailed plans and facility preparation plans with citizen participation methods) in 1980. Designed for the formation of small areas with a quality environment, the system gave local governments additional authority for community planning. In response to the popularity of Machizukuri, several local governments introduced their own community development ordinances in addition to the Detailed Plan System. Kobe and Setagaya, for instance, established Machizukuri ordinances and promoted participatory community planning on a neighborhood scale, followed by many other municipalities around the country which conducted similar experiments. Since then, the individual systems supported by various funds, local governments, and government agencies to assist Machizukuri have diversified and continued to expand. Nevertheless, the government has until today not put into force any comprehensive and fundamental law to support Machizukuri. However, from another point of view, this lack of legal frameworks has in a way enabled a diversity of parties to provide freely a variety of assistance services for citizens to choose.

A critical moment in the spreading of the Machizukuri movement occurred in the 1990s through two national events. In 1994, hundreds of citizens and professionals interested in participatory planning gathered in Kahoku-cho, a small town in the Kochi Prefecture, and participated in the first "Waku Waku Nationwide Workshop Meeting." Two years later, a second event took place in Kitakyushu, with over 1,000 participants from all over the country. It can be said that these epoch-making events contributed to the spreading of Machizukuri and the workshop method nationwide.

The popularity of the movement reflects a growing sense of crisis at the community level in Japan, including the fear of disintegrating human relationships in the face of penetrating global economy. As a result, since the 1990s, "Machizukuri" is widely used in Japan to describe various citizen activities to rebuild the bonds within local communities.[1] The notion of "Machizukuri" has been applied to a wide range of activities including social welfare programs, health, sports, culture, public relations and information services, historical preservation, environmental conservation, small neighborhood business, problems of homelessness, and revitalization of community.

After the Hanshin-Awaji Great Earthquake in 1995, over 1 million people from all over Japan gathered to support the earthquake victims as a volunteer work force. The phenomenon had a great impact on Japanese society. It aroused an active citizen movement to push for the enactment of the NPO Law in 1998, a legislation that was introduced by the Diet members. The Law brought about an important social reform, by formally recognizing the status of non-profit organizations (NPOs). By autumn 2009, there were an estimated 38,800 NPOs engaging in a broad range of activities. About 40 percent of them register Machizukuri as one of their activities.

With the failure of the government's economic policy that led to the bubble economy in the 1980s and a long recession in the 1990s, Japanese citizens' consciousness has shifted from dependence on the government to a model of collaboration that involves civil society and the public sector. Administrative reform and distribution of authority was still in progress in the 1990s. Since 2000, the policy aiming at creating a small government has accelerated the collaboration among NPOs, businesses, and the government. The introduction of the "Care Insurance System" in the welfare sector, for example, has promoted the participation of NPOs. About 60 percent of all NPOs declare welfare activity as one of their missions. Besides the central government, local governments also adopt a policy that regards NPOs as undertakers of administrative policy. Various issues surrounding the relation between NPOs and governments have been a subject of intense discussion.

Along with the growing number of NPOs, there is also an increasing number of foundations and private companies with programs for supporting NPOs and organizers of Machizukuri activities. These programs have become one of the most effective systems to promote participation of people and Machizukuri professionals and support independent management of organizations. With the enactment of the NPO Law, social reform, and funding support from foundations and businesses, citizens' initiatives have gained wide acceptance since the 1990s. These developments have contributed to the growth of Machizukuri activities around Japan.

Over the past nearly half century, unique characters of Machizukuri have gradually emerged. Machizukuri is not a movement preceded or prompted by the legal systems. Instead, it is a sum of activities that citizens have been engaged in to improve their everyday life and the environment that their lives rest on. In contrast, the urban planning practice in Japan, with a history of approximately ninety years, is a system institutionalized by experts and government bureaucrats. As shown in Table 12.1, prepared by Yukio Nishimura (Nishimura *et al.* 2005), the comparison between the Machizukuri approach and the legal city planning system clarifies the unique characteristics of Machizukuri.

Development of Machizukuri in Setagaya

The Tokyo metropolitan area today has a population of nearly 30 million. Located southwest of the center of Tokyo, Setagaya is one of the twenty-three special wards in Tokyo, with a population of approximately 800,000. Within Setagaya, the southwestern part is an established residential area with mainly middle-income households of middle-aged and elderly residents. The northeastern area, with a high risk of earthquake and fire, in contrast, is densely populated with collective rental houses and residents of young white-collar workers and university students. Here, various citizen activities have emerged since the 1960s. In the 1980s, the ward government of Setagaya established the Machizukuri Ordinance and founded a City Design Section inside the government. Using various workshop and participatory design methods, a number of small parks and community street projects became the testing ground for Machizukuri.

In 1992, the ward government further introduced the Machizukuri Center Plan, building on the participatory planning experiences from the late 1980s. A Machizukuri

Table 12.1 Differences between Machizukuri and the legal city planning system

Machizukuri	vs.	Legal city planning
governance by residents	vs.	governance by law
community-based	vs.	atom-like individuals
human as inherently good	vs.	human as inherently evil
non-experts in the majority	vs.	experts in the majority
horizontal, priority given to community	vs.	vertical, priority given to professional
bottom-up	vs.	top-down
by example and agreement	vs.	regulation by compulsion
common law	vs.	written law
gradualism	vs.	structuralism
originality and invention	vs.	following precedents
transparent and discreet	vs.	fair and equal
individualistic and flexible	vs.	standardized and stiffening
open and frank	vs.	closed
aiming at the highest	vs.	securing the lowest
integrative approach	vs.	analytical approach
residents' initiative	vs.	resident participation

Source: Nishimura *et al.* (2005).

Center was set up to support participatory planning. In addition, the Machizukuri Fund was created and overseen by a steering committee to support Machizukuri activities. The Machizukuri Center was managed mainly by the professionals who had studied and practiced urban design and participation in Germany and the United States. The center offered many opportunities for residents to study the workshop method and to participate in the design of community facilities.

One of the programs that the center managed is the "proposal solicitation program," which utilizes the Machizukuri Fund to encourage local citizen initiatives. With successful results, the "proposal/open competition method" has since spread nationally and opened the window of opportunity for citizens to propose initiatives and activities based on their own wishes. The system of financial support under the program differs significantly from the vertical hierarchy of the government administrations. About twenty projects are supported each year in Setagaya. Each can be funded for three years. Usually half of the funded organizations have continued their activity after the funding is finished. Since the inception of the program, about 180 organizations have continued their activities. These activities have in turn developed numerous social networks within and outside the area. In addition, there is a network of professionals developed through the participatory projects. Together, we see layers of various social and professional networks developed in the Setagaya area.

In an expanding field of Machizukuri activities, the numerous networks developed among people and between different organizations have produced mutual benefits. These networks can be regarded as social capital. Furthermore, they have expanded the concept of public realm in Japan. In the following, I will focus on the case of Tamagawa Machizukuri House and the impact of its expanding activities and networks on the notion of public realm at the community level in Japan.

Case study: Tamagawa Machizukuri House

Tamagawa Machizukuri House (TMH) was founded in the spring of 1991 by three experts in community design, each being a resident of the Tamagawa area, located in southern Setagaya. Tamagawa is a residential area with some 200,000 residents. For the past fifteen years, TMH has focused its activities on a neighborhood of about 900 households where TMH is based. The neighborhood was a typical high- and middle-income residential area in Tokyo. At the start of the 1990s, a number of real estate businesses began to purchase and subdivide properties in the area for sale. The quality of the neighborhood declined rapidly with shrinking property sizes as well as reduced green foliage. The deterioration of the community has caught the attention of local residents. To address the issue, TMH has developed a mission to maintain the quality of the local living environment while improving community well-being.

The first task TMH took up was designing a small park with the participation of local people, which led to the organization of a volunteer group of citizens who have since taken care of the management of the park (1992–1994). Then TMH started running a community garden utilizing a municipality-owned site in the neighborhood (1992–1998) and later (1995–1998) promoted citizen participation in the designing of a daycare center built on the same site by the city, prompting the start of a volunteer organization to support the management of the center (1998–).

Simultaneously, to arrest the subdivision of properties by real estate companies, TMH established a residents' conference on the living environment (1997). The conference worked out a proposal on land use and architectural regulation in the area, which was submitted to the city office. The city office later adopted the proposal as an area plan based on the Urban Planning Law (2000). In 1995, TMH decided to extend until 1999 its activities to help rebuild the area afflicted by the Hanshin-Awaji Great Earthquake,[2] and at the same time took part in the movement to promote the introduction of an NPO Law into Japan. The law took effect in 1998 and TMH was recognized by the law as an NPO in 2000. The following introduces a selection of projects that demonstrated how NPOs such as the TMH expand the notion and practice of the public realm at the community level in Japan.

Day Home Tamagawa

Day Home Tamagawa (1998–; Figure 12.1) is a social welfare facility developed by the local government with citizen participation. The space is used not only to provide daily support for elderly people, but also for other citizen activities. On the first floor, a space for citizen activities is available. Tamagawa Machizukuri House uses the Day Home to hold a bazaar every spring (2005–), an event for collecting unused utensils, accessories, and books from families supporting the House activities. The items are then sold to cover part of TMH's management expenses. The event also provides opportunities for information exchange between local residents as well as for fundraising for the Green Commons Fund (see below). These activities help transform an ordinary social welfare facility into a new public space in the community.

Saburo Miyamoto Museum

In 2003, TMH took part in the designing of the Saburo Miyamoto Museum, an annex to the Setagaya Art Museum. The design of the annex was completed through the participation of the local community. Specifically, TMH helped the museum expand its community networks and worked as a coordinating organization to help realize proposals from citizens in the museum programs. In one proposal, for example, classical music lovers in the community formed the European opera music club in 2007 and hosted several events. The events were attended by not only community members but also people from outside the community. Through the participatory programming, the museum becomes a new public realm that supports diverse cultural activities. In addition to individual projects, the museum also supports meetings of neighborhood groups. The expansion of the community network in turn generates opportunities to foster Machizukuri.

Green Commons

TMH started its "Green Commons" activity in 2007. The establishment of the program began in an effort to preserve a site in the neighborhood that had been purchased by a real estate company. In the area, eighty houses have been rebuilt in the past eight years. Trees on a site are usually cut down according to the institutional way of Japan when a property is sold or redeveloped. The preservation effort began

Figure 12.1 Day Home Tamagawa. Photograph by Yasuyoshi Hayashi.

with a focus on saving a zelkova tree on the site, a tree vivid in the memories of local residents (Figure 12.2). Later, the community residents began a discussion about changing the habit of cutting down trees as properties are sold and redeveloped. To do so, residents have started fundraising activities to create a Green Commons in the community, to preserve trees from twenty hectares of private lots. The fund will be utilized to preserve trees through the collaboration of residents, site owner, and developer. As the program began, the developer has become a member of

Figure 12.2 At the Green Commons, local residents want to preserve this zelkova tree (circled). Photograph by Yasuyoshi Hayashi.

Figure 12.3 Model of the Green Commons development. The new plan is to relocate the tree (circled) to the plaza by the road. Photograph by Yasuyoshi Hayashi.

TMH, and contributed to the fundraising effort. They disclosed the revised plan of a new building that involved demolishing the old building. The new plan will replant and preserve the tree in a plaza by the road (Figure 12.3). Related to the Green Commons program, TMH is currently developing the idea of "commons of garden trees." The program is to create a method to make garden trees loved by residents into a property of the community with consent of the owner.

Community Café Engawa

The third group of activities involved opening up private spaces in the neighborhood to create small community gathering places. One such example is the Community Café Engawa (Figure 12.4). "Engawa" is a kind of open terrace in a traditional Japanese house, a place where people would pop in, sit around, and talk freely. In this project at the TMH itself, a wooden deck was created to function as an engawa, connected with an indoor café. The space has been used for various activities of TMH and the community. The café has often been used as a meeting space for non-profit organizations. For example, the meetings of the NPO network in Setagaya City were held at the café. On a more regular basis, the café functions as a quiet gathering place in the community. Following the example of Community Café Engawa, a nearby bookstore named Mikamo rented a house and opened

Figure 12.4 Community Café "Engawa." Photograph by Yasuyoshi Hayashi.

it to the community in 2006 as Reading Space Mikamo, a reading and "hobby meeting" place for the neighborhood citizens (Figure 12.5). The bookstore's quiet environment offers relaxing and fruitful time for community residents and visitors. It also functions as a small gathering place in the community. To expand the use of private properties, the Setagaya Machizukuri Center has established a "wisdom and practice team" for the utilization and conservation of valuable private properties.

Community assets and the creation of a new public realm

In Japanese society, the term "public realm" refers predominantly to public facilities and sites that are built, owned, and managed by the administrative authorities. Under Machizukuri, a new type of public realm has emerged through two mechanisms. The first is through transforming the existing authority-owned spaces into new "common properties" managed by and accessible to citizens, based on citizen participation and consensus. The second is by encouraging citizens and businesses to take action on their own and open up their private spaces for community use. The citizen actions in both cases are pillars in the creation of a "new public" and constitute an important goal of Machizukuri.

As demonstrated in the case of Tamagawa, Machizukuri is an activity that can

Figure 12.5 At the Reading Space "Mikamo," a small group of local women gather for craft activities. Photograph by Yasuyoshi Hayashi.

create gathering places and "common properties" inside communities. These are places where citizens can relax and connect with each other. The activities also form networks that are open not only to the community members but also to the outside world. Machizukuri utilizes existing resources close to residents to improve their amenities and resolve problems in their everyday life. Successful results contribute not only to the physical realm but also to the social assets of the area. For example, participatory design of small parks not only improves the design and use of neighborhood space, but also stimulates children's creativity and sense of ownership. The processes of small projects in turn create new networks in the area, an important social outcome in itself. The newly created networks in the area can empower people with the ability to undertake further activities and initiatives. Through the process, people who participate in these activities and initiatives may create bonds and mutual trust that can in turn heighten the possibilities for creative collaboration. The bond between people with different kinds of expertise and resources will improve their efforts in ways that we cannot expect from a typical neighborhood. This body of networks, bonds, and assets in the area can be described as the power of community.

Notes

1   Similar concepts have also emerged in Taiwan and South Korea, borrowing elements of the Machizukuri movement in Japan.
2   The Hanshin-Awaji Great Earthquake (a.k.a. Kobe Earthquake) occurred on January 17, 1995. Approximately 6,434 people were killed, and 300,000 people were left homeless.

Bibliography

Nishimura, Y., Minohara, K., Kubota, H., Isikawa, M., Kitazawa, T., Murosaki,Y., Hayashi, Y., and Jinnai, H. (2005) *Cities as Public Spaces*, Tokyo: Iwanami (in Japanese).

CHAPTER 13

Niwa-roju

Private gardens serving the public realm

Isami Kinoshita

Over the fences, the tree branches grow. In spring, cherry and plum blossoms turn the streets into scenic landscapes. Green leaves of large trees cast shadow on the summer sidewalk. In autumn, ginkgo and maples create colorful pictures like a gallery corridor. In the dry winter season, persimmon, oranges, and other fruits form mellifluous scenery.

In Japan, harmony with neighbors has been a traditional way of life. But this kind of community consciousness has been weakened by rapid economic development in the modern era, in which a materialistic consumer society has emerged. Meanwhile, the residential site has changed from open to closed, as enclosures formed by cement blocks can be seen everywhere. With this transformation, communication between neighbors has been in decline, and as a result, neighborhood crime watch and mutual support for social welfare became everyday challenges.

The typical Japanese residential townscape is composed of single houses and private gardens along the streets with fences or walls standing between the street and the private parcels. The edge of the private parcels facing the public space has a somewhat public role. Even though the fence is part of the private domain, the surface of the fence has a public meaning. It shapes a part of the public streetscape. The fences and walls are similar to building façades in historic towns in Europe in the way they shape the townscape. However, compared with European cities, the consciousness of the private landowners in Japanese cities tends to focus on privacy and individual rights rather than contributions to the public landscape. This is one of the reasons why the Japanese townscape is in chaos in the recent time.

Is the public realm only limited to the street right of way? Do the private lands along the street have any public functions? What would be the role of the property edge facing the public space in today's Japanese cities? Is there any middle ground between the public and private spheres? May we consider semi-public or semi-private areas as a new public realm?

In this case study of the Kogane neighborhood in Matsudo city, I want to focus on the area between streets and private lands. Specifically, using the idea of *niwa-roju*, I want to focus on the contributions of private gardens to the public realm.

The concept of *niwa-roju*

Niwa-roju is an idea that conceptualizes the use of private gardens to complement public streets in place of planting street trees in a public right of way. The word was created with my students through the community design studio work in the Kogane district of Matsudo city, where we have been working for several years (Sekiguchi *et al*. 2005). *Niwa-roju* is a wordplay on the concept of *gai-roju* (trees lining a street). In contrast to the word *gai-roju*, *niwa-roju* means using the trees (*ju*) in private gardens (*niwa*) along the street (*ro*). But it includes not only trees in the gardens but also flowers and other vegetation on private lands that may also include parking spaces. With tree branches, leaves, and fruits hanging over the fences, this greenery has qualities and functions that contribute to the improvement of the streetscapes and townscapes.

In Japan, there are many streets with not enough width for planting street trees. In such cases, the contribution of private gardens and vegetation, such as hedges, trees, and flowers, to the streetscape in effect creates a new public realm that contrasts with the typical streetscape with standardized street trees. However, there are still some common barriers that prevent the use of the private landscape for the public, such as concrete-block walls and other tall walls that stand between the street and private gardens. The idea of the *niwa-roju* is to break through such barriers by making them transparent, such as opening a hole in the wall or lowering the height of the wall, and to enhance the relationship between the street and private greenery. In addition, this idea applies not only to the physical environment, but also to the involvement of people by engaging them in the remaking of public realm.

In the novel *Utopia*, Sir Thomas More (1925: 71) describes the ideal city of Utopia using the tale spoken by the fictional traveler Raphael Hythloday about the city Amaurot as follows:

> They set great store by their gardens. In them they have vineyards, all manner of fruit, herbs and flowers, so pleasant, so well furnished and so finely kept, that I never saw thing more fruitful nor better trimmed in any place. Their study and diligence herein cometh not only of pleasure, but also of a certain strife and contention that is between street and street, concerning the trimming, husbanding and furnishing of their gardens: every man for his own part.

It is interesting that the notion of Utopia is closely connected with the act and scenery of gardening by its residents. Ebenezer Howard's idea of "Garden City" also uses the word "garden" to represent the idealized life in the countryside similar to More's Utopia. In the Edo era, the downtown of the capital city Edo (now Tokyo) was said to be a kind of garden city, composed of small gardens and potted plants in townhouses (Kawazoe 1979). At the time, people enjoyed the different plant markets, such as the Asagao Ichi (Morning Glory Market) in Iriya and the Hoozuki Ichi (Ground Cherry Market) in Asakusa, to see, buy, and bring home the plants. The people from the countryside came to live in downtown Tokyo, and they made their neighborhood of houses and streets by themselves, as well as planting vegetables in vacant lots to continue their rural way of life (Yanagida 1929). The idea of *niwa-roju* may play a similar role in today's Japanese city to empower and engage people again through gardening, if we could break through the boundary of the public street and the private gardens.

Understanding *niwa-roju* in Kogane

The neighborhood of Kogane was formerly a post town in the Edo era (1603–1864). Located on the historic Mito Kaido, it served as one of many resting stops for travelers between Edo and Mito. Since the late nineteenth century, this small town on the periphery of Tokyo has undergone a number of significant changes. In 1896, the railway from Tokyo divided the town into north and south. During the 1960s, widespread housing estate developments in the greater Tokyo region resulted in demographic and physical transformation of the area. In the 1990s, a high-rise redevelopment project around the local train station led to the latest change in the neighborhood, as supermarkets and a department store attracted business away from the local shops along the historic main street (Hou and Kinoshita 2007). Today, while the historical townscape has become increasingly unrecognizable as a result of urban development, there is still a high number of private mansions and gardens along the historic main road that indicate the history of the area (Figure 13.1).

The large number of private gardens and the changing streetscape in Kogane provided the context for this research. To understand the phenomenon of *niwa-roju* in the district, we conducted interviews in thirty-five gardens along the historic street about the management of the gardens and the residents' consciousness concerning the neighborhood townscape. The interviews were conducted by ten students from Chiba University under the direction of two faculty members. The interviews lasted for one to two hours each, with watching, drawing, asking, listening, and noting. Based on field observations, we also classify the different boundaries such as fences, hedges, and walls between the street and each private garden according to the following characteristics: *penetrative vs. opaque*, *low vs. high*, and *natural vs. artificial*. We also checked each tree with branches overhanging the property boundaries as well as notable trees seen from the streets by pedestrians.

Figure 13.1 The contemporary streetscape of Kogane. Photograph by Isami Kinoshita.

The gardens of the old clan families each come with a long history. Most gardens were made in the traditional Japanese garden style composed of stones, rocks, and well-manicured trees. For the maintenance of a garden, an owner would pay from 1 to 5 million yen per year to a gardener. The good maintenance of the garden was necessary to impress guests. If a garden was not kept in good condition, it would bring shame to the owner. But today such tradition is in a crisis as the younger generation often like to change their gardens into Western-style grass lawns, or even convert the gardens into apartment buildings to avoid paying inheritance tax later. Many gardens also face the problem of management as aged people often live alone or as couples only. Garden maintenance becomes difficult if they are not able to pay for gardeners and have to tend the gardens on their own. This situation has increased recently and will become more so in the future.

For example, in one specific case in Kogane, there is a garden with a special character made by an old woman according to her taste. She had planted the trees that she bought at the traditional green market at the temple every year for the last forty years. After she died, the garden had been maintained by her husband alone, in memory of his wife. As such, the garden embodies the personal history and the private world of the couple. In this case, maintenance of the garden would not be a problem so long as the husband is in good health. But what will happen if he is not able to work any more because of some health condition? How will this special garden be managed by others? If the site is not open to the public, it is difficult to get any support from the public. Since the memory of the trees and plants of the garden was a very private one, wouldn't it be disturbed by access to the public? In the context of the personal history and the human relationship with the plants, the plants and the space have special values. How can we bridge between this personal realm and the public realm? These are issues to consider under the idea of *niwa-roju*.

In another case in Kogane, this following episode was revealed to us. An old woman whom we interviewed had just come back from the hospital a few days before after a cancer-related operation. Her private garden is called "the Grandma Garden" (Figure 13.2). Chrysanthemums of different colors and types are planted in this garden. In the blossom season, the garden was very attractive for the pedestrians walking along the sidewalk. The fence between the sidewalk and the garden is very low. Therefore, rich conversations between strangers walking on the sidewalk and Grandma have often occurred. The absence of Grandma from her garden during her operation brought anxiety to the people who regularly walked by the garden. During the interview, she explained how the garden gave her opportunities to get to know many people, such as a photographer who one day gave her beautiful photographs of her garden taken during the beautiful flowering time of the chrysanthemums. That was one of the reasons that she started her gardening work again as soon as she came back from the hospital.

Lastly, there is another case in which the owner set a bench in front of her garden that became a place of many conversations. In this case, the bench opens the border between the street and the private garden, enabling communication between strangers and neighbors.

From the interviews and observations at each garden, we also found the following tendencies and characteristics. The Japanese-style gardens in Kogane are

Figure 13.2 Students interview a woman in "the Grandma Garden." Phtograph by Isami Kinoshita.

often enclosed by walls, but with several trees that can be seen from the street. The gardening activities are often led by the male head of the household. The gardens become an important part of the street scenery especially during cherry and plum blossom time. The traditional gardens require costly maintenance by gardeners. Nevertheless, the owners are often proud to keep them beautiful and are honored if people look at their garden from the street. Historically, the plants in the garden have come from the green market that has taken place once a year at the temple for more than 100 years. But nowadays there are also gardens with planting done in the style of Western gardens, such as English-style gardens. These gardens are tended mostly by women. With lower fences, the gardens can be seen more easily from the street.

Realizing *niwa-roju*

After the initial research, the students made proposals to break through the boundaries between the street and private gardens as a realization of the concept of *niwa-roju*. The proposals included ten different types of street–garden interfaces, focusing on fences, gates, green ornaments, and open gardens, ranging from simple to complicated interventions. After students presented their proposals to the residents, the residents had to choose their favorite one among the ten proposals. The one that was eventually selected by the residents was titled "Communication through the Gardens."

The result shows that the residents approve the idea to empower communication in the public realm using their gardens. The enhanced human relationship is important to safety and to ensure that hedges and lower fences can be sustained. As such, *niwa-roju* provides an important bridge between the private realm and the new public realm.

Figure 13.3 Before
(top) and after (bottom)
the "Drawing a Future
Vision" experiment.
Photographs by Isami
Kinoshita.

In 2006, a series of four workshops were held to create a vision of the neighborhood streetscape using the concept of *niwa-roju*. With the participation of students from the local junior high school and primary school together with the residents along the street, the workshops involved "Drawing a Future Vision" and coming up with ideas to replace the cement-block walls. A decision was made to experiment with covering the walls between the street and private gardens using green colored sheets for a couple of weeks (Figure 13.3). The purpose was to simulate the replacement of cement-block walls with hedges and to invite reactions from the residents. The overall reaction was not bad, but the approval was also not very strong. The reason might be that the simulation of the hedges was not entirely successful. Nevertheless, this event was useful to make the residents become more aware of the issue and think more about their townscape. The final workshop involved making a model and synthesizing and evaluating the different ideas.

The Takahashi house pocket park

Building on the concept of *niwa-roju*, the case of the Takahashi house pocket park is an amazing case in Kogane in which a private carport was converted and opened to the public as a pocket park through students' studio work involving local primary school kids. The project was a result of a collaborative design studio between the University of Washington and Chiba University in 2003 in which the students produced a number of design proposals to improve the streetscape in

Figure 13.4 Before (top) and after (bottom) creation of the Takahashi house pocket park. Photographs by Isami Kinoshita.

the neighborhood. The idea of creating a public space caught the attention of one landowner, Mr. Takahashi, who decided to give up his carport and make it a pocket park for the community (Figure 13.4). He also paid for all the materials. The construction was carried out by the Chiba University landscape architecture students, together with Kogame primary school children and a builder from the neighborhood. The land is still privately owned but it is now open to the public. As such, it suggests a new type of public realm.

This idea of converting a carport into a small public space might be a good one to consider in the aging society of Japan. When people become too old to drive a car, they may not need their carport any more. If private carports could be opened as a public space, it would also be very helpful for the elderly people walking on the street because they need places to sit down and rest.

The residents along the street in Kogane were very encouraged by the making of the Takahashi house pocket park to join in improving the neighborhood streetscape. Motivated by the project, the local community development organization (Kogane No Machi Wo Yokusuru Kai or "Yokusuru Kai") subsequently proposed to the Prefecture Office to remove the telephone poles along the street and put the cables underground. This proposal was accepted by the Prefecture and the feasibility study was conducted in 2005. Furthermore, the Yokusuru Kai had been organizing workshops for making neighborhood design guidelines with the participation of the neighborhood residents. In the guidelines, the idea of *niwa-roju* was introduced to encourage other landowners to apply this idea in their private gardens (Figure 13.5).

Figure 13.5 Children receive a tour of a private garden. Photograph by Isami Kinoshita.

Conclusion

Niwa-roju is a new word and concept for utilizing private gardens to improve the townscape and street environment in place of *gai-roju*. There are two factors in recent trends that enable such an idea in Kogane. One is the recent model of Western (English) gardens, which has enhanced the consciousness of the residents (mainly women) in favor of showing private gardens to the outside world, rather than the Japanese gardens that tend to be seen only from the inside, closed to the street. The other factor is that the trees in the traditional gardens have matured and can be seen from the street, thus playing an important role in the neighborhood townscape. The species of trees are similar because they were all once bought from the annual green market at the temple. The narratives of each garden and its owner show the background of human attachment to the plants and garden. Such narratives are important assets and human factors in the community that may enable collaborative maintenance of the gardens once the owners become older and contribute to the improvement of the neighborhood townscape. More than just vegetation along the road, *Niwa-roju* can become a tool for community improvement and for defining a new public realm.

Bibliography

Hou, J. and Kinoshita, I. (2007) 'Bridging Community Differences through Informal Processes: Reexamining Participatory Planning in Seattle and Matsudo', *Journal of Planning Education and Research*, 26 (3): 301–313.

Kawazoe, N. (1979) *Tokyo No Genfukei Toshi To Denen No Koryu* (Original Landscape of Tokyo – Interaction of City and Country), Tokyo: NHK Publisher.

More, T. (1925) *Utopia*, Robinson, R. (trans.) London: Macmillan.

Sekiguchi, Y., Odaira, T., Sakushima, Y., Dohi, C., Hikita, J., and Kinoshita, I. (2005) 'NiwaRoJyu: Penetrating of Personal Life, Architectural Institute of Japan Competition – the Development and Control of the Urban Architecture (Honorable Mention)', *AIJ Journal*, 120 (1534): 38–39.

Yanagida, K. (1929) *City and Country*, Tokyo: Asahi-Newspaper Publisher.

CHAPTER 14

Farmhouses as urban/rural public space

Sawako Ono, Ryoko Sato, and Mima Nishiyama

In Japan, the population decline caused by reduced agricultural production has resulted in a marked increase in the number of vacant houses in rural areas. In the meantime, the urban baby-boomers reached their retirement age around 2007. It is highly expected that a large population may move to rural areas from the city in the coming years. With an opportunity to increase the rural population, both national and municipal governments have offered programs to promote a new lifestyle in rural areas for the aging urban population. They encourage people in the city to move to rural areas. To provide them with housing, many local governments have set up vacant farmhouse reuse programs that offer information, mediation assistance, and subsidies for repair. How can the private farmhouses be converted for public use and other new functions? What would this mean to the social and spatial fabric of rural towns and villages and their relationships with urban residents in Japan?

The opportunity of reusing the rural farmhouses faces two main challenges. First, the government programs regard the houses as objects with only material values while neglecting the owners' personal and emotional attachment to these buildings. Most farmhouse owners are therefore reluctant to lease or sell their houses, even though the houses remain unoccupied. The owners do not feel comfortable about outsiders taking over their properties and fear losing control of the houses. Second, many vacant farmhouse owners live in the city. For them the house is the center of their roots, a place where they grew up, and a place that embodies generations of family history. It is a thread that connects them with their home villages. Therefore, they do not wish to reliquish control of their properties.

The purpose of this chapter is to examine the potential for the reuse of the rural farmhouses for new social and community purposes and, in the context of Japan, how such uses connect city residents with their counterparts in the countryside. We begin by reviewing the current situation of the farmhouses and issues concerning the existing government programs, before examining two recent cases of conversion.

"Country living"

Both the national and local governments in Japan have raised concerns about the population decline in rural areas since the 1980s, and have been encouraging city people to return to and settle in the countryside with moderate success. Currently, they are trying to extend the policy to attract the large number of retiring baby-boomers. One such policy is a nationwide action called "One Million People Homing and Circulating Campaign," with a Campaign Support Center set up in 2002. The center's main task is to provide information and guidance on country living to city people who are interested in relocating to the countryside.

As the term "Circulating" suggests, the policy promotes a lifestyle in which people spend a certain amount of time (one to three months at a time) in the countryside while keeping their regular residence in the city. They call this new lifestyle "dual residence" (MLIT 2005). This policy has been adopted as a strategy to solve the problems facing both the rural areas and the cities. In rural areas, it is feared that a large decline and rapid aging of its population will cause an expansion of deserted areas especially in the villages and towns outside the local core urbanized areas. In the meantime, the people's demand for country living has been emerging in cities. It is believed that dual residence in the countryside provides city people with more leisure-oriented and spacious housing. It is also expected that the local economy will be strengthened with expenditure on necessaries and housing. Both the national and local governments have offered various programs to realize this policy.

The programs, however, have two flaws. The first is that, in desperation to attract city people to the countryside, often only the positive aspects of country living are being promoted to the outsiders. An image of a village as an ideal place to live with peace and joy has captivated especially the educated city people in Japan. The scenic natural environment has been a focus of promotional campaigns as a place blessed with abundant natural products and filled with people of warm and simple spirit. Consequently, the difficulties that face rural areas are often hidden. Therefore, even those programs that profess to understand country living tend to display only the charms of the countryside. We can see it in the monitoring tour program for dual residence sponsored by the Ministry of Internal Affairs and Communications in 2006 (MIC 2006).

The selected sites under the program were all remote small villages where local people had been working hard, with considerable success, to have city people come to visit as tourists. Additionally, the monitoring tours joined by city participants covered only the programs that had already been well organized. With colorful events, plenty of good food, and warm hospitality, the participants from the city were naturally satisfied with the well-organized programs. The events were designed to entertain the guests from the city, while the hosts, local people, worked to provide them with leisure activities and to present their places as tourist attractions. The main purpose of these monitoring tours was to give the city people a chance to communicate with the locals. However, it is doubtful that visitors got a taste of a real local life that includes not only the attractions but also its problems, and that local people got any idea from the city people about how to improve their life. Communication here occurred mainly on the surface.

Second, the programs are carried out without inputs from the local community. The project of the Ministry of Agriculture, Forestry, and Fisheries under the dual residence policy is to build allotments with accommodation in rural areas. The allotments were intended to provide the first step for city people to settle in the countryside. The purpose was to involve city people in farming activities, especially in places where it is inadequate to operate mechanized agriculture. With subsidies from the national government, many municipal governments have established such allotments in rural areas. Most of them consist of twenty to thirty lots each with a bungalow and some vegetable plots. However, despite the attempt to integrate city people into a local community in this project, the allotment sites are often separated from the village proper through the development of a new site. The abandoned farmland and farmhouses remain unoccupied. Therefore, contrary to the original intent, the allotment seems to be primarily a place where the city people simply enjoy leisure in the rural area without interacting with the rural community or addressing issues of the local economy.

Reuse of farmhouses

According to research on reuse of vacant houses by the Ministry of Land, Infrastructure, Transport, and Tourism in 2006, the number of vacant houses in rural areas will increase rapidly from 3,260,000 in 2003 to 4,600,000 in 2020 with 18 percent of houses vacant. However, the owner's motivation to lend their houses for other uses is very weak. Only six out of eighty-five vacant house owners have agreed to lend their houses. Eighty percent of the owners who do not lend their houses have no intention of lending their houses. The reason is that they use the house on special occasions such as the New Year holidays and Buddhist memorial services when their families return home from the city, and they keep their Buddhist altar where the ancestor spirits are enshrined. To meet the conditions for lending, the tenants have to be trustworthy, or information on the tenant must be available beforehand. In addition, the house can be used only when the owners are not using it (MLIT 2006).

These results show a strong attachment of the homeowners to their houses. They have inherited their houses from generation to generation together with their farmland. The houses have been the center of their life and they have been maintaining them through hard work. Even though no one may live there regularly, the ancestors' spirits stay. Therefore, they feel uneasiness about outsiders utilizing their properties. In addition, the owners have a responsibility towards their community. If they introduce tenants who act against the community, it will be their fault.

To promote the utilization of vacant houses, some local governments and citizens have established a system called "Akiya Bank" (Vacant House Bank), an information system for both the owners who intend to sell or lend their houses and people in the city who are interested in living in rural areas. Akiya Bank is helpful especially in rural areas where real estate business is often absent. In addition, the individual house owners regard the information to be reliable because the system is conducted by municipal governments or citizen organizations. However, this system still has shortcomings. For example, in order to avoid being involved in potential troubles with individual contracts, the system leaves the negotiation process to only the parties concerned. In order to make the Akiya Bank system more effective, the information provider should work as a medium between the owners and the applicants as well as between newcomers and the local community.

Today, despite the weak support among most house owners and the difficulties in facilitating the utilization of vacant farmhouses, there have still been a broad variety of reuses. According to research on the conversion of old folk houses in the Kanto area in central Japan (Nakata *et al.* 2006), 96 of 203 cases are cultural facilities such as museums, interpretive centers, and libraries; sixty are commercial uses such as restaurants, galleries, souvenir shops, and tourist information centers; and thirty-five are community facilities such as community centers and community interpretive centers. Furthermore, some others have been converted into accommodation facilities, providing guests with an experience of rural life through interpretive programs. Welfare facilities such as nursing homes have also been seen in a small number as the newest examples. How these cases come about is unknown, but since these data were collected through local governments and chambers of commerce, they represent a concern and interest by the local municipalities and communities. We have found similar evidence in other rural areas throughout Japan.

Case one: Rokusuke – interpretive center for country life

Chiba Nature School is a non-profit organization (NPO) working for rural area improvement in the Chiba prefecture. The school has been planning to convert an old farmhouse and the estate in a small village in southern Chiba into an interpretive center to run programs for city people to experience the country life. The owner moved to the city several years ago and the house fell into ruin without any occupant. Chiba Nature School got a lease in 2003. In April 2006, they organized a workshop to get to know the place. Guided tours in the village conducted by the local people showed workshop participants features of the village (Figure 14.1). In the shade of the woods, there were hidden historical monuments. A stream looked good for having a water mill. A splendid view of the Pacific Ocean from a hilltop caught their breath. Although abandoned rice paddies indicated depopulation and aging of the community, they were convinced of the potential of this land as a prototype of a rural landscape. After having local delicacies for lunch, they made a vision map of the house and its surroundings.

This workshop was held as a part of a *satoyama* symposium. *Satoyama* means originally the forest managed by local agricultural communities used for daily life and agriculture. It provides young and fallen leaves used as fertilizer in the rice paddies, and wood for construction, cooking, and heating, as well as grass for feed and thatch. More recently, it means a rural landscape that has been shaped through centuries of agricultural use. It contains a mosaic of mixed forests, rice paddy fields, vegetable fields, grasslands, streams, ponds, and reservoirs for irrigation (Kobori and Primack 2003). Today, population decline and lifestyle change are considered as the significant factors in the disappearance of *satoyama* in the Japanese rural landscape. Since the 1980s, conservation of *satoyama* has been implemented throughout the country. As a part of this movement, the Chiba prefecture enacted a *satoyama* ordinance in 2003. Since then, they have held a *satoyama* symposium every year to discuss the issues related to rural area conservation and improvement of *satoyama*. In this symposium, the house is regarded as the center of rural life.

The house has been well known among the village people as Rokusuke for a long time. Rokusuke is the title of the family as well as the house. In a village the people

Figure 14.1 View from Rokusuke. Photograph by Sawako Ono.

distinguish a family from others by the house titles because there are so many families with the same family names. A title name includes the family, the house, and its estate. It indicates that all of them have been recognized as a fundamental unit in the local community, with the house being at the center. By retaining its title, the house could maintain a kind of personality that attracts the visitors and is known to the locals. The family tomb also stays on the site. This enables the owner's family to maintain a connection with this place through their regular visits to the grave several times a year. Although the owner is not intimately involved with the Chiba Nature School's projects, he often comes to see the progress. The Chiba Nature School also talks with him when it improves the house.

With a government grant, Nature Environment Conservation and Formation Project Grant, by the Ministry of Agriculture, Forestry and Fishery, the Chiba Nature School started to repair the house. The estate lies on a hillside along a road. It consists of the thatched-roof house, a gate with barns, a storehouse, a front garden, backyard woods, a bamboo grove, vegetable gardens, and a family graveyard. Some fruit trees grow at the corner. This is a typical farmhouse in this region. When Chiba Nature School took over the house, the house and its surroundings were in a terrible shape. The school restored the ruined roof first.

Thatched roofs were so common in rural areas that they became an essential feature of a rural landscape. However, few of them remain because slate roofs have replaced them since the 1960s. Thatched roofs had been a product of community cooperation. All the villagers used to participate in rethatching work including gathering thatch in the village common. This tradition does not exist any more,

Figure 14.2 Thinning a bamboo grove. Photograph by Sawako Ono.

Figure 14.3 Catching breath after work. Photograph by Sawako Ono.

and also the village common for growing pampas grass has turned into woods in a few years. The thatched roof is a good example that shows the interaction between nature and people in rural areas. Therefore, the workshop for rethatching was a good opportunity for the participants to learn about the maintenance of traditional folk houses and get their hands on the house.

The bamboo grove requires thinning every year to get light and air inside. This task has been efficiently incorporated in farming life until recently without being recognized as maintenance. This was done through picking bamboo sprouts in spring for food and cutting down mature plants for various uses in autumn. At Rokusuke, the long-time abandonment left the bamboo grove untouched so that it was overgrown. The workshop participants cut down bamboos and removed them from the grove (Figures 14.2 and 14.3). The number of participants was eleven. Some were from Chiba Nature School, some from a local company; also included were a man from a nearby city, and a couple from a neighboring village. The local company that approves the project sent four employees to every workshop. An elderly couple who have been regular participants of this workshop live in Yokohama and have a business in downtown Tokyo. They bought a house in the neighboring village and stay there on weekends. They are practicing, so to speak, the concept of dual residence.

The former head of Rokusuke was a local historian and a man of influence. So the community people care for the house. They watch Chiba Nature School's project expectantly. However, they have not taken an active part in it initially. The local people are skeptical about anything new that brings change, and the local community usually closes its door to outsiders. In Japan, it is hard for a newcomer to be accepted as a community member. Chiba Nature School tries to get community people involved in the project. One of the staff lives in Rokusuke, attends community meetings, and takes part in the neighborhood festival. The school asks community people to act as instructors. The interactions have just been starting, and it is bound to take time to develop a sustaining relationship.

Case two: Aramaki-tei and Numata-tei – rental farmhouses for short stays

Located in Satomi, Ibaraki prefecture, Aramaki-tei (Aramakis' house) and Numata-tei (Numatas' house) are rental farmhouses for short stays run by the NPO Yugaku. Satomi is a village located two and a half hours by car north of Tokyo. With the historic route from central Japan to northern Japan passing through this village from the ninth century to the early twentieth century, the village has flourished as a gateway in this region for a long time. As the modern highway to northern Japan took another route, Satomi is now a village left behind by industries, forestry, and agricultural production. NPO Yugaku was formed to manage these two houses in 2007. Aramaki-tei is located along the main road in the center of the village, and Numata-tei sits in secluded woodlands facing farmland.

After working for years in big cities, Mr. S., the director of the NPO, returned to Satomi to take over the family's lumber business. After returning to Satomi, he also worked for the village to set up Michino-eki (Roadside Station), a roadside rest spot unified with a farmers' market, and became its director. One day he was asked by the village to start a vacant farmhouse reuse project when the owner of Aramaki-tei, an eighty-year-old woman, asked the town to lease the house. She lived in a cottage beside the main house by herself and worried about the future of the main house, which was unoccupied after her son moved to the city with his family. Mr. S. had visited France to see green tourism and knew about the tourist farmhouses there.

Figure 14.4 Tatami rooms of Numata-tei. Photograph by Sawako Ono.

Figure 14.5 Fireplace of Numata-tei. Photograph by Mima Nishiyama.

He had an idea for a membership-based rental farmhouse business, and started it with a few neighborhood residents in 2002. They got a US$20,000 subsidy from the village and provided the same amount themselves as the starting funds. After spending one year in repairing and renovating the house by themselves, they opened it in 2004.

Mr. S. put the information on a website with the catchline of "Would you like to enjoy the leisurely country life?" It brought guests from cities such as Tokyo, Kashima, and Hitachi. They recruited about forty members who brought 400 guests in a year. The house was filled with guests almost every weekend, half of whom were return visitors. Watching their project working well, a neighborhood resident asked them to take care of another vacant house, Numata-tei, in 2007. Taking this opportunity to solidify the business, they together formed NPO Yugaku. The board of directors consists of thirteen people. Nine of them are from the community and four live in Tokyo.

Both Aramaki-tei and Numata-tei are folk houses with tatami rooms, a fireplace, an earthen floor, and a traditional kitchen and bathroom (Figures 14.4 and 14.5). In addition to the main house, Aramaki-tei has a cottage and three storehouses, and Numata-tei has a barn where NPO Yugaku's office is located. The earthen floor of Numata-tei is large enough for a piano and a screen, so that the visitors as well as the community people can enjoy a concert and a movie here.

At both places, only one group occupies the house at a time. They spend the days freely as they like as if they are at home. The number of guests varies from four to twenty. At first, Mr S. treated the guests with a feast because the hospitality in a village meant full entertainment. However he soon realized the heavy workload. The feast also gave the visitor a false sense of the countryside, that everything there is free of charge. So, soon afterward, he offered the guests "hospitality without special entertainment," and charged them for extra services.

Mr. S. expects the visitors to enjoy the slow local time and experience daily life in the country including the landscapes, the way of life, the people, and the products, as well as the problems that the countryside faces right now. The old folk house serves well for this purpose. The space with earthen and wooden materials and a soft light through paper sliding doors soothes the guests, who have busy lives in the bustling big cities. The visitors at first tend to act as tourists visiting sightseeing spots in the village, but as they come to the house over and over again they begin to conduct more ordinary routines. They stroll in the village, cook local products with wood, or just stay in the house. Ninety percent of the visitors cook by themselves, although the NPO offers a catering service by the neighborhood volunteers. Cooking with wood using a traditional brick oven is one of the attractions that the house provides.

A variety of groups have stayed in the house, including families, friends, coworkers, hobby groups, and a university student seminar. It often happens that a family that stays by itself on the first visit is accompanied by its friends or relatives the second time. The farmhouse was originally built for a big family and community gatherings. The spacious guestroom had accepted many people during family ceremonies such as weddings and funerals. On such occasions, many people worked together in the big kitchen to provide the guests with food and drink. In addition to the householder's kith and kin, people from the community participated in the event. The front yard was big enough for a community gathering. But, as a large house, a farmhouse is rather inconvenient to live for daily life. This is one of the reasons that many younger people prefer to live in a modern house, or build a new house beside the old one and leave the old house unoccupied. As the houses are now occupied by large groups of people, they recover an original function of the house as a gathering place. In contrast to the old days, however, neither community residents nor blood relatives are the main participants in this gathering any more, but rather people who come of their own volition from outside the community. The old folk house thus has a new role in the contemporary social context.

Through the rental farmhouse project, Mr. S. knew the area itself is a treasure for the community. The village landscapes have been the ordinary and accustomed surroundings for the villagers for centuries but they are new to the visitors. The farming landscape is a result of efforts by the villagers' ancestors. Their hard work through many generations has resulted in the landscape today. It is hard to estimate their merit at a monetary value. He thinks the villagers have to cherish them. Therefore, to Mr. S., community improvement is not about developing the area with new facilities but about improving and preserving its way of life and the local environment.

On one hand, city people need to come to know the countryside, not only because the countryside gives them leisure but also because it is their lifeline. It provides everyone with food, water, and other necessary resources. On the other hand, the villages need to be in touch with cities to adapt to the changes in contemporary society. Mr. S. has a plan to increase the number of rental farmhouses that bring extra income to the farmers in the village. If they supplement their income by renting their houses to city people without having too much extra work, they can still focus on their main work – farming and forestry – while maintaining an improved quality of life in the rural area. He intends to create a new business model starting with a successful rental farmhouse in Satomi and popularizing them throughout Japan.

Conclusion

The two cases above represent efforts to reuse vacant farmhouses by local NPOs and to imbue their original role, as the center of life and a place for gathering, with new functions and meanings. Rokusuke has been converted to become a place for interpreting rural life. The house is not just for one family but also for many people outside the community. It generates activities that give city people in particular a chance to experience real country life and to work for rural landscape conservation. Aramaki-tei and Numata-tei are gathering places. Similar to Rokusuke, they do not serve just close kin or the community people as in the old days but are also open to a variety of people, especially those from the city. In both cases, the only requirement for participation is that participants are interested in rural life.

The second case seems to be more successful than the first one. We can see two reasons. The first is that the director of the NPO is rooted and lives in the community besides having experience of city life. He is familiar with the way of life and people in the community and has personal relationships with them. He also knows well about current movement outside the community. Therefore he can work as an intermediary between the city and the country. It is easier for him than outsiders to get community people involved in the project. The second is that the NPO gains funding for their project through their activities. With their own funds they can work more freely.

As gathering places for the urban and rural populace, they provide a bridge between the cities and the countryside. A farmhouse is an essential element of the rural landscape, *satoyama*. Because the rural landscapes have been shaped through an elaborate system by both people and natural processes, when the farmhouses are revived as the center of rural life again, it also brings the rural landscape to life.

Bibliography

Kobori, H. and Primack, R. B. (2003) 'Participatory Conservation Approaches for *Satoyama*, the Traditional Forest and Agricultural Landscape of Japan', *AMBIO: A Journal of the Human Environment*, 32 (4): 307–311.

Ministry of Internal Affairs and Communications (MIC) (2006) *Era of Dwelling for Communication.* Online. Available HTTP: http://www.soumu.go.jp/c-gyousei/2001/kaso/pdf/kouryu_kyojyu.pdf (accessed 1 May 2007).

Ministry of Land, Infrastructure, Transport, and Tourism (MLIT) (2005) *Significance of Dual Residence and a Framework of its Strategic Support Plan*. Online. Available HTTP: http://www.mlit.go.jp/kisha05/02/020329/01.pdf (accessed 1 May 2007).

—— (2006) *Survey on Vacant House Reuse to Promote Dual Residence*: Online. Available HTTP: http://www.mlit.go.jp/kisha/kisha06/02/020707 (accessed 1 May 2007).

Nakata, S., Kaneda, A., and Katsumata, H. (2006) 'A Research on Conversion from Old Folk House (in Case of Ibaraki, Tochigi, Gunma, Chiba, Saitama, Niigata, Nagano and Yamanashi Prefecture)', *Journal of Architecture and Planning*, 606: 79–84.

PART FIVE

UNCOVERING

CHAPTER 15

Urban Archives

Public memories of everyday places

Irina Gendelman, Tom Dobrowolsky, and Giorgia Aiello

In the face of economic globalization, some scholars argue that we live in an increasingly placeless world. Market forces can destroy and rebuild decontextualized places of consumption, creating a "geography of nowhere" (Zukin 1991, Kunstler 1994). Superstar cities compete to attract the investment capital of globe-trotting elites who are not tied down to one particular geographic region (Gyourko *et al*. 2006). Urban centers, therefore, become luxury commodities, which are attractive for their unique character but at the same time can be easily substituted for each other. In this process, cities essentially become global neighborhoods that require intense marketing in order to gain a competitive edge in attracting high-income buyers. The resulting rapid development threatens alternative histories embedded in the materiality of the urban environment.

In this chapter, we discuss how the Urban Archives – a digital archiving project that we have created and developed – contributes to documenting, preserving, and telling the stories of places that get ignored, overlooked, or marginalized. We treat the city as a laboratory to research diverse and often unconventional forms of urban expression in an attempt to understand the complex relationships of power that exist in our everyday surroundings.

We view everyday, material aspects of space as manifestations of underlying cultural values and explore the meanings of public, private, and liminal spatial narratives in order to actively participate in the shifting (re)definitions of public spaces. Documenting ephemeral communication in the urban environment, we glean insights into local histories and cultures. We investigate networks of visual expression (e.g., graffiti and advertising) in both static and dynamic forms. Not only do these networks yield temporary and permanent artifacts, but their participants range from official authorities to illicit actors. In sum, we analyze the city as a diverse spectacle composed of interwoven signs, competing stories, diverse actors, and social boundaries in constant flux.

By combining technology and institutional infrastructures with the study of vernacular urban texts, the Urban Archives challenges two related issues in the representation of memories in the contemporary city. On one hand, institutional archives tend to focus narrowly on traditional forms such as "historic" architecture or official documents. On another, emerging types of populist documentation on the Internet lack consistent annotation. We utilize emerging technologies such as tagging, metadata, and geolocation, with accessible media – digital photography and artifacts – and academic methods to map landscapes, annotate their semiotic content, and analyze their meanings.

Urban Archives: a short history

We started the Urban Archives in 2003 as graduate students (in the Information School and the Department of Communication at the University of Washington [UW] in Seattle) interested in urban environments, ethnography, and visual communication. Of particular fascination were ephemeral artifacts that are often overlooked or ignored by institutional collections and by conventional scholarly research about cities. We began gathering our data by exploring the city on foot, observing the everyday images that form Seattle's cultural landscape in a cacophony of visual signs. Our tools were digital cameras and our early collections consisted of graffiti and ghost signs (the vanishing, old painted advertisements on building façades).

Once our eyes acclimated to the city as a hodgepodge of communicative genres, and with the help of a team of undergraduate assistants, we began to compile a list of categories that could organize the multitude of texts in the urban visual landscape: graffiti, ghost signs, prohibitive architecture, official signage, etc. One of our students, for example, identified a category that she called Yard Art. She found fascinating contemporary examples of how people use private property around their own homes to carve out a space as a venue for public expression. In another project, we assigned students to research Seattle's Aurora Avenue. The students photographed street signs and conducted archival research in order to situate the newly gathered data into a historical context. At the same time, as with *The Ave is Back* mural project, we continued our own research alongside our students, learning from one another and sharing our findings in the classroom and, publicly, through the project's website.[1] We were energized by the opportunity to craft categories of urban texts for the archives and, most of all, by the sudden academic license to explore aspects of the built environment that had previously been disregarded as derelict or irrelevant. Our team of urban archivists sensed that important discoveries lay among the low-brow explorations of alleys, walls, and urban decay.

Eventually, we realized that in order to keep track of our growing data we needed a repository for the digital images as well as a system of metadata, or information about the images. The University of Washington Libraries' Digital Collections was our logical solution and fortunately a willing collaborator. It had the server space to hold our photographs, an existing database infrastructure, and a desire to grow its digital collections. Aside from storage and classification, we would be able to display our archives publicly online. One requirement of the Library's system was a controlled (standardized) vocabulary for the metadata. In developing this scheme to organize our images, we further refined the process of categorizing urban texts. We will revisit metadata later, after we introduce the three case studies mentioned above that exemplify our project.

Case study one: Yard Art

When space is contested, people often use their own property to publicly express identities, political views, and complaints. We defined Yard Art as such modification, intentionally made to residential façades or the private property surrounding them, which may include decorations, works of art, or political signage. Over a period of ten weeks, our student LeeAnn Robison documented "famous" or spectacular yards that were locally known in various Seattle locations. She primarily found these spaces through word of mouth, reporting that, once she told people about the project, inevitably someone would say, "did you see the yard on such and such street?" A saturation point was reached when she started to come across mention of the same notable yards. Selecting four yards as her sites, she visited them multiple times, documenting and recording changes to their exhibits.

Photography was essential as a method of data gathering and analysis. The photographs helped us identify patterns and order to what appeared fragmented and chaotic from the street. We looked over the photographs, transcribing any writing and viewing the entire image of words and objects as a unified text. Additionally, LeeAnn searched recent local newspaper articles and government documents for mention of the spectacular yards, uncovering that some of the most radical of these genres were indeed contested spaces, teetering on the verge of vanishing

For example, one yard (Figure 15.1) was intensely decorated with found objects and signs made from surfaces that lent themselves to writing and painting. On closer inspection, objects such as rocks, wood, and hubcaps were found to be carefully arranged in orderly patterns, often to form larger images. Many surfaces were covered in poignant writing. The writing on various pieces of fencing, for

Figure 15.1 Found objects outlining the shape of a train engine. Photograph by LeeAnn Robison, Urban Archives Item Number 20050311LAR0048.

instance, read "underground railroad," "you got to pay for using us as your mules," and "just like you kill my 1st nation tribe for our home landz [sic] now you kill arabz [sic] for their landz [sic]." In her research, LeeAnn found out that the city, responding to neighbors' complaints about the disorderly yard (detrimental to property values), pressured the yard owner, an elderly African-American and Cherokee woman, to "clean up" her property. This move angered and further provoked the artist to post additional signage on her property, confronting city officials.

In order to avoid bad publicity, the city decided, for the time being, to turn a blind eye. This inattention allowed the woman to voice her protests, but kept them from becoming any more public (via the media) than they already were in the neighborhood. The powerful words and images were easily brushed off as irrelevant largely because the neighbors and the city perceived the medium as an eyesore of the neighborhood. In documenting and archiving this type of Yard Art, we agree with the deputy director of Seattle's Museum of History and Industry, who told a Seattle newspaper that "such images could help historians decades from now 'take the pulse' of the city in 2005" (Frey 2005).

Case study two: Aurora Avenue

Another disregarded urban space that we found intriguing is Aurora Avenue, the busy thoroughfare that cuts across several neighborhoods in north Seattle. We conducted this study with the undergraduates Naraelle Barrows, Arin Delaney, Edith Fikes, and Ingrid Haftel. In this case, we combined ethnographic fieldwork and visual data collection with extensive archival research. A busy thoroughfare lined by run-down motels and strip-mall businesses, and an urban area that is considered an eyesore by many, Aurora Avenue is never featured in popular travel literature about Seattle (see Aiello and Gendelman 2007). However, the thoroughfare is also a living, yet fast decaying, slice of Seattle's visual landscape and, more broadly, US history. Part of the former US Route 99 (now Highway 99), Aurora once was Seattle's only "speedway" (Dorpat 1988) until the completion of Interstate 5, which has been the West Coast's main highway since 1968. Aurora saw its heyday in the late 1950s and early 1960s, when most of the businesses – motels in particular – and neon signs that line the road were built in the midst of the post-war economic boom and in anticipation of the 1962 Seattle World's Fair.

The neon signs mark Aurora Avenue as an historic area with a nostalgic, kitschy character. Signs for businesses such as the Pink Elephant Car Wash (Figure 15.2) and Puetz Golf are examples of well-kept landmarks in Seattle's vintage Mom & Pop commercial landscape. On the other hand, derelict places such as the Villia del Mar Motel (Figure 15.3) or the Bridge Motel – which was given over to the development of townhouses and turned into a huge site-specific installation by local artists before being demolished in the summer of 2007 (Edwards 2007) – remind us that the era that originally conceived the majority of these neon signs is over. Over the past two decades, Aurora's motels have primarily been homes for transients and settings for crimes such as prostitution and drug dealing (Sullivan 2008). City authorities and neighboring homeowners have pushed for and welcomed the uptake in development and, in some cases, the razing of these establishments.

Figure 15.2 Pink Elephant Car Wash. Photograph by Naraelle Barrows, Urban Archives Item Number 20060130NKB0004.

Figure 15.3 Villia del Mar Motel. Photograph by Naraelle Barrows, Urban Archives Item Number 20060130NKB0012.

Our interest in documenting and studying Aurora Avenue, then, was sparked by an urgency to confer enhanced visibility and permanence to urban spaces that are most often kept hidden in the public presentation of a city. By the same token, we were quite aware from the onset that the texture of decay and the retro, "Americana" aesthetic of neon signs also constitute the appeal of such places as Aurora. Last, it seems such landscapes are increasingly destined to vanish.

In addition to adding nearly 200 annotated, mapped photographs to the Urban Archives collection, the undergraduate students involved in the project researched the history of Aurora's development in the municipal archives. Finally, with the creation of a project website (http://urbanarchives.org/projects/aurora/aurora.html), the students connected the historical and contemporary discourses regarding the aesthetic qualities and flaws of Aurora Avenue with underlying social and economic issues. This illuminated the power-laden processes of defining what is worthy or unworthy of appreciation and preservation.

Case study three: The Ave is Back

In 2002, the City of Seattle embarked on a project to renovate University Way NE, colloquially known as "the Ave." This street runs parallel to the University of Washington's main campus – one block away from it – and constitutes the main commercial thoroughfare of the University District neighborhood. It has been one of Seattle's alternative business districts, and UW's "campustown," since the early 1900s, shortly after the university moved to this location in 1895. As a result of its proximity to the university as well as its varied businesses, this street features an eclectic mix of students, residents, street people, and visitors. It is a high traffic area, both pedestrian and automotive, with a highly visible streetscape.

The Ave's renovation resulted in complete repaving, new sidewalks, and quaint new street lamps. It was perhaps an attempt, through municipal reinvestment in infrastructure, to spark commercial and public reinvestment in the street. Unfortunately, this renovation did not fully rectify the widespread presence of vacant storefronts. One such storefront was located prominently on the corner of NE 45th Street and the Ave, essentially the main crossroads of campustown.

Partially to advertise the improvements and partially to mask a prominently vacant property, a large, colorful mural was pasted across the length of the empty store's windows. It read, "The Ave is Back" in giant letters. Its background panels featured images of flowers, fruit market stands, historic views of the street, insets of local landmarks, and buzzword text such as "Alive," "Progressive," and "Diverse" (Figure 15.4).

Made of vinyl and having been pasted on top of the windows, it was especially susceptible to accepting marks. Local taggers and citizens wasted little time in annotating this mural. Some played with its elements, drawing faces on images, for example, or adding word balloons making George Washington's statue say things (Figure 15.5).

Others disregarded the background altogether; these marks seemed to stand out in a third dimension against the mural's lithography. Still others affixed stickers. One sticker expressed hope: "beer store . . . make it happen." Another sticker protested:

> Recall, arrest, and hang Mayor Greg Nickels. He's a corrupt, conceited, self-promoting, pompous, piece of shit. This street improvement project was a big fat waste of taxpayers' money.

The mural was an illuminating and entertaining record of public conversation.

Figure 15.4 45th St. view of mural. Photograph by Tom Dobrowolsky.

Figure 15.5 Close-up of George Washington graffiti. Photograph by Tom Dobrowolsky.

Although its official authors included the city, the university, and the chamber of commerce, the mural's subsequent annotations by unsanctioned authors transformed its original, one-dimensional message into a rich, layered document exemplifying the diversity of street-level discourse. The mural is long gone, its vacant storefront now a functioning business. The collection of insurgent marks, expressing the voices of illicit writers, disgruntled citizens, and the politically powerless, has been wiped from the landscape.

Our project, however, has preserved visual records of this conversation. This documentation can be combined with a 1955 photo of the corner from the UW's Special Collections, which shows it to be a Martin & Eckmann Clothiers store. Conversely, a contemporary photograph will show it as an American Apparel store. Our photographs, then, illustrate an incarnation in between, an illicit one, at this storied corner.

Studying the city

Jacobs (1961: 6) writes that "cities are an immense laboratory of trial and error, failure and success in city building and city design. This is the laboratory in which city planning should have been learning and forming and testing its theories." The Urban Archives takes this advice to heart, extending the study of the city into visual, cultural, communication, and information studies. Accordingly, we view public spaces as complex, living laboratories. Fieldwork is paramount to our research. We reflexively observe the streets, interacting not only with spaces but with the people using them.

In this laboratory, the camera and notebook are our primary instruments. Jakle (1987) introduced the simple concept of sight-seeing as a way to study visual landscapes: touristic behavior "involves deliberate searching out of place experience" (p. 8). Pedagogically, we encourage such behavior as a starting point for investigations into public spaces. We first examine sites without a definite question or plan. This mimics how visitors parse unfamiliar landscapes and make sense of their surroundings. Since most of our students have familiarity with and access to cameras and are eager to walk the streets in search of data, photography becomes an especially keen pedagogical instrument for studying the city. Photography introduces students to ethnographic research in relation to three key aspects of well-rounded scholarship: selecting and collecting field data, annotating and processing visual data that can be accessed by other researchers, and, ultimately, critically analyzing collected and archival data.

From the outset, archiving photographs and artifacts has been an important component of the project. Ostensibly, such documentation is not so novel. Graffiti writers and admirers, for example, have infiltrated the web with galleries and forums devoted to writings on walls. However, these sites contain little description, contextual annotation, or geolocation. Thus, they have little use for research beyond displaying entertaining pictures. In recent years, photo-sharing sites such as Flickr have come to the fore, allowing users to organize photographs, add them to communal albums, place them on maps, and tag them with keywords. Although Flickr's rudimentary classification tools are robust, the site still fails to ameliorate archivists' worst nightmares about the ambiguous nature of the tagging (folksonomies) and the uncertainty of the archives' stability (the images are often hosted on proprietary servers).

In consideration of this, since libraries are some of the most reliable places to store information for long periods of time (Foote 2000), our collection is housed in library archives. Moreover, we apply standardized metadata to the materials.

We employ a faceted classification scheme that offers the flexibility of free-tagging with the rigor and quality control of a standardized vocabulary. Current researchers debate possible new terms before inclusion in order to best gauge how future researchers may access them. In this way, we add value to both the materials tagged as well as the tags themselves; we make them useful for a larger number of users. Systematic methods allow us to address the shortcomings that we have identified with ubiquitous digital photography, popular sharing sites, and the lack of planning for long-term preservation.

Our data and analyses are not meant for our use alone, nor are they to be packed away from public view. Digital technologies allow us to easily share our data, reflecting significant trends in collaborative scholarship, and focus on collective intelligence. Visitors have contacted us with corrections, photographs, and new information about our images and the metadata. For example, one author, of a text documented by our collection, emailed us explaining the origins of his idea. Others have decoded faded signs or graffiti or offered their own images. And, in an insurgent gesture apropos of the digital era, a graffiti writer annotated some images in our Flickr group with tags identifying some texts in the photographs.

These occurrences demonstrate the potential that collective knowledge could bring to our archives. More importantly, they mimic ways in which people communicate and construct public memory in the built environment. Urban Archives has merely tapped into the power of new media in facilitating exploration of liminal spaces.

Space, memory, and dialectic

Insurgent spaces are often impermanent precisely because cultural authorities and institutions have not sanctioned them. For this reason, it is important to document and archive these ephemeral spaces, which may disappear before their importance is noted.

Our interest in impermanent and unsanctioned dimensions is rooted in the recognition that archives are not neutral, nor are their biases necessarily intentional. Rather, this inherent bias is a consequence of a larger social structure. As Zinn (1977: 15) states, "the existence, preservation, and availability of archives, documents, records in our society are very much determined by the distribution of wealth and power." As a consequence, the "impotent and obscure" (Zinn 1977: 16) are most often excluded or diminished to irrelevance in archival practices. On the other hand, both institutional archives and their publicly visible counterpart, museums, are extremely powerful tools for the production of knowledge and collective memory among the members of an imagined community (see Anderson 1983). Dickinson, Ott, and Aoki (2005: 88) write that "[h]istory museums are a popular way for US Americans to engage the past, and more importantly, they are perceived by the public to be the most trustworthy source of information about the past." However, in the act of collecting, exhibiting and (re)presenting artifacts, history museums select, recontextualize (and often decontextualize), and ultimately also actively interpret and "anchor the transient character of memory" (Dickinson et al. 2005: 89).

Arguably, online digital archives of both past and contemporary artifacts are, not unlike traditional museums, "sites of remembering and forgetting" (Dickinson *et al*. 2005: 89; see also Foote 2000), as they engage equally in acts of documentation, archiving, and display or exhibiting by way of the web. In this sense, online institutional archives – with their ability to both preserve and display – play a major role in shaping collective memory as well as setting the agenda for what should be seen as worthy of documentation and remembrance (Foote 2000).

Although our project may not yet be able to affect the shaping and consolidation of collective memory at the scale of a city, the Urban Archives is an effort to contribute to the creation of public memories by illuminating everyday urban texts that would otherwise be effaced or relegated to the status of curiosities or sub-cultural expressions in the increasing number of online folk photo collections (such as Flickr), blogs, and homepages dedicated to the various aspects of our urban landscapes including graffiti, vintage signage, and yard art. In a time when personal memories are systematically shared with others through digital recording and social networking practices, to the extent that they become part and parcel of the broader cultural fabric (van Dijck 2007), it becomes all the more crucial to embrace and mobilize the power of archives (Jimerson 2003). We therefore render popular yet often unsanctioned urban texts accessible and searchable in ways that promote the development of further academic and expressive knowledge about our cities.

In addition to the academic utility of classifying and displaying images within a highly organized information system, our digital archives create a virtual "space" for everyday materials found in the built environment. By preserving them digitally, we extend the lives of ephemeral street texts, allowing them to continue speaking as documents long after they have been removed from the physical landscape. On one hand, particular sub-sets of images may be considered detailed documentation of specific times and/or spaces – Aurora Avenue, for example. On the other hand, moving the representations (photographs, scans, etc.) of artifacts from their original physical environment into this virtual space allows us to reconsider and recontextualize their meanings in novel ways. The digital archives as a whole transcend the limitations of space and time by connecting themed images across disparate locations, as with images of Yard Art in other countries or documenting landscape evolution through time as with The Ave Mural project.

Although physical archives have provided this utility to some degree, digital archives provide quicker and more easily reconfigurable access to different combinations of images. Digital space is infinitely malleable. Unlike physical objects, digital ones can simultaneously belong to multiple virtual sets, collections, and exhibits, for example. These configurations can be derived by users on the fly as well as pre-packaged into "canned collections" by archivists.

Furthermore, online archives provide greater access to a wider audience. For example, a street painter in Chicago may view and copy a text from Seattle. Additionally, different archives may link to one another's materials. In the end, the networked space of online archives, combined with promiscuous hyperlinking, extends ideas across physical distances that could not have been as readily accomplished otherwise.

We might conceptualize these networked, online spaces as sort of *fourth places*, albeit more asynchronous than Oldenburg's (1989) *third places*. Given our ability to geocode photographs with location metadata, we can ameliorate the initial feeling of placelessness in the online environment by mapping their embedded geodata and reconstructing the spatial placement of the photographed artifacts. This ties virtual space back to tangible places in the built environment.

Conclusions

Though critique of development and globalization often turns to placelessness, Escobar (2001: 147–148) argues that we should also consider the "existing local production of place and culture of the local; not from the perspective of its abandonment but of its critical affirmation; not only according to the flight from places, whether voluntary or forced, but of the attachment to them." Critical affirmation of place, in the face of global interests, can be uncovered by studying informal and vernacular uses of space that are often overlooked as too insignificant in comparison with larger and more formal urban projects. It is therefore imperative to compile a significant body of data of these missed, sometimes unauthorized, and at times illegal urban texts in order to examine how people rebel, speak out, or try to assert control of their built environment.

Naturally, as a site for the creation and preservation of public memories, the Urban Archives is not exempt from the problematic nature of acts such as collecting, exhibiting, and (re)presenting (Dickinson et al. 2005). Some of our decidedly low-brow subjects and sites of study, however, provide a balance to the collections of high-brow museums and archives. Our project supplements these collections to help paint a more complete story of places. Jimerson (2003) writes that we need to let go of the notion of an archive as a temple or a prison of information and employ its power for social justice. Indeed we see the documentation and public academic analysis of contested urban spaces as a way to contribute to debates of public interest. As a result of our graffiti research, for example, we have been able to share our data and take part in media discussions about contested policies related to urban revitalization.

With the emergence of new technologies, the academy faces new challenges and opportunities in the way that we can contribute to public life. DeRuyver and Evans (2006: 945) survey "the digital landscape of online primary sources" in American studies and write that there is a lack of transparency of the digitizing processes that underlie digital humanities projects as well as widespread digital illiteracy among scholars in the humanities at large. Through their overview, they advocate for the development of a generation of scholars that is much more in tune with the technologies, processes, and languages at work in the digitization of primary sources.

In line with this observation, the New Media Consortium in collaboration with EDUCAUSE released a report (Horizon Report 2008) about the key emerging technologies likely to impact teaching, learning, and creative expression in higher education. The report predicts that emerging technologies such as mobile devices including cell phone cameras, easy-to-use web applications such as Flickr, ways to "mashup" data (such as combining images and maps), and collective intelligence harnessed through wikis or shared tagging are changing pedagogy. As the

EDUCAUSE report emphasizes, "[t]he academy is faced with the need to provide formal instruction in information, visual, and technological literacy as well as in how to create meaningful content with today's tools" (Horizon Report 2008: 6). We have tried to illustrate how our project attempts just that. The combination of institutional resources, digital technologies, and collaborative/dialogic pedagogy allows us to create meaningful and polysemic content about our urban spaces where (re)presenting, or the act of interpreting the artifacts/data, becomes a potentially multiplicitous endeavor, as the database is available for anyone to use for their own research at http://www.urbanarchives.org.

Note

1   http://www.urbanarchives.org showcases our research projects, links to a collaborative wiki, our blog, a search portal to the UW's Digital Collections, and other resources.

Bibliography

Aiello, G. and Gendelman, I. (2007) 'Seattle's Pike Place Market (De)constructed: An Analysis of Tourist Narratives about a Public Space', *Journal of Tourism and Cultural Change*, 5 (3): 158–185.

Anderson, B. (1983) *Imagined Communities: Reflections On the Origin and Spread of Nationalism*, London: Verso.

DeRuyver, D. and Evans, J. (2006) 'Digital Junction', *American Quarterly*, 58 (3): 943–982.

Dickinson, G., Ott, B. L., and Aoki, E. (2005) 'Memory and Myth at the Buffalo Bill Museum', *Western Journal of Communication*, 69 (2): 85–108.

van Dijck, J. (2007) *Mediated Memories in the Digital Age*, Stanford, CA: Stanford University Press.

Dorpat, P. (1988) 'From Byway to Speedway', *Seattle Times and Seattle Post-Intelligencer*, 18 December, p. 26.

Edwards, H. (2007) 'Artists Bid Farewell to a Seedy City Landmark', *Seattle Times*, 15 September, p. 4A.

Escobar, A. (2001) 'Culture Sits in Places: Reflections on Globalism and Subaltern Strategies of Localization', *Political Geography*, 20: 139–174.

Foote, K. E. (2000) 'To Remember and Forget: Archives, Memory, and Culture', in Jimerson, R. C. (ed.) *American Archival Studies: Reading in Theory and Practice*, Chicago: Society of American Archivists.

Frey, C. (2005) 'Students Create Urban Archive, Preserving Graffiti for Posterity', *Seattle Post Intelligencer*, 8 December, p. 1A.

Gyourko, J., Mayer, C., and Sinai, T. (2006) 'Superstar Cities', National Bureau of Economic Research Working Paper No. 12355. Online. Available HTTP: http://www.nber.org/papers/expecting/w12355 (accessed 24 August 2007).

Horizon Report. (2008) *The 2008 Horizon Report*. New Media Consortium and EDUCAUSE Learning Initiative. Online. Available HTTP: http://www.nmc.org/pdf/2008-Horizon-Report.pdf (accessed 29 January 2008).

Jacobs, J. (1961) *The Death and Life of Great American Cities*, New York: Random House.

Jakle, J. A. (1987) *The Visual Elements of Landscape*, Amherst: University of Massachusetts Press.

Jimerson, R. C. (2003) 'Archives and Memory', *OCLC Systems and Services*, 19 (3): 89–95.

Kunstler, J. (1994) *Geography of Nowhere: The Rise and Decline of America's Man-Made Landscape*, New York: Simon & Schuster.

Oldenburg, R. (1989) *The Great Good Place: Cafés, Coffee Shops, Community Centers, Beauty Parlors, General Stores, Bars, Hangouts, and How they Get You through the Day*, New York: Paragon House.

Sullivan, J. (2008) 'Prostitutes, Drugs Chased from Aurora Corridor by Group's Patrols', *Seattle Times*, 17 January. Online. Available HTTP: http://seattletimes.nwsource.com/html/localnews/2004129652_gain17m.html (accessed 28 April 2008).

Zinn, H. (1977) 'Secrecy, Archives, and the Public Interest', *Midwestern Archivist*, 2: 14–26.

Zukin, S (1991) *Landscapes of Power: from Detroit to Disney World*, Berkeley: University of California Press.

CHAPTER 16

Funny . . . it doesn't look like insurgent space

The San Francisco Bureau of Urban Secrets and the practice of history as a public art

Jeannene Przyblyski

> Situated at the intersection of art, activism and everyday life, the San Francisco Bureau of Urban Secrets specializes in identifying the cities of mystery, desire, and dreams hidden within the utilitarian infrastructure of a complex and changing metropolis.
>
> —SFBUS Mission Statement

> psychogeography: The study of the specific effects of the geographical environment, consciously organized or not, on the emotions and behavior of individuals.

> psychogeographer: One who explores and reports on psychogeographical phenomena.
>
> —Guy Debord (Knabb 1989: 45)

The work of the San Francisco Bureau of Urban Secrets is often described as "whimsical" or "quirky" – two words that would seem at odds with a revolutionary, or insurgent, or even just plain "critical" agenda. Among other projects, the Bureau formulated a perfume based upon the smells of San Francisco (*Urban Essence*, Figure 16.1 – which remained available to the general public for several years, until its maker actually smelled someone wearing it), and proposed to provide the San Francisco Planning Department with the only definitive, quantitative accounting of urban quality of life to be achieved by polling every single one of its citizen (*The Deeply Subjective Survey of Urban Goodness* – ongoing, and, like many urban planning initiatives, of potentially infinite duration).

Yet the Bureau was founded at a moment of explicit urban contestation, when an influx of speculative capital, fueled by a rapidly expanding Internet industry, wrought almost unbearably rapid change in the city. The infamous "dot-com boom" of the 1990s left many San Francisco residents feeling like strangers in their own town. This sensation of "alienation" had real consequences for the many workers, teachers, artists, non-profit organizations, and small businesses displaced by skyrocketing real estate costs, and it generated an intensive period of political

Figure 16.1 *Urban Essence: The Scent of San Francisco (Don't just live it. Wear it!)*, multi-sensory media project, 2002–2007. Photograph by Jeannene Przyblyski.

activism and engagement.[1] But it also provided a special opportunity for artists and others to re-engage with the city as an unstable temporal construct, rather than an ostensibly "permanent" agglomeration of bricks and mortar. It provided a special challenge to consider the "state of emergency" of the present circumstances as immediately historical, and hence to engage immediately with the whole history of the city, its triumphs and its disasters up to that point (and beyond), as a "battlefield of representations" in which every image produced by the "powers that be" (capital, in other words, in all its guises) could be appropriated, repositioned, and counter-interrogated by those on the margins of power.[2] The dot-com boom, in other words, provided an unusually urgent wake-up call to urban denizens, lulled to complacency by the dream state of urban spectacle, to reckon with the dynamic interplay between the ineluctable pull of eternal return (the sensation of history as "ever the same") and the potential counter-movement of the revolutionary act, however ephemeral or impossible to sustain; which in some cases might just include the act of writing urban history, but differently.

Since 2001, the Bureau has staged art and other interventions directed toward visualizing these different histories, asking participants to engage in the process of rebuilding the everyday skills of landscape literacy and the ability to read cities as palimpsests of historical and cultural texts that have all too often been obscured by the numbing demands of negotiating everyday routines: getting to work or school on time, doing the shopping, finding a parking space, tuning out the other riders on the bus, standing in line for one thing or the other. For all its quirkiness, the Bureau's specialty is not the purposeless play of flash-mob pillow-fights and other typically arbitrary, mostly silly gestures that attempt to reanimate the public realm, but rather a purposeful play, in which the conditions, practices and technologies of life in a particular urban context both compel "business as usual" and, *at the very same time and in the very same guise*, shape a set of possibilities for alternative experiences of historical awareness. At the root of the Bureau's projects is the conviction that enabling participants to rediscover the eloquence always already latent in the public realm as a repository of competing histories will reawaken in them a heightened awareness of the ways in which the form and quality of social experience are enabled and constrained by the forms and qualities of public spaces. The practice of "psychogeography" in this sense is conceived not in terms of the pure indulgence of individual desire (whatever that might be) mapped against the regimentation of the modern city (and the psychogeographer who is satisfied to engage in "drift" merely for drift's sake is a very poor practitioner indeed), but as a counter-mapping of the city's existing architecture and modes of urbanism, that itself becomes a form of insurgent activism. Here are a few examples.

Case study one

Travels with Carlos & Anza: A Brief Explorer's Guide to a Few Missing Monuments, Jeannene Przyblyski, with Mitche Manitou, commissioned in conjunction with *Monument Recall: Public Memory and Public Spaces at SF Camerawork*, San Francisco (2004). Missing monuments (plexi-glass, wood and metal), take-away, printed traveler's guide, and associated inserts and updates

> With the aid of old maps, aerial photographs and experimental derives, one can draw up hitherto lacking maps of influences, maps whose inevitable imprecision at this early stage is no worse than that of the first navigational charts; the only difference is that it is a matter no longer of precisely delineating stable continents, but of changing architecture and urbanism.
>
> —Guy Debord (Knabb 1989: 53)

Travels with Carlos & Anza traces the convergence of the historical and political pasts of San Francisco during the eighteenth-century age of Spanish exploration and the twentieth-century dot-com boom, extending the Juan Bautista de Anza National Historic Trail federally administered by the National Park Service to include a series of selected sites commemorating the continued inscription of Anza's presence on the civic landscape of San Francisco (Figure 16.2). The project's starting point was a

Figure 16.2 "Anza Evicted!", collateral postcard following on the exhibition of *Travels with Carlos & Anza: A Brief Explorer's Guide to a Few Missing Monuments*, 2006. Photograph by Jeannene Przyblyski.

controversy over the placement of two bronze monuments: an equestrian statue of Anza, who opened an overland route from Mexico to Alta California in 1776, and established the settlements of the Presidio of San Francisco and Mission Dolores; and a standing statue of King Carlos III of Spain, who commissioned the expedition. The statues had to be removed from their original downtown location after the 1989 earthquake, but their proposed reinstallation near historic Mission Dolores was blocked by neighborhood-based anti-gentrification activists in 2001.

Using old and new maps, historic and contemporary photographs, and such staples of interpretive guides as the chronological timeline, *Travels with Carlos & Anza* retells the story of Anza's fortunes in San Francisco in such a way as to ask its readers to consider, simultaneously and critically, the histories of imperial colonization and the decimation of native populations in the Spanish age of exploration, and of urban gentrification and displacement in the Internet age. Although the project was initially conceived for an exhibition in 2004, by adding updates and inserts to the original publication the Bureau continued to track the fortunes of the two monuments through their eviction from storage at a city-owned service yard in 2006, the ensuing backlash against the city's apparent disregard for Anza's legacy led by "Los Californianos" (the organized descendents of the original Anza expedition, who hold an annual commemorative ceremony in San Francisco), and the "final," at least as of this writing, reinstallation of the monuments at Lake Merced, where Anza had previously made camp 230 years ago.

Case study two

Welcome to the UGB Trail, Jeannene Przyblyski, with Mitche Manitou, commissioned in conjunction with *Monument Recall: Public Memory and Public Spaces at the Art Gym*,

Marylhurst University, Portland (2005). Public art proposal/ narrative map, community outreach brochure, and promotional buttons

> The element of chance is less determinant than one might think: from the dérive point of view cities have a psychogeographical relief, with constant currents, fixed points and vortexes which strongly discourage entry into or exit from certain zones.
>
> —Guy Debord (Knabb 1989: 50)

When we pull our cars over at a roadside monument marking the westward expansion of the United States along the Oregon Trail (or the Anza expedition for that matter), we are honoring land-use initiatives that have receded far enough into the past to have made the transition from the discourses of land mapping and management (topographical surveys and claim-staking, parcels and easements, homesteading, town-making, agricultural entitlements, grazing rights, etc.) to historical narratives of exploration and adventure usually featuring visionary land barons, heroic acts of fortitude, and hardscrabble legions of pioneers. But is it possible to see contemporary debates over environmental sustainability, open space preservation, and property rights as part of the same story? This question was uppermost in the Bureau's mind when we were invited to do a site-specific project in Portland, Oregon, several

Figure 16.3 "Welcome to the UGB Trail", community outreach brochure accompanying the exhibition of *The UGB Trail: Sites & Monuments*, 2005. Photograph by Jeannene Przyblyski.

months after the 2004 passage of Measure 37, a statewide ballot initiative requiring market-rate compensation to private property owners for "takings" resulting from regulatory zoning (Figure 16.3). The chief target of this initiative was the Portland Metro Urban Grown Boundary (UGB), a cornerstone of progressive urban planning in Portland that seeks to protect agricultural and open space and contain "sprawl" by concentrating development within a prescribed, already urbanized footprint.

After only thirty years, then, the UGB was beginning to look like history. The Bureau responded by proposing a public art project commemorating the UGB, complete with community outreach materials, distinctive logo, and a series of historical markers (modeled on real estate signs). Beginning at the end of the historic Oregon Trail, cutting through New Urbanist villages along the Portland Metro rail lines in Gresham and Orenco Station, spanning "revitalized" (and condo-ized) downtown Portland, as well as edge developments and farmsteads at Hillsboro, and ending in the outer metropolitan Portland suburb of Tigard, where the current headquarters of the property rights group Oregonians in Action was identified as the proposed future site of The End of the UGB Trail Interpretive Center (funds pending), the newly historic UGB Trail would encompass the original legacy of uncompensated takings from native American tribes exiled to the Grand Ronde Reservation outside Portland, and the contemporary battles over land use and speculation being waged in the courtroom and at the ballot box. Closely imitating the cast of characters typical of westward narratives (Tom McCall as the visionary "green" governor of Oregon in the 1970s, Dorothy English as the gritty twenty-first-century granny whose retirement nest egg was threatened by restrictive zoning), the UGB Trail asked Portlanders to see their city as once again a new frontier, and to consider which side of the fence they were on. As of this writing, the jury is still out on the effects of Measure 37.[3] Like most frontiers, the UGB remains a moving target.

Case study three

Comings & Goings: 2 Backwards Journeys thru Lands End, Jeannene Przyblyski, with Mitche Manitou and Ryan Verzaal, commissioned by *Southern Exposure, San Francisco for So-Ex Off-Site (2007)*. Temporary trailhead for time travelers, reversible artist's book/wayfinding guide and audio podcast

> Even the topologies and tropes used to describe the "place" where memory is stored in the brain imply erasure. Over the centuries, this "place" has been imagined as a waxen tablet, an electrical trace, a closer sparking on a network, a library made of eroding fabric, a mental theater with painted doors. In practically every version, the site is "built" from a highly malleable substance, or moves along a very slippery trail. Memories tend to efface easily, or lose track.
> (Klein 1997: 14)

The phrase "National Parks" in the United States more often than not conjures visions of the majestic façade of Yosemite's Half-Dome or untrammeled alpine meadows at the foot of the Grand Tetons (to be sure, these visions might be the subject of another essay on wilderness as insurgent public space). Increasingly, however, the National Parks Service (NPS) is the chief federal custodian of collective memory in the country, with a string of urban parks and national historical sites (including the Washington Mall) under its jurisdiction. Over the last thirty to forty years, as post-modernism, multiculturalism, and identity politics have recast the academic practice of the humanities, the NPS has engaged in a critical internal dialogue over the forms and methodologies of history most appropriate to its evolving, contemporary mission.[3] At the same time, the NPS has seen its budget slashed repeatedly, with resources for historical and interpretive work especially constrained. Ironically, at the very moment that the NPS is challenging itself to open national trails, and the national pathways to memory that these trails represent, to a multiplicity of voices and experiences, it increasingly finds itself unable to afford to practice any history at all beyond the most basic mandate to "preserve and protect." It is sometimes difficult to see these budgetary cuts as anything other than a federally sanctioned instrument of collective forgetting.

Comings & Goings: 2 Backwards Journeys thru Lands End steps into the breach, by working across the jurisdictions of the alternative arts space, the non-profit park conservancy organization, and the National Park, using the pretext of art to question what sorts of histories remain visible (and audible) in a National Park landscape once settled, then ruined, and now in the process of being restored to nature. Following the Coastal Trail on the westernmost edge of San Francisco ("Lands End") from the ruins of Sutro Baths (a Victorian pleasure ground and public pool) to Sea Cliff (an exclusive residential enclave) – and back again – participants can retrace the Bureau's steps, equipped with an audio podcast and a reversible wayfinding guide (Figure 16.4). Different aspects of the trail's rich soundscape, both present and

Figure 16.4 "Sutro Baths, Stop I or VIII" (depending on whether you are coming or going), printed wayfinding guide accompanying *Comings & Goings*, 2007. Photograph by Jeannene Przyblyski.

1897 – Sutro Baths, incompletely.

past (human voices, bird calls, fog horns, rocks tumbling in a landslide, a steam locomotive, carnival sounds), become the "hooks" for a series of short vignettes and meditations asking participants to imaginatively project themselves backwards and forwards in time, exploring different conditions of historical awareness even as they learn something about the landscape's history. Just as importantly, however, *Comings & Goings* served as the pretext for a series of cross-community events, bringing arts community members to the Golden Gate National Parks during a series of onsite-art experiences and walking tours, bringing Park visibility to the Mission-district location of Southern Exposure, where a community-based, bilingual "trailhead" was installed to raise awareness of the Park as an open space amenity amongst the area's largely Latino residents, and opening up opportunities for stewardship and other forms of participation across art, environmental, and neighborhood organizations (Figure 16.5).[4]

Figure 16.5 *Comings & Goings* "Trailhead for Time Travelers" installed in the storefront gallery of Southern Exposure, Mission District, San Francisco, 2007. Photograph by Jeannene Przyblyski.

Living and learning the city

> The construction of situations begins on the ruins of the modern spectacle. It is easy to see the extent to which the very principle of the spectacle – nonintervention – is linked to the alienation of the old world. Conversely, the most pertinent revolutionary experiments in culture have sought to break the spectator's psychological identification with the hero so as to draw him into activity . . . The situation is thus made to be lived by its constructors. The role played by a passive or merely bit-part playing "public" must constantly diminish, while that played by those who cannot be called actors, but rather, in a new sense of the term, "livers," must constantly increase.
>
> —Guy Debord (Knabb 1989: 25)

In the end, what do we hope you might take away from these case studies in the context of an interdisciplinary anthology on "Insurgent Public Space"?

Bureau projects usually combine the tactics of *dérive* (drift) and *detournement* (redirection) first articulated by the Situationist International in the 1950s and 1960s with a updated practice of public history anchored by different signifiers and representations of the publicness of space: the public monument, the planning boundary or zone, the urban national park and its trails.[5] The Bureau believes that the methodologies of art and politics are also profoundly useful methodologies for historical practice.

In conjunction with the Situationist tactic of *detournement*, Bureau projects typically turn on the play between instrumentalizing aesthetics and aestheticizing instrumental protocols that so preoccupied the Weimar cultural historian and critic Walter Benjamin in his essays on the role of art as a form of counter-engagement against the aesthetic politics of fascism.[6] This is a purposefully tactical form of mimetic play, interacting with the administrative codes of municipal government, the strategies of bureaucratic information-organization, and the voice of officially sanctioned public history to pry open a space of possibility for different narratives and experiences.

Bureau projects generally emphasize research and dialogue with administrators, experts, stakeholders, and project participants, facilitating collaboration and the cross-fertilization of perspectives, and activating the public as co-conspirators. At the end of the day, there are not a lot of opportunities for passive spectators in Bureau productions.

Increasingly Bureau projects seek to engage more than just the sense of sight. Smell and sound, texture and touch are also site-specific. When technology is used (cell phones, iPods, and the like), it is used intermittently, meant to be both turned on and turned off, acting not as a virtual surrogate, but as a portal to a more fully embodied experience of place.

Bureau projects tend to be produced for a given exhibition or venue, but take a more open-ended view to the question of the project's completion, acknowledging the ways in which making history is always unfinished business.

Quirky? Maybe so. But then again, what's not radical about quirkiness? With such conviction in mind, the San Francisco Bureau of Urban Secrets will continue, perversely and even whimsically, to seek the wrong (aesthetic) tool for the right (instrumental) job – not in the "white cube" of traditional gallery space, but in a dynamic urban context that makes and remakes meanings out of the very processes of living and learning the city.

Notes

1 For a study plotting the nexus between art and progressive politics during the dot-com boom, see Solnit and Schwartztenberg (2002).
2 For a brief and cogent discussion of the keywords "ideology" and "spectacle" as they relate to the contested representational regimes of urban life, see Clark (1984: 6–10).
3 In 2007, Oregon voters approved Measure 49, which overturns and modifies many of the provisions under Measure 37.
4 For an overview of NPS approaches to historical interpretation and the challenges facing the organization, see Pitcaithley (2007).
5 Most recently, the Bureau produced *A Lover's Line thru the Presidio* (2009), a multimedia project that remapped the most direct route out of the former military base and now national park as a detoured path charting the historical play of human desires whose traces remain inscribed, sometimes just barely, in the contemporary landscape. *A Lover's Line thru the Presidio* was awarded the 2009 Award for Media Excellence by the Association for Partners for Public Lands.
6 For an excellent collection of Situationist writings in translation, see Knabb (1989), from which most of the epigraphs in this essay were drawn. For a scholarly discussion of Situationist practices and modernist urbanism, see Sadler (1999).
7 See, in particular, Benjamin (1986: 220–238), 'The Author as Producer.'

Bibliography

Benjamin, W. (1986) *Reflections: Essays, Aphorisms, Autobiographical Writings*, New York: Schocken Books.
Clark, T. J. (1984) *The Painting of Modern Life: Paris in the Art of Manet and His Followers*, Princeton, NJ: Princeton University Press.
Klein, N. (1997) *The History of Forgetting: Los Angeles and the Erasure of Memory*, new edition, New York: Verso.
Knabb, K. (1989) *Situationist International Anthology*, Berkeley, CA: Bureau of Public Secrets.
Pitcaithley, D. T. (2007) 'On the Brink of Greatness: National Parks and the Next Century', *George Wright Forum*, 24 (2): 9–20.
Sadler, S. (1999) *The Situationist City*, Cambridge, MA: MIT Press.
San Francisco Bureau of Urban Secrets (2004), *Travels with Carlos & Anza: A Brief Explorer's Guide to a Few Missing Monuments*. San Francisco Bureau of Urban Secrets.
—— (2005) *Welcome to the UGB Trail*, San Francisco: San Francisco Bureau of Urban Secrets.
—— (2007) *Comings & Goings: 2 Backwards Journeys thru Lands End*. Online. Available HTTP: http://soex.org/jeanneneprzyblyski.html (accessed 20 July 2009).
—— (2009) *A Lover's Line thru the Presidio*. Online. Available HTTP: http://www.presidio.gov/experiences/lovers (accessed 20 July 2009).
San Francisco Bureau of Urban Secrets official website (2009) Online. Available HTTP: http://www.bureauofurbansecrets.org (accessed 20 July 2009).
San Francisco Bureau of Urban Secrets on Facebook (2009) Online. Available HTTP: http://www.facebook.com/group.php?gid=51152062 951 (accessed 20 July 2009).
Solnit, R. and Schwartztenberg, S. (2002) *Hollow City: The Siege of San Francisco and the Crisis of American Urbanism*, New York: Verso.

CHAPTER 17

Mapping the space of desire

Brothel as a city landmark, Wenminglo in Taipei

Yung-Teen Annie Chiu

A cultural landscape is often the site of unresolved cultural differences and conflict. As culture and history are often reinterpreted and contested in cities, the space of an insurgent site is thus the materialization of competing urban histories. This chapter examines the cultural conflict and contestation concerning the preservation of Wenminglo in Taipei. Wenminglo is the name of a brothel house (Figure 17.1). The building was designated by the Taipei city government as a historic landmark in 2006. In the case of Wenminglo, what began as the sex workers' protest movement in Taipei evolved into an effort to make the brothel a city-designated historic building. The movement began with the abolishment of licensed prostitution in the government's effort to "clean up" the city back in 1999. Wenminglo was one of the buildings where the group of sex workers once worked. It later became the home of an NGO group: "Spring Every Day" or formally the Collective of Sex Workers and Supporters (COSWAS; see http://coswas.org/02sexworker/4storyofbailan/578#mo re-578). This material and discursive transformation prompts the questions: Whose culture and history should be preserved in a city? Can a brothel be part of the urban

Figure 17.1 Wenminglo is one of the row houses in the otherwise residential-looking Guisui Street in Taipei. Photograph by Yung-teen Annie Chiu.

collective memories? Who has the right to erase the culture of others? How can such memories and buildings be preserved in the city?

This chapter discusses how preserving a building that seems to represent the underclass's irresponsible sexual acts challenges the urban middle class's value system as well as the mainstream historical preservation discourse. It is argued here that the preservation of history that some would like to forget is an important part of a cultural discourse. In such cultural discourse, the changing interpretation of a historical event would continue to challenge the present value system. Through such cultural discourses, the cultural heritage is thus something that reshapes the cultural values of the society and from which one continues to learn.

Through first the preservation of the building, second the debate concerning social, cultural, ethical, and moral values, and finally the issue of public and private ownership, the Wenminglo case has challenged the usual historical preservation discourse in architecture, which is predominantly male- and class-oriented and focusing on prestigious landmarks. The case of Wenminglo addresses both the complexity and alternative possibilities for answering the primary questions of the preservation discourse: what is the culture value, and whose culture needs to be preserved?

"The (hi)story we tell of the city is also the (hi)story we tell of ourselves" (Rendell 2002: 2). Eric Halbwachs points out that the invention of a tradition occurs for three reasons: first, "to establish social cohesion within a group"; second, "to instill a series of values, beliefs and behaviors within different members of a society"; and finally "to legitimize authority of a sovereignty or a nation" (Boyer 1994: 310). Boyer argues that historical preservation often solidifies the traces of the past into a unified image in order to restore an intactness that has never been. "A designer focuses on the context of a landmark or a historic district, thus becoming the architect of theatrical stages sets that have little to say about the memory of place" (Boyer 1994: 373). These are the theoretical concerns that prevail in this chapter.

This chapter begins by discussing the significance of Wenminglo in challenging the existing social, ethical, and moral values regarding sex in the context of class. Focusing on both the preservation of the building and the right of the sex workers to save their workplace as well as their place in the society, the second part of the chapter examines the search for new interpretations and management of cultural heritage. Finally, the chapter discusses the outcomes of a participatory design workshop in prompting new attitudes toward both the conservation of the historical building and re-examination of conservative social values in the city.

Wenminglo historical preservation project: a culturing process

What does historical preservation means? What cultural value is being preserved or challenged that would serve to justify the questioning of ethical and moral value systems? Wenminglo, historically a space of legal prostitution, serves as the site of such inquiry. The preservation of Wenminglo has become a public concern long before it was designated as a historical building. Yet it is still the living quarters of the building owner and managed by the NGO group that advocates for legalizing prostitution in Taipei. Inside the realm of the private sphere of home is also the interior of the "public space" in the city. Further complicating the issue is that the land belongs to the Taiwan Bank, a government-owned yet privately controlled institution that regards itself as the private owner. The rental status of the house also made its public ownership even more ambiguous. As the place has been used as a leased property for the past forty years, can COSWAS claim the collective memories of the site, and is the organization able to serve as the steward of the place?

The movement to designate the site as a historical landmark has challenged the conventional discourse of historical preservation, and is itself interesting at three levels. First, it is not just the building or the architectural merit of the façade or interior elements that is deemed controversial. The designation would also effectively create a domino effect that helps to highlight the historical geography of desire: the red-light district of early colonial Taipei.[1] The second deals with the concept that historical sites are often considered to be the jewel of the city and often have to be culturally accepted in the society, especially by the dominant middle class. Although places such as prostitution museums do exist in places such as Denmark, in an East Asian city such as Taipei, sites such as Wenminglo that seemingly celebrate an "immoral act" between men and women are not "culturally" accepted. Culture is to be learned and explored. But often the right of interpretation is in the hands of the government, even if the site has been continuously lived in by residents and not subject to the control of the "public agency." The preservation of Wenminglo, the moral and ethical values, and finally the preconceived idea of historical buildings as public space all have to be challenged and renegotiated through a new "culturing process." Such culturing process has the potential of producing and creating a more diverse Taipei.

The historical geography of desire in Taipei

Wenminglo is located in Tadaocheng, an area popularly known in Taipei as one of the oldest and most traditional districts. The name Tadaocheng originally means "the big rice field." But for a long time the area was better known as a main commercial center in the city, settled by early immigrants from China. Since the late 1980s, Tadaocheng has also been the site of an intense battle for historical preservation. In the end, the preservationists won the fight, and the area was designated as one of the first historic districts in the city. However, the layers of sexual desire as represented by the brothel houses have been a missing element in the official narrative of the historic district. In the past forty years, many brothel houses have been transformed into high-class clubs, while others have been demolished. The legitimacy of such spaces of desire has been completely neglected in the historical preservation discourse.

Many of these sites have been invisible, until they were uncovered by the few research projects undertaken in the past several years. Some sites have served as the focus of "memory projects," which means that the physical buildings no longer exist. Through photographs and interviews, recent research has helped to sketch and outline the life that took place in those spaces. In an old, dilapidated urban district, the buildings represent a culture or sub-culture that is to be uncovered

Figure 17.2 Entrance to the ground floor of Wenminglo, currently used as a therapy center run by the Collective of Sex Workers and Supporters (COSWAS). Photograph by Hong-Lin Yen.

Figure 17.3 Foyer of Wenminglo, where licensed prostitutes once greeted the clients. Photograph by Hong-Lin Yen.

and rediscovered. For some of the designated sites, the built structures only exist in pictures, and what remain physically may only be a few columns. The remembering and recalling of the past make these landmarks reappear and resurface.

In the case of Wenminglo, the building is fortunately not only intact but also still in use (Figures 17.2 and 17.3). The focus of so-called "reconstruction" then is not on the renovation of the building but rather on the recovery of stories and meanings. Although the building itself may not have unique architectural significance, the designation of the building as a historic landmark prompts the possible preservation of the red-light district and simultaneously a reinvestigation of the historical geography of desire in Taipei; this includes the hotels and bars, where high- and low-class prostitutes linger and in many ways parallel the economic prosperity of the city.

Buildings such as Wenminglo represented the commercial prosperity of Tadaocheng. They also help to paint a clearer picture of the lives in the early days of this commercially booming district. In the heyday of Tadaocheng, the sex industry was thriving, as revealed in the common street saying with respect to the area: "Without seeing the Yi-ji (prostitutes that sing and dance), you didn't come to Tadaocheng." In terms of the actual activities and buildings, although Tadaocheng once had at least ten brothels in business, they are often invisible from the outside. In fact, from the street, they look just like any mixed-use shop-houses. There are no visible signs or posts that advertise the businesses. As one informant described the milieu of one of the brothels, "it is about twenty to thirty *ping* (900 square meters) in size, not so luxurious, one bedroom, one dining room, and one sitting room, with few painting on the walls, the décor is simple and demure."

The district of Tadaocheng is not only the site of early economic development in Taipei, but also the site of the early democratic movement in Taiwan. As such, how one interprets the history of the site can be a contested issue. What is to be seen or highlighted becomes an important issue in the future planning of the district. Without the discursive transformation of desire, in treating sex as part of everyday life in early Taipei, the memory of licensed prostitution would be in direct competition with "democracy," "localization," or any other politically correct discourses in Taiwanese society.

The continuation of the public–private space

Just as legalized prostitution challenges the boundaries between legal and ethical, public and private, the preservation of a brothel as a public landmark also presents a set of unique predicaments. The land of Wenminglo is owned by the Taiwan Bank, a bank that belongs to the state but is at the same time a private company. In short, the bank is free to sell the land, as it often does by auctioning off properties to private corporations or individuals. But, because it is regarded as a private exchange, the transactions are not under the jurisdiction of the government authorities.

Sitting on the bank-owned land, the building structure of Wenminglo itself is owned by an eighty-year-old couple. The Taiwan Bank leases the land to them and continues to own the site beneath the building. This has been the case for the past thirty-odd years. The couple has in turn leased the first floor to the brothel, while retaining the second floor as their living quarters (Figures 17.4 and 17.5). The third floor was once rented out as well, but is now in a dilapidated condition. Around the area, the ownership of many buildings is also shared by the publicly owned, privately run Taiwan Bank and private individuals. The complexity of the land ownership makes the landmark designations more symbolic than substantive. Not the bank, the private owner, nor the City's Department of Cultural Affairs has complete rights in regard to the programming or the future use of such a site. This creates complexity but also opportunities for renegotiating the programming of the building space, a culturing process. In the meantime, the space has been fully

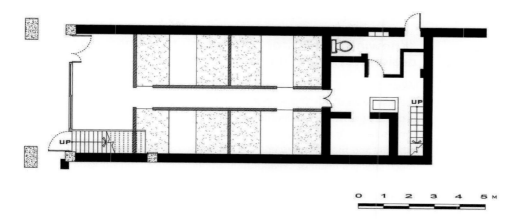

0   1   2   3   4   5 M

Figure 17.4 Floor plan of Wenminglo showing partition of rooms. Source: COSWAS.

Figure 17.5 The view down the corridor showing the simple partition of rooms and the boundary between privacy and access. Photograph by Hong-Lin Yen.

utilized by the NGO "Spring Every Day" as its therapy center while the space upstairs is still used by the building owners.

"Knowing" the history of Wenminglo: a participatory design workshop in historical preservation

Wenminglo as a case of historical preservation could not have come this far without the ten years of the movement for legalized prostitution before it. Begun first as protests against the abolition of legalized prostitution, the movement later focused on discursive transformation and overcoming the stereotype that prostitution is ethically and morally unacceptable in society. The preservation effort that emerged much later is a result of collaboration among the planning students, academia, and the sex worker activists. The work focused on the culturing process of how and what to preserve in the building. Through workshops and lectures, a preliminary programming of a "street for desire" was generated.

One such workshop was held in August 2007 as an attempt to find new solutions for the preservation of Wenminglo. The workshop was a part of the project funded by the Taipei Department of Cultural Affairs to identify new uses for the historical landmark. Rather than focusing on the technical aspects of the structure, material, or control of humidity, the workshop team sought to involve the public in the process of articulating the future uses and programming of the site. In close collaboration with COSWAS, the workshop was an attempt to better understand the past history of the site and the present urban problem, as well as to remedy the cultural ignorance of the general public. Working together with the former sex workers, the workshop participants looked for future alternatives in transforming the brothel house into a "real" public space.

Led by myself, one of the workshop teams explored the layers of interior ceilings inside the brothel by first tearing it down (at least a portion of it), and thereby revealing the different time periods in which the building has been used: from the colonial era to the present time. To create a new historical interpretation and a new way of seeing, while not disrupting the ongoing therapy sessions that still occupy the space, the interior ceilings provided an ideal setting for design interventions and reinterpretation of memories. A visitor would experience the space by viewing and reading the ceilings by lying on the bed, just as a prostitute would be looking up while she worked. By using the existing steel structure and replacing the ceiling tiles, workshop participants designed new storyboard mock-ups that would tell stories in the new brothel museum (Figure 17.6). As the visitors lie down on the beds, the ceilings became the visual focal point to learn about the stories of the sex workers, their past and present.

Another team, led by the artist Mali Wu, created an installation art project focusing on a "back alley lifestyle" that parallels the life of the brothel: both often lie in darkness. By using simple two-dimensional black cut-outs to create the silhouettes, the installation highlighted the alleyway's ambiguity as both public and private space. The third team, led by C. M. Mu, took a more conventional urban design approach by identifying new programs for Guisui Street, where Wenminglo is located. Rather than focusing on a single building, the team believed that the entire street should be investigated and redesigned as a whole. The street would be renamed as the "street of desire," where different forms of recreation from drinking tea to touring an eco-museum of the sex workers become components of a program to revitalize the neighborhood.

Conclusion: brothel as public space

Through the workshop, new questions have been raised, and preliminary answers have been attempted. Specifically, the workshop produced public art installations that tried to challenge the stereotype and raise the consciousness of the back alley, as well as the creation of a visioning plan for a "street of desire" that includes

Figure 17.6 The ceiling interpretive installations and the participating students in the workshop. Photograph by Yung-teen Annie Chiu.

leisure programming at different levels, making the area part of a so-called "cultural industry zone."

The preservation project that originated with the movement for advocating the rights of the sex workers has been a long journey in questioning the right to one's culture and the right to one's place in the city. It challenges what is to be preserved collectively as urban memories. If urban planning is to "know the city" (Rendell 2002), a creative answer or discursive transformation in neo-liberal historical preservation in the city must include retentions of the memories of everyday lives, and concretization of a culturing process that includes people of all classes, work types, and genders. The answer might be not necessarily to preserve everything, but to engage in the public process and discourse, vis-à-vis exclusion in the name of morality or ownership.

As the boundary between public and private in today's society becomes increasingly unclear, creating a new public sphere requires more ingenious solutions. The workshop is one such small experiment. As a fragment of the urban past, Wenminglo reflects more than it records. Perhaps through embracing and learning from the moral and spatial ambiguity of Wenminglo, the city would reconcile itself historically, in the present, and toward the future.

Note

1 Taipei, along with the rest of Taiwan, was colonized by Japan from 1895 to 1945, during which time sections of the city were designated as entertainment areas.

Bibliography

Boyer, M. C. (1994) *City of Collective Memory: Its Historical Imagery and Architectural Entertainments*, Cambridge, MA: MIT Press.
Rendell, J. (2002) *The Pursuit of Pleasure: Gender, Space and Architecture in Regency London*, New Brunswick, NJ: Rutgers University Press.

CHAPTER 18

Spatial limbo

Reinscribing landscapes in temporal suspension

Min Jay Kang

The situation of Taipei's Shezih Island has always been pending and ambiguous. A spatial conundrum. When this originally isolated and clearly demarcated island was forced to be appended to the city and turned into a peninsula, its relationship with metropolitan Taipei evolved into an ambivalent tango of "ruptured association."[1] The shaping forces of the island's spatial form emerged, on one hand, from the natural erosion of the adjacent rivers and the constant shift of physical boundary due to tidal flow, and, on the other, from the state apparatus's operation, which suspended capital influx.[2]

The lag of planning implementation deferred the process of irreversible landscape transformation,[3] yet the construction moratorium of more than thirty-five years also ironically suggests the inability of the government to solve the perplexing problems of flooding on this fragile sandbar. However, a more apparent yet comparatively obscure force shaping Shezih's cultural landscape can be found in the daily practice of grassroots community that has been accumulating layers of cultural implications on the land as time gently undulates and lapses.

Shezih Island is located at the convergence of the Keelung and Tamshui Rivers, and mirrors the similarly fated Zhoumei agricultural settlement across the river. As one meanders back and forth on this island's haphazard and almost irrational routes, random images of old and ramshackle buildings, farmhouses, walk-up flats, grocery stores, sheet-metal patched factories, betel-nut stalls, vegetable gardens, corner temples, illegal structures, schools, ruins, aged trees and vines, oil drums, and garbage carelessly pop up and fade out. The road circling the island is often charged up by gravel and heavy-duty trucks vibrating the shallow ground and, like so many other "guerrilla motorcades" scurrying around the borders of the city, they secretly bring in discarded materials while taking away local resources and quietly transform the subtle details of the island's landscape. The footpath trailing the embankment ridge cuts across the silver grass and mangrove, and the sprawling wetland inhales and exhales migratory birds, tidal crabs, and urban excretions in a relaxed pace and rhythm. The road and embankment sever the originally contiguous sandbank and settlement, and on the small opening near the shore a few shiny red plastic stools and a wide variety of abandoned chairs are scattered in front of a small temple. Senile men and nonchalant women sit laid back, smoking and drinking tea. In the shade of a banyan tree, humble huts in dim lights insinuate some hidden engagement. Small boats mooring by the wooden pier paddle the silt, awaiting the high tide (Figure 18.1).

For all that it is, Shezih Island is not merely an evocation of pre-modern nostalgia, nor is it just a yet-to-be-developed piece of land suspended in the city owing to unresolved property rights issues. It is also not simply a spread of illegal and informal building under the restrictions of the construction moratorium, or a place of conscious conservation action resisting the development mode of the capitalist city. Oscillating between Shezih's microscopic settlement fabric and the capacious scale of globalization that has transformed the city proper, there exist a political reality of the local and a structuralist proposition of contemporary spatial dialectics intimating the intercourse of state rationality and the ubiquitous sweep of capitalism.

Yet either scale of analysis alone is not quite adequate to elucidate the stagnant-cum-implosive landscape of Shezih. The semi-island is very close to the city but, just this arm's length away, it is doomed to spatial segregation and discrimination derived from involuntary choices of development deferral. If contrasting with other underused spaces of suspension outside the city limits or in the rural areas, Shezih Island, under specific restrictions of city zoning and a forlorn development lag, reveals another dimension of urban paradox: the glittering and glamorous city life and the reality of high-speed, high-concentration, and high-volume traffic shuttles

Figure 18.1 Traces of daily life in the suspended condition of Shezih Island. Photographs by Min Jay Kang.

through the nearby elevated Zhoumei Highway every day, and such a fact deepens the unsettled conundrum of Shezih, a disarticulation from the neighboring city's rapid urbanization under the manipulation of both natural forces and state power. The residents on the island self-mockingly refer to themselves not as a legitimate child of Taipei city, but as, quoting one of the neighborhood chiefs' vivid expression, "exiled citizens of an outlaw state independent of Taiwan," having no choices but to adopt an attitude of living on the island that is skeptical of outsiders yet at ease with whatever comes their way.

The territorializing of *dehors*, the bordering of out-there

Under such vague and pending circumstances, the residents of Shezih could not even mobilize themselves to determine their own future actions. Nonetheless, confined by a multitude of legal restrictions over the years, the apparently dead-end dilemma evolves into a slightly anarchic carefree zone where state authority and capital are nearly irrelevant. Its suspended and undecidable condition (or a pre-condition of post-determinacy), compared with a pure geographic fringe, is even more akin to the spirit of urban exile.

Spatial ideology and subjectivity of a place become rather obscure in Shezih, but within its enclosed geological framework an open imagination of *dehors* (Deleuze 1988) may be "folded" out. Following the train of thought from Maurice Blanchot and Michel Foucault to Gilles Deleuze, *dehors* refers to a "non-thinkable" philosophical vagrancy and transferability without boundaries or forms (Foucault 2003) – an ontological substance challenging Hegelian dialectics through "negativity without use" (*negativité sans emploi*). *Dehors* is, like death, which does exist but which no one can really describe, more remote than the outside yet more immanent than the inside.

That is, what *dehors* intends to depict is not a physical space, and any interpretation of *dehors* as a specific space indeed reduces and preposterizes the essence of such philosophical thinking. But if one considers the locus of suspended development and marginalization as a "conscious return to space" regarding *dehors*, and ruminates the intent of *dehors*, which "brackets off" our ideological construct and breaks down the binary demarcation of us *vs.* the strange others, refuses to completely give meanings in general discursive language, and incessantly seeks for the uncharted surface in the crevices of "in-betweenness," then the spatial connotation of *dehors* may strike a critical alarm on contemporary goal-oriented planning paradigms that at times worship rationality but at times embrace nostalgia or local historical researches which monopolize interpretations relying on linear diachronic descriptions. The conceptualization of *dehors* may also stimulate necessary explorations of aesthetic consciousness while facing the complex dimensions and sometimes discomforting realities of urbanity and identity politics: can *dehors* implicate a different kind of aesthetics beyond the traditional norm of order, "city beautiful," or historical appreciation, yet strive to grapple with the ontological inquiry into complexity?

Using *dehors* as a way to conceptualize the spatial relationship between Shezih and Taipei, we may perceive that this drifting island banished by time conceals certain philosophical/aesthetic imaginations that continuously transgress established ideologies and planning politics when its pending status is prolonged into normality. The territorializing of *dehors* or the bordering of out-there is at best a temporary status/site of the spatial return aforementioned, and is always fabricated in the open process of spatial narrative yet unable to sustain a predetermined meaning.[4] Literary and pictorial representations of the *dehors* landscape that do not fawn upon those in power take a sojourn in this field of philosophical nomadism to register real sensation and perception outside the realm of discursive language, before they are again pinned down to fixed norms and meanings by domineering authorities.

Spatial differ(a)nce and the "uninspired" insurgence

T. S. Eliot opens his epic *The Waste Land* (1962) with the voice of a caged old sibyl who wants to die but fails and is eventually turned into a powerful and inconceivable being by the vicissitude of time. She is forbidden to reach the very end, and neither can she reinvigorate her long lost youth. Her dying (or caught between life and death) status immortalizes her decaying physique and everlasting becoming. The sibyl personifies the Waste Land.

Derrida uses another metaphor to fathom the suspended condition of "in-betweenness": as kitschily portrayed in different folklores and cultures, the zombie reifies the anxiety of boundary collapse and transgression from life to the greater beyond (Collins and Mayblin 1996). The incompatibility of life and death is strangely settled in the horrendous and unresolved form of the zombie; it is both alive and dead, and it is neither alive nor dead. The daunting characteristics of the zombie lie in its own "indeterminacy" and its defiance of order within recognizable and categorical boundaries. The logic of binary opposition that sustains the core values of metaphysics and the rational world subordinates the possibilities of indeterminacy, yet the undecidable dark matters always find their niches in the fluid and flexible in-between.

Comparing Eliot's sibyl with Derrida's zombie, however, reveals a drastic difference between two striking images. The former is much too conscious of her existence so that her pain at failing to meet her final demise or return to the origin becomes her very strength; the latter is a corpse with no soul, mind, or gender, which deconstructs the general belief in subjectivity and will. Both images metaphorically unveil the nuanced facets of investigating landscape in temporal suspension when its intended progress is "in limbo."

The concept of limbo appears in Catholic as well as in Taoist religion, and in either belief the extramundane region is further divided into various levels for post-mortem souls with different ante-mortem human deeds and sins waiting to be judged or reincarnated. Limbo also carries the meaning of "border" (or anything joined on) and "prison" (a state of confinement and exclusion till release). It has a spatial connotation in both imaginary and physical senses, and at its core it is a space constructed by a particular dimension of time.

From a specific lens, spatial limbo echoes the territorializing of *dehors* and implies places that are lagging behind and left out of public investment and care over and above private capital venture for development. The locus of spatial limbo has its past history and multiple layers of stories to tell, and it is not often vacant or devoid of human activities. But, as time evolves, the ownership of land and properties grows to a magnitude of extreme complication. And, in many cases, the demarcated public land may be encroached upon by private uses if the land is not yet developed according to the land-use plan (Figure 18.2).

As a consequence, the border between public and private becomes fuzzy and ambiguous. It may not be a lively place in terms of activity intensity, but it is by no means a dead space. Its stagnant feel and comparatively slow pace of daily rhythm sometimes recalls the spatial patterns of the pre-modern period (not necessarily romanticized). It is blessed (or cursed) with an organic incrementalism that becomes less and less likely to be planned in the modern city. Different immigrants (mostly social underclass or first generation settlers) move in or squat in and adapt themselves to the limited resources of the environment, together making up a social network of mutual interdependence in the border zone (Figure 18.3).

Figure 18.2 The courtyard wall-houses under the gigantic funnels encroach incrementally on the defunct Naval Fuel Plant in Hsin-chu. Photographs by Min Jay Kang.

In spatial limbo, there is an ineffable sense of uninspired insurgence. In the line of community planning, we often expect the grassroots insurgent power to capsize the top-down dominant control or institutional enforcement, as if the "public" realm of a democratic society can thus be won over and claimed. The legitimacy of the public, from this perspective, is therefore inseparable from the citizens' autonomy or actions or resistance, but it is easy to ignore the fact that the Western concept of the public is far too remote and abstract for those disempowered citizens who simply have no resources or motivation to fight or counter-oppress from the bottom up. In many cases, they do attempt to resist but fail, and then they retreat to a condition of bare subsistence, indifferent to the idea of insurgence. At the development limbo of the capitalist city, the deep-seated belief in the will of the people and the ardor of revolution can be gradually expended and relegated into some sort of awkward jargon.

In most cases of activism and insurgency, the conscious resistance is a thrust of passion and consumes tremendous energy to maintain; yet the paradox is that, once it is "maintained," it is often sanctified with a nearly religious zest and cut off from day-to-day practice. Or, when it comes down to everyday life, the act of resistance fades into history and becomes a story or urban fable, and the passionate social movement marches on to another front of the resistance battlefield.

The status of spatial limbo reflects relentless social realities of uninspired

Figure 18.3 Squatters and immigrants of various origins and periods make up the social network of Keelung's Ho-ping (Peace) Island. Photographs by Min Jay Kang.

insurgence that lack a serious drive to enlighten the glorified public, yet the collective private life continues understatedly and follows a less enforced rhythm in a less maintained or managed or manipulated condition, whereas the "public" sets disciplines and rules to serve the public good in general. The gesture of the public and the assumed public interest in a modern democratic society inevitably evolves into a kind of censorship and institutional control, and the claimed public sometimes raises a threshold of exclusion without even being noticed.

Between unreachable hope and infinite despair, "strange" religions settle and infiltrate into the subconscious of the place. Faith, in a spatial limbo such as Shezih, is straightforwardly equated with a particular type of religion that does not quest for the meaning of life but offers conceivable protection and short-term remuneration for the hardship of living or, better yet, brings perceptible good fortune. Quite contrary to the peaceful and eternal heaven blessed by the only and mighty God, the spatial limbo is a sanctuary embracing all deities and denizens and ghosts in a mundane world. The seats of gods and the shelters of ghosts find comfortable niches along the daily routines of ordinary people and are closely interwoven into the hodgepodge fabric of the local landscape, regardless of any land-use planning or regulation (Figure 18.4).

In many ways, the spatial limbo is a place made of uncompromising differences in a collective instead of a common mode, and it confronts all kinds of conflict, fear, and desire without modernist aggrandizement. It does not pretend or make any effort to be more than what it already is. At first glance, the traditional dimensions

Figure 18.4 "Strange" religions seep into the subconscious of Taipei's Wo-long squatters' village, which is situated between the old cemetery and the high-speed transit lines. Photographs by Min Jay Kang.

of the public are embarrassingly missing in the spatial limbo, but it is perhaps a truer epitome of the public itself.

If we employ Jacques Derrida's (1982) word play of differ(a)nce and coined terms "defer" and "differ" to explore the landscapes in temporal suspension, then its "gerund" (both verb and noun) situation caught between time and space, physical entity and action, and existence and fabrication, or the "indeterminacy" thus referred to, may curiously provide clues to understanding places and landscapes of limbo status that have rarely been touched upon by past urban planning rationality. Differ(a)nce is a non-existing and untranslatable word either in English or French, which can only be comprehended and gestured in the context of grammatology: an act lagging behind spoken language (connoting phonocentrism as well as logocentrism). It is a conscious deliberation to question the legitimacy and predominance of real-time presence, while reminding us to investigate the "trace" of presentation (which is "necessarily present in its necessary absence": Collins and Mayblin 1996).

Through the act of reinscribing the spatial limbo, it may no longer be deemed to be a diametric opposite of forward development or just a backlash against urban planning. As the spatial gap has its own spatial dimension, so does the temporal gap have its own dimension of time. The deferred space becomes a space of differ(a)nce. It is not attached to a fixed meaning or norm, and it is always becoming, even if each inscription about it must somehow meet a temporary narrative end.

Wetland as a metaphor or cultural ecotone as a planning undertone

The landscapes of spatial limbo may exhibit an anarchic and dynamic equilibrium comparable to a wetland (Figure 18.5). A wetland is often situated in the interzone between distinctive ecological environments. It is in constant transition and hardly ever stable, and consists of many habitats for different species of plants and animals, insects and microorganisms, but the entire composition is not, metaphorically, dictated by a singular force or species. A wetland is shaped by gradual natural processes rather than a dominant exogenous power exerting on the landscape at a particular time. In between distinctive habitats, species vie for their territories in an identifiable ecosystem where they live differently and more dangerously than on their own independent turfs. A wetland can be a microcosm of the world, but it is not the world per se.

This ecotone exists in the leftover area of the greater world, yet the more wetlands are allowed chances to survive on their own terms, the richer the world can be. A wetland does not strive to replace the world, nor expect to set a standard value for the world to achieve. It is a kind of paradigm in which differences coexist on a daily basis, yet it can be easily eliminated if its shaping forces are contained or manipulated because it is comparatively fragile and ambiguous. A wetland is evidence of collective tactics instead of a common plan: some migrate, some squat, some respond to the change of time and tide, and each feeds on the biological chain. Life and death mingle, and death is easily transformed into nourishment for

Figure 18.5 Living "in between" – from biological ecotone to cultural ecotone, from spatial limbo to constructed ecotone. Photographs by Min Jay Kang.

the living. It deserves to be appreciated as an alternative social network as well as a cultural landscape pattern that can shed a light on modern-day planning.

A constructed wetland is a human endeavor to simulate the form and mechanism of a natural wetland. It is by definition planned, but aiming to conserve the utmost diversity and complexity of the micro-ecosystem with minimal maintenance input. If a wetland can be planned and constructed, what does it imply for urban planning's treatment of spatial limbo?

Once it comes down to urban planning, fallow or underused space is often criticized as the outcome of poor planning and implementation. The interpositions of discourse and institution eventually step in to resolve the "problems" of spatial limbo and rectify the deviation of space. Under the logic of land-use zoning, every urban space has its own general features, and those that belong to the argument of history will return to publicly acknowledged preservation (followed by all sorts of reprogramming of museumization, adaptive reuse, and regeneration) and those worthy of development are just awaiting an opportune moment for a public or private agency to arrive and carry out the projects in compliance with the law.

Public and rational consensus (in which minority opinions tend to be sacrificed and overlooked) decides almost everything. Putting aside those areas that have already been demolished and renewed in Taipei, we can still see how Skin-peeling Alley (Bo-pi-liao) in Wan-hua (Mankah), which has similarly been subject to a construction moratorium for more than half a century, was reprogrammed as a center for local culture study in a rather taken-for-granted manner after all the original residents were evicted. And the squatter village of Treasure Hill (Bao-zang-yen) hanging likewise at the water's edge, after being reclaimed and rezoned as a preservation area by the "progressive" Bureau of Cultural Affairs of Taipei, is now on its way to being gradually made into a cohabiting community for social housing and arts according to the vision of "progressive" planning, which helped to legalize the status of some of the squatters. It is to be expected that the original feel of self-autonomy and anarchy will find little space to breathe in the planned mode, no matter how socially progressive its new program may be.

There are also other preservation projects turned into museums on various scales and inevitable commercialized spaces due to management strategies following the governmental requirement of a self-sufficient OT (operate–transfer) mechanism. The invisible hand of the institution is always present when the meaning of an underdeveloped urban landscape is redefined through reprogramming, and this raises the question: is it unfortunate or the opposite for Shezih Island to be in its current situation of limbo and differ(a)nce?

If Shezih Island is not content to simply live and let die in the future, then imagine it as an extension of a biological ecotone into a constructed cultural ecotone. Gessner's (2005) literary account vividly translates "those rich, overlapping areas, those unstable, non-categorical places that aren't one thing or another" into the context of literature:

> Just as biological ecotones are areas of great species diversity and biological density, of intense life and death, so literary ecotones are the places where words come most alive. These edges – between genres, between science and literature, between land and sea, between the civilized and wild, between the earnest and comic, between the personal and biological, between urban and rural, between the animal and spiritual – are not only more alive, but more interesting and worthy of exploration. And it is only here, in these places in-between, that we are able to make maps complex enough to mirror the uncertain and often chaotic fluidity of our true, confused selves.

Similarly, the imagined cultural ecotone is nothing short of a cross-boundary adventure. The planner of a cultural ecotone may recognize the territories of different inhabitant species as well as values and aesthetics of the spatial limbo without romanticizing or aestheticizing the living condition of the inhabitants, and allow time to shape or dissolve the cultural boundary (instead of functional subdivision of land-use zoning) of the ecotone. If any of the public or institutional programs is needed to be implemented, it should be deliberately meshed into the routine of everyday life – a public–private mix. The planner may also play the role of a species inhabiting a vacant piece of land (not any socially higher or lower than the other species) to engage in the landscape narratives of the ecotone.

A "fold" of the spatial limbo

Spatial discourses often converge to focus on the vision of the government or the role of the local community's life experiences and autonomous empowerment in the consequential contention of spatial meaning and planning actions. Philosophical and aesthetic reminders in light of this appear to be rather trivial and unimportant. *Dehors* indeed is omnipresent (therefore, development or preservation or abandonment of space may not make any difference in terms of *dehors*), but the temporary territory of *dehors* (or, plainly, the laissez-faire and anarchic spatial condition that is curiously connived at by the government) is shrinking under various forces of incorporation and assimilation.

Deleuze employed the analogy of the Ship of Fools cast out in the ocean during the Renaissance to approach Foucault's *dedans* which is a "fold" from *dehors* and is "more profound than the inside." The insane are confined in the core of utmost freedom and openness, and shackled at the intersection of infinity. The insane are the ideal travelers and an imprisonment of an endless journey, according to Deleuze. At *dedans*, the insane signify the "thinking" about the other, but not based on some humanistic morality or condescending social concerns for the disempowered minority. It is not about giving justice, but an ontological reflexivity about the human condition bounded by physical space and measurable time. It is our futile yet desperate attempt, while confronting uncertainty and indeterminacy in the "chronotope" (Bakhtin 1981), to make transitional meanings of who and when and where we are out of nameless chaos.

The shackles of time have not been unchained from the isolated Shezih even when it was made a peninsula. The travelers at the core of the utmost freedom and openness continue to roam in the endless journey.

Notes

1 The island of Shezih became home to a few immigrant families from mainland China in the Ching Dynasty when its initially calabash-shaped land stabilized. During the Japanese colonial period, this backwater area was the major supplier of the capital's vegetable produce. Then it lost the primary role to other agricultural fields down in central Taiwan when the North–South Freeway was completed in 1978; the dumped soil from the freeway construction also filled in the stream at its southern border and thereafter annexed the island to the city (Wang 2001).

2 According to the Flood Control Plan of the Taipei Region of 1970, Shezih was designated as a flood buffer zone. Ever since, except for illegal constructions, the development of the entire island was restricted (yet the general survey of 1993 indicated that, of 969 buildings on the island, illegal ones comprised 44.7 percent of the overall stock). The plan was revised again in 1993, including the revision of a proposal for a "porn industry special district," which highly irritated local people, and a controversial plan to shrink and raise the island to the level of 9.65 m at the same time. In 1998, the finalized plan intended to turn Shezih into a desirable land of entertainment, leisure, and livability, yet the mode of land expropriation could not persuade the approximately 10,000 islanders and the plan was withheld again till today.

3 The district policies of heavy embankment, ground level upraising, and rezoning, alongside strict prohibition codes of construction and development before actual planning implementation, impede large-scale exploitation by the private sector.

4 Note that Maurice Blanchot defines narrative as a motion toward a certain point. This point is not merely unknown, unrecognized, unfamiliar, but moreover it seems

to have no reality outside or before its motion. But it is so predominant that all attractions of narrative are thus derived and the narrative cannot even begin before reaching this point. Only narrative and its predominant motion can proffer the space that renders the point real, powerful, and attractive.

Bibliography

Bakhtin, M. M. (1981) *The Dialogic Imagination: Four Essays*, Emerson, C. and Holquist, M. (trans.) Austin: University of Texas Press.

Collins, J. and Mayblin, B. (1996) *Introducing Derrida*, Duxford, UK: Icon Books.

Deleuze, G. (1988) *Foucault*, Hand, S. (trans. and ed.) Minneapolis: University of Minnesota Press.

Derrida, J. (1982) *Margins of Philosophy*, Bass, A. (trans.) Chicago: University of Chicago Press.

Eliot, T. S. (1962) *The Waste Land and Other Poems*, New York: Harcourt, Brace & World.

Foucault, M. (2003) *La pensée du dehors*, Wei-Hsin Hong (trans. into Chinese) Taipei: Hsing-Ren Publishers.

Gessner, D. (2005) 'On Living In-Between', *Ecotone: Reimagining Place*, 1 (1). Online. Available HTTP: http://student.uncw.edu/dfc1532/issues/spring-2005.html#From_the_Editor (accessed 7 January 2010).

Wang, Z. (2001) *On the Vicissitude of Shezhi*, Taipei: Shezhi Cultural and Educational Foundation.

PART SIX

CONTESTING

CHAPTER 19

Public space activism, Toronto and Vancouver

Using the banner of public space to build capacity and activate change[1]

Andrew Pask

"Plan to leave cars on public space opposed" reads the headline. The sentence is set in Times New Roman typeface with its bold capital letters broken over three lines: a proclamation the width of a single column sitting on the front page of the paper. The ensuing article leads with a quote from Curtis Guild, "a civic worker," who makes his case up front: "Further encroachment on the common should be stubbornly resisted by all those who love our beautiful city." A paragraph later we find that Mr. Guild is also part of the Boston Common Society, a citizen's group waging a now-public battle with the city's automobile "club" over the latter's proposal to use a portion of the greenway for parking.

In recent years these sorts of stories have started to show up in media reports and blogs from around the world on a daily basis – and key word searches of "public space" in newspaper archives show an exponential leap in the number of articles since the mid-1990s. The specifics are often different, but the themes remarkably similar: citizens' groups, grassroots collectives, sometimes even local governments themselves, leading a charge to create public space where it does not yet exist, to reclaim it from where it was lost, and to rejuvenate it from states undesirable or incomplete.

Coincident with this growth in the use of the term has been an enlarging awareness (and resulting dialogue) around the importance of "public space" – termed as such – as part of municipal planning processes, grassroots organizing, and community development initiatives alike. "Public space" is seen as a constituent element in ensuring positive social relations and well-being (Dines and Cattell *et al.* 2006), as well as a more robust opportunity for social inclusion in cities and communities (Eberle and Serge 2007: iii[2]) – not only for the general public, but also for populations where the potential for isolation and marginalization is higher. The term is understood to have multiple literal and metaphorical meanings (Brodin 2006) and is conceived as: a component of democratic health (see Habermas 1962/1989, through discussion of the public sphere), a site facing the threat of corporate incursion, and, concomitantly, an antidote to an increasingly privatized physical (and mental) landscape (e.g. Klein 2000: 35–38), and a space of refuge for all residents of urban centers that comes generally – though not exclusively – without an admission fee.

In the process, "public space" has become a mobilizing term around which many activists and organizations have coalesced. Sometimes "public space" is the focus, and other times it is incidental but nevertheless important. Mr. Guild's group, for example, was focused on an intensely local, immediate, and personal effort – protecting the green space between Lafayette Mall and Tremont Street – but it is the type of effort that many groups today, in urban centers large and small, can relate to.

What makes the work of the Boston Common Society and its fight such an interesting starting point is that it took place in October 1914.[3] For activists today, this makes it a mildly sobering but nevertheless helpful way to start to contextualize urban activism and current advocacy work around public space. In this chapter, I try to paint a picture of how current work in two Canadian cities – Toronto (starting in 2001) and Vancouver (starting in late 2005) – is helping to push the notion of "public space activism" still further, moving engagement beyond a polyphony of specifics (this park, that sidewalk) and on to a more comprehensive narrative of whole (the city's public space).

The transformation of public space and public space activism

Conventional planning theory, as taught in planning schools in North America (and about North American cities), suggests that citizen-led planning and advocacy – the type that results in a push for neighborhood-scale development, greater pluralism in the process, demands for local parks, sidewalks, libraries, childcare, etc. – began in the 1960s and 1970s, when the influence of the modernist-infused "planning technocrats" began to wane.[4] This notion – though reflective of a substantial growth in citizen planning activities – obscures a genealogy of "insurgent planning" that stretches back in time a considerable way.[5] It is clear from the article on Boston Common (and others like it from newspaper archives and community bulletins in other cities) that conflicts over public space (as a component of the urban environment) are part of a larger and ever-changing history of insurgency and resistance.

Since the turn of the millennium Toronto and Vancouver have both seen the formation of citizen-based public space advocacy groups – groups whose focus is on public space (as a concept, in a general sense, writ large, etc.). What makes these groups, and others like them, different from the Citizens Assembly of 1889, the Boston Common Society of 1914, or any of the other initiatives that followed them, is the way that "public space" as a banner – a unifying concept or *modus operandi* – has been employed. In the former, the notion of public space is the key driver, manifested as a source of focused activity in various places around the urban environment. In the latter, the focus is on a particular space, which may or may not be referred to as "public space" (usually not – which, in fact, is why the Boston Common example is so interesting).

In other words, "public space" has now become an end in and of itself, or, as Mark Kingwell has termed it, "the age's master signifier" (Kingwell 2008: 1). It is no longer just about the park or the waterfront – it is about those particular areas as part of a bigger picture – as points of connection to other spaces and the public that uses them. Far from this being daunting or problematic (Kingwell decries the signifier as "a prison" that is "loose", "elastic" and "variously deployed") I would argue that it is an extraordinarily effective unifying concept *and* rallying cry that has enabled an increase in the appreciation of civic issues, community spaces, and the everyday experience of the cities in which we live.

Before getting to the specific work of these two organizations, I want to try and contextualize this change in a fuller fashion. I believe the creation of self-conscious, self-reflective "public space" activism is a fairly novel invention that, although it has existed in many different ways – and in the work of diverse groups and collectives such as the Open Spaces Society, Project for Public Spaces, the Billboard Liberation Front, Reclaim the Streets, among many others – is also a product of fairly recent times.[6] My thesis here is that a distinction needs to be made between three different and overlapping uses of the idea of "public space activism": something that is a product of historical changes in terminology, as well as variations in the scope of what gets treated as public space.

Public space before it was public space

There is a substantial and long-standing body of activities connected with public space and with insurgent activities connected with these spaces in which the term "public space" is not actually used (either because it was not in common parlance at the time, or because other terms were used instead). This is often the case with historical conflicts over the commons, enclosure, etc., but it also characterizes many examples of recent activism as well.

Connected to this is a tendency for present-day journalists, scholars, and activists to frame these past activities and insurgencies as being related to "public space" – thus inserting the term into the situation as a descriptor, albeit (sometimes) an anachronistic one. A recent work by Peter Goheen (2000) that explores community involvement in waterfront planning in nineteenth-century Toronto is an example of this, as are the following:

> The heritage of the reclaiming of public space, the "commons" themselves, can be found much further back in British history, to a group of radicalised landless commoners who occupied St. George's Hill outside London in 1649. These were the "True Levellers" or "Diggers";
>
> (Social Centre Stories 2008: 1)

and:

> [I]t was this public space [the "middle ground" created by print technology and its readership] and its potential for fostering popular enlightenment that John Milton . . . set out to defend in November 1644 when he published his attack on the licensing of the press in *Areopagitica*.
>
> (Rahe 2008: 182)

There are a lot of good examples of these sorts of assessments, each reflecting a contribution to the reappraisal of the role of public space in our social history. Many past conflicts are now being "fitted in" to the larger narrative around the public realm – which adds richness, as well as increasing breadth – to our present-day understanding of the term.

"A" public space (singular) before it was "public space" (holistic and all-encompassing)

There is a second category of reference to *specific* projects, issues, and interventions, as being connected with the public realm and in which the lead actors engaged in the project (and not the academics who are looking upon it from the present age) use the notion of public space as a way to mobilize, foster understanding, etc. Here, the crucial distinction is that it is specific projects that are seen as "an example of/ type of" public space, and that the mobilization uses the idea of public space in the context of a specific issue. Public space, here, is (part of) the rationale for a specific intervention, and it is generally subsumed into the specifics of the matter, rather than the other way around. For example, a park, square, or plaza that is imperiled is seen as "an important public space" and thus worthy of attention. This category defines the early use of the term "public space," as well as innumerable contemporary applications. From this approach, public space is less a unifying concept and more a descriptor of something else; a part, not a whole.

Interestingly, a search of various databases suggests the historical use of "public space" is narrower than one might think, given the present-day breadth of the term. The Boston Common story is one of only a few media headlines from the period between 1850 and 1950 that employs the phrase. Legal databases suggest a similar paucity: the first case law reference to "public space" that appears in the Canadian courts dates back to 1916,[7] but then the expression does not show up again for several decades.

These dates are helpful because they serve to establish the modern etymology of the term "public space" and its usage. Collectively, this seems to suggest that "public space" as a concept has effectively and quickly grown in prominence only in the last three or four decades – and only substantively (based on counted references to the term) in the last ten to twenty years.[8]

Public space-related activism as "public space" activism

It may seem like an unnecessary diversion to bring in the aforementioned sections, but, in order to appreciate the change that has taken place with regard to insurgency around public spaces, it is helpful to see the shift to a more focused "public space activism" – versus the work of the Boston Common Society, Surveillance Camera Players, or Critical Mass – as being more than just semantic. It is actually an operational difference, which is what makes the work of groups such as the Toronto Public Space Committee (TPSC), Vancouver Public Space Network (VPSN), and others showcased in this volume a bit of a departure from what preceded them.

What this means is that "public space" has now become a driver of social movements and activism in its own right – and a particularly strategic one at that. As an umbrella concept for previously disparate areas of activism, "public space activism" is, by default, forging strategic linkages, mobilizing people not otherwise connected with activism, and providing a more accessible and generalized language for advocacy and citizen engagement. Perhaps most importantly, the movement links together formerly "siloed" elements: people engaged in street reclamation, guerrilla gardening, parks advocacy, disability activism, counter-surveillance, anti-billboard lobbying, street artistry, progressive urban planning and design, and more. And rather than this being a problem because it makes the term public space too "loose" or "slack," it is actually a spectacular means of forging linkages and creating a highly networked umbrella social movement. In fact, the decision to seek out and build these linkages reflects a very conscious choice on the part of groups such as the TPSC and VPSN.

"Public space" activism in practice: the VPSN, the TPSC, and their activities

The Toronto Public Space Committee was formed in 2001, though it got its formal organizational momentum a year later. The Vancouver Public Space Network was conceived in 2005 but also got its formal start a year later. In both cases, there was a series of catalyzing events. For the TPSC founders it was, first, the prospect of a video billboard overlooking the city's largest green space, followed quickly by the City of Toronto proposing a new anti-postering bylaw (Figure 19.1). In Vancouver, the initial events featured a Hummer marketing campaign at the local library (Figure 19.2), a police proposal to install CCTV downtown, and a plan amongst friends to undertake a guerrilla gardening project. In both cases, rather than focusing exclusively on the specifics of the different issues, an attempt was made to sew the initiatives together with the thread of "public space." It worked.[9]

Over the ensuing years, the specific projects of the TPSC and VPSN have undergone some changes, though many of the core initiatives are still in place. Tables 19.1 and 19.2 provide an overview of the main areas of activity for each group. Organizationally, the TPSC and VPSN differ in their approach inasmuch as the TPSC has tended to structure itself as a series of sub-committees working on specific focused campaigns (e.g., anti-postering bylaw, the potential non-compliance activities of Viacom) whereas the VPSN has focused its organizational energies on the creation of working groups covering broader portfolios (e.g., corporatization, urban design, transportation), which have then taken on specific issues and projects. In addition, the VPSN has also created a number of more centralized internal working groups that operate across the network on matters of organizational planning, communications, volunteer development, and special events.

From the activities outlined above, it is clear that there are points of overlap and distinction between the organizational structures of the two groups. The focus of many TPSC campaigns continues to be the larger issue of corporatization, whereas the VPSN has branched into areas such as urban design work and community gardens. Both groups work on billboard issues and guerrilla gardening. And in both cases there is the same spirit of "if it's public space, it's fair game" in terms of potential activities. There is, in fact, a cross-pollination of ideas between the

Figure 19.1 Street posters in Toronto. One of the motivations for starting the TPSC was the proposed anti-postering bylaw, which would severely curtail the use of public space for poster messaging. Image from Vancouver Public Space Network.

Figure 19.2 Hummer promotion on the plaza outside Vancouver's central library. Concern about the corporatization of public space led to the formation of the VPSN. Image from Vancouver Public Space Network.

groups. Whereas billboards and carnivalesque ideas around transit parties migrated westward from TPSC, the VPSN's work on exploring the public space aspects of civic naming rights and municipal CCTV projects traveled eastward.

With both the VPSN and the TPSC there is the further recognition that, organizationally, the groups themselves must function as a sort of public space, operating both in the public realm (meetings are usually held in public facilities, and are open to the public), and in a fashion that is as close to democratic as possible. This means a strong emphasis on consensus decision making, transparent planning processes, and an attempt to encourage a diverse array of participants and volunteers.

Table 19.1 Toronto Public Space Committee – key campaigns

Campaign	Description
TTC TV	Video ads on Toronto's public transit system
Viacom contract violations	Non-compliant street furniture and advertising
Monster garbage bins	Advocacy against ad-infused trash receptacles
Anti-postering bylaw	Street postering bylaw advocacy
Downtown de-fence	Program to encourage voluntary removal of chain-link fences
Ad Trucks	Advocacy against mobile billboards
Billboard Battalion	Billboard variance monitoring
Thanks for Riding	Cycling promotion and support
Art Attack	Installation of temporary street art on top of street furniture advertising
Guerrilla gardening	Gardening in public space
Human River	Buried waterways
City for Sale	Civic sale of naming rights

Table 19.2 Vancouver Public Space Network – working groups and key areas of activity

VPSN working group	Areas of activity
Corporatization	Advocacy around civic naming rights; non-compliant billboards
Democratic Spaces	Civic and provincial elections; major policy discussions and debates
Greenspaces (4 working groups)	Parks; community gardening; community composting; guerrilla gardening
Mapping & Wayfinding	Amenity and issue mapping; guerrilla wayfinding projects
Public Art	Street art; public space films; public art policy
Surveillance & Security	CCTV; private security; community policing
Transportation	Bicycle infrastructure; walkable communities; public transportation
Urban Design	Review of major planning projects; evaluation of public spaces; design competitions
Organizational Development	VPSN operational and strategic planning
Communications	Website; ebulletins and backgrounders
Events	Public transit parties; park celebrations; tabling and community events
Volunteer Coordination	Volunteer training and skill matching

TPSC and VPSN as agents of "insurgency"

The idea of insurgency poses an interesting question for public space groups because it suggests that there is a single actor, or set of actors, against which these groups operate. In practice – at least with the TPSC and VPSN – it is more complicated, even dialogic. The concern is less with "the state" or "private interests" or "corporations" than with "threats to public space." This means that there is a more fluid playing field with the key power brokers operating in the public realm. In Vancouver, the

VPSN has regularly and vigorously deputed against civic policies, projects, and regulatory measures that it feels are detrimental to the city's public space (Figure 19.3). At the same time, the network has not only supported proactive measures, but collaborated with the city and cosponsored events (Figure 19.4). The dialogue, then, is one of specifics – a fact that is enhanced by a local government that, being composed of numerous departments and agencies, is in some cases less monolithic in its thinking than might be supposed.

Public space activism in Vancouver and Toronto is far from anarchistic in nature. In fact, public space activists have made a habit of using various state-driven mechanisms to advance their causes: deputations, encouraging participation in public workshops, etc. in addition to mobilizing media and other more conventional forms of advocacy and activism. Indeed, some of the major work undertaken has been around getting the state – local governments in Vancouver and Toronto – to enforce regulation that is already in place. The very discourse of "publicness" serves to invoke the idea of the state-as-agent in matters of the public realm.

As a form of insurgency, both the VPSN and TPSC attempt to work within the framework of regulations and policies, but take great liberties in exploring the full latitude of possibilities that exist in this framework. With the private sector, the response is similarly one of particulars. Both organizations recognize that "corporations" are not monolithic either, and that private enterprises that play a role in the urban public space in both cities can take on very different values

Figure 19.3 Cover of the VPSN's *Public Space Manifesto*, which was produced for the 2008 municipal election. Image from Vancouver Public Space Network.

and approaches. This is as apparent in architecture and urban design firms, as it is for developers, manufacturers, store owners, business associations, and the like. Thus, where the VPSN has worked with various developers in an attempt to create community gardens, it has also targeted other outdoor signage companies for their installation of billboards, non-compliant or otherwise.

In both cases, the more fluid nature of the VPSN and TPSC activities is defined by a philosophical approach that seeks to "ensure the 'public' in public space."[10] The insurgency is both proactive and reactive, but the targets are not always as fixed, binary, or archetypal as they were in the past.

Shortcomings and opportunities

As much as there are advantages to the new public space activism that has come about, there are limitations too – or at least areas that need attention. Having spent some time trying to rationalize this new form of public space activism I want to conclude by looking at some of the issues that have come up in the work of the

Figure 19.4 Jury selection from the VPSN's *Where's the Square?* Design Ideas Competition, which sought to generate discussion (and proposals) around the idea of a new central gathering place. Design by Mark Ashby & Greenskins Lab.

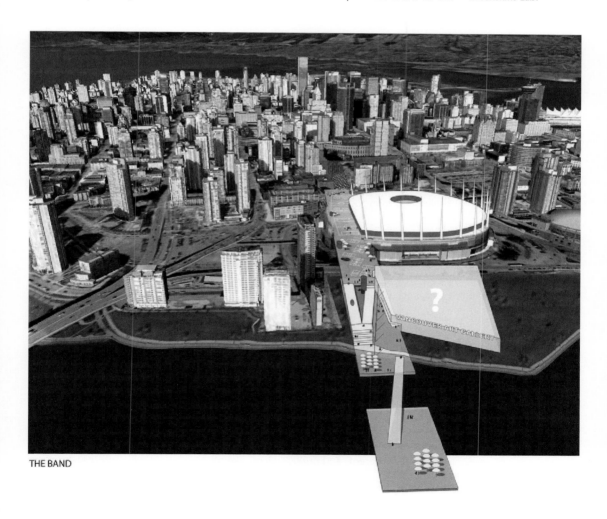

THE BAND

TPSN and the VPSN, or that have been directed at proponents of "public space" more generally. Undoubtedly there are more, but the five I will look at here relate to ensuring diversity and inclusiveness, breadth, conflicts over "public space," funding, and downloading.

Breadth of work

The first is an obvious one: the sheer scope of issues that can potentially be taken on is far more expansive than would otherwise be the case with a single-issue focus. This requires a judicious allocation of volunteer resources, but also a bit of a balancing act. There has to be a resilient enough organizational structure so that the organization can expand its work appropriately, manage its volunteer resources, and still retain a strong sense of overall coherence. In the case of the VPSN, regular organizational development meetings and planning work help with this, as do regular scans of emerging issues.

Ensuring diversity and inclusiveness

In their recent work on cultural diversity and urban public space, Low, Taplin, and Scheld make the case for amenity planning that is more inclusive and reflective of the changing demographic nature of our cities (Low *et al*. 2005). We can broaden this still further and say that there is a need for an inclusiveness that speaks to the same ethnocultural and economic diversity that exists in the broader community. Ideally, the work of the VPSN and the TPSC aspires in a similar fashion, though in practical fact, the results have not always been as cosmopolitan as might be ideal. This is not to say that members of either group are homogeneous by any stretch. Meetings and activities bring out a range of ages, ethnicities, and other populations. There is, however, more work to be done to ensure that this inclusiveness is further broadened to include a wider variety of ethnocultural and economic cohorts.

Conflicts over "public space"

When Mark Kingwell referred to public space as a prison, he did so in part because of the pervasive application of the term. He laments its deployment "to defend (or attack) architecture, to decry (or celebrate) civic squares, to promote (or denounce) graffiti artists, skateboarders, jaywalkers, parkour aficionados, pie-in-the-face guerrillas, underground capture-the-flag enthusiasts, flash-mob surveillance busters and other grid-resistant everyday anarchists" (Kingwell 2008: 18). This is a nice but overwrought way of saying that ideas over what constitutes public space can be normative (a *good* use of space, a *bad* intervention) and that people can have different opinions over this. However, far from being problematic, I think it is actually one of the strengths of the concept. It is open for discussion and debate and is loose enough to inspire a variety of opinions, whether laudatory or denunciatory. Semantic overload in the term only occurs if its many uses become mutually incoherent, and public space – like other rich points in our urban lexicon –

is no Tower of Babel. No one ever faulted art (or "art") for having the same capacity to inspire contradictory responses.

Funding

Lots of people like to volunteer on public space issues; in fact, a few years ago, the TPSC received media recognition and an award for "best volunteer organization." This is good, because sadly, there are very few Canadian funding agencies that have a mandate to fund holistic and integrated public space activities. The result is that both the TPSC and the VPSN are entirely volunteer-driven and sustained through a combination of sweat equity, private donations, and some small social enterprise undertakings (with the lion's share being the first of these three items). At present, public space, as a holistic entity, is the type of concept that falls through the cracks in grant programs. This creates a disadvantage when it comes to undertaking major projects, but it also inspires a fair bit of creative thinking.

Downloading

The last few years have seen a considerable amount being written about downloading and devolution: upper tier levels of government transferring responsibilities for various types of service provision down to local governments (without transferring the concomitant funding resources to properly manage the program). What is less apparent is the potential for public space activists and organizations to pick up the slack when overburdened (and/or unwilling, as the case may be) municipal governments decide they are unable to undertake the sort of rigorous consultations, policy, guideline and bylaw analysis, and community planning work that might otherwise be reasonable to expect on matters of importance to the public realm.

Conclusion

As an organizing principle and rallying cry, the notion of public space opens up and makes visible the connections between many different types of space: buses, sidewalks, community gardens, civic consultations, the visual environment, and more. It helps to clarify linkages, common threats, and opportunities for engagement within and between these and other aspects of the urban environment. The public space activism that has emerged in Toronto and Vancouver in the last few years is founded on this integrationist approach, taking public space as an overarching, comprehensive, and multilayered concept – a holistic thread that links many types of physical and conceptual spaces. Projects themselves may be more specific in scope (as with the TPSC's postering campaign or the VPSN's recent Ideas competition for a new public square) but they are always nested inside the larger framework of public space and always communicated in this fashion.

Public space activists in the Toronto Public Space Committee and Vancouver Public Space Network have taken the opportunity to forge a variety of collaborative networks, and drawing on these linkages has become a way to advance a common discussion and mobilize previously fragmented groups/initiatives into a more unified response. The result has been a sophisticated, dynamic set of linkages among artists, academics, cyclists, civil libertarians, economists, armchair urbanists, and citizens of all stripes and affiliations who place emphasis on the livability of the urban environment and the role that the public realm plays in fostering this.

In this way, "public space" has become the leading article in a new, more inclusive, more integrated phrase of civic advocacy. This process of "scaling up" has been part and parcel of a reconceptualization of public space such that (1) individual projects related to "a" public space are seen as part of a larger whole; (2) a public space "whole" is, by virtue of these connections and linkages, greater than the sum of its parts. By extension, this approach leads to the forging of further ties, and the recognition that (3) the health and well-being of "a" given public space (a park or plaza, etc.) is intrinsically linked to the overall livability of the city. Conversely, a threat to public space in one area (a trend toward privatization, a state of disrepair, etc.) is reflective of a threat to the city's public realm as a whole.

Notes

1 I am indebted to Dave Meslin of the Toronto Public Space Committee, as well as Dale Duncan and Matt Blackett of *Spacing Magazine* for their insights on the growth of public space activism in Toronto.
2 Note, for example, p. iii: "Public space, in the sense of a widely shared public core, plays a central role in the limited urban discourse about social inclusion. Such public spaces are settings that bring people with differing backgrounds together for civic celebrations or to act as the symbolic centre of a city."
3 The article is entitled 'Plan to Leave Cars on Public Space Opposed' and is found on the front page of the October 17, 1914, edition of the *Christian Science Monitor*. To date it is the oldest example of the use of the term that I have discovered in news media.
4 See for example Davidoff (2003); Friedmann (1987).
5 In truth, it is impossible to say exactly how far back citizen-led involvement in matters of local urban planning, architecture, and city building goes. For one, the boundaries of what constitutes "citizen-led" or "involvement" are not as clear as one might think. On a second note, many of the individual and collective voices that have directly or indirectly lent their voices to the shaping of cities on this continent and elsewhere have simply disappeared into the mists of time.
6 The present-day, holistic public space activism of the Toronto Public Space Committee (TPSC) and Vancouver Public Space Network (VPSN) owes much to the preceding work of a diverse array of theorists, writers, artists, citizens' committees, grassroots organizations, and radicals. Of these, some of the most immediate organizational threads come from the work of issue-oriented groups that were active from the late 1960s onward. Here, notable examples include the various anti-freeway groups that were active in a number of cities (including Toronto and Vancouver); the Billboard Liberation Front (founded in the US in 1977 and a precursor to the emergence of "culture jamming" in the late 1980s); Reclaim the Streets (which emerged in the UK in 1991 and spread to other cities around the world); the decentralized cycling collective Critical Mass (which began in San Francisco in 1992); and the Surveillance Camera Players (who use street theatre to highlight the troubling proliferation of public and private CCTV, started in New York in 1996). Issue-specific urban activism was also infused, particularly in the late 1990s and early 2000s, with the work of anti-globalization/global justice organizations that provoked discussions around the interrelated concepts of public/private and global/local. Finally, public space activism also has a strong planning and design-related component; one that draws on the work of Jane Jacobs and William Whyte as well as organizations such as Project for Public Spaces (started in New York in 1975) and Portland City Repair (founded in the late 1990s). A useful review of the Toronto chapter of Reclaim the Streets – some of

whose members ended up involved with the founding of the Toronto Public Space Committee – can be found in Smith (2004).

7   See *Elliott* v. *Fraba* (1916), in which Judges Meredith, Riddell, and Lasten oversaw the proceedings. The reference in question is as follows: "while the day-light was still sufficient in a public space, where there were persons on foot and persons in carriages, the defendant ran down, with his motor carriage, a young woman, who was standing by the side of a driving-track on grounds used for public purposes."

8   The same holds true even when planning literature is factored in. In fact, a search of the Library of Congress and several university databases suggests that the first time "public space" worked its way into the title of a book was as recently as 1973, with the publication of Lyn Lofland's *A World of Strangers: Order and Action in Urban Public Space.* And thereafter it appears only intermittently throughout the 1970s, with growing frequency in the 1980s before going large in the 1990s and 2000s.

9   In the case of the VPSN, it also helped that a number of the VPSN members were well acquainted with the work of the TPSC. This enabled the latter to act as a precedent.

10 This phrase is used regularly in presentations and workshops given by the VPSN and also reflects the essence of the TPSC philosophy as articulated by Meslin, Duncan, and others – and in particular in conversations I had with these two during the fall of 2007.

Bibliography

Brodin, J. (2006) 'The Structure of Public Space', paper presented at the annual meeting of the Midwest Political Science Association, Palmer House Hilton, Chicago.

Christian Science Monitor. (1914) 'Plan to Leave Cars on Public Space Opposed', 17 October, p. 1.

Davidoff, P. (2003) 'Advocacy and Pluralism in Planning', in Campbell, S. and Fainstein, S. (eds.) *Readings in Planning Theory*, Cambridge, MA: Blackwell Publishers.

Dines, N. and Cattell, V. with Gesler, W. and Curtis, S. (2006) *Public Spaces, Social Relations and Well-being in East London*, London: Joseph Rowntree Foundation.

Eberle, M. and Serge, L. (2007) *Social Inclusion and Urban Form: An Exploratory Research Study*, Ottawa: Canadian Mortgage and Housing Corporation.

Elliott v. *Fraba*. (1916) *Ontario Supreme Court – Appellate Division, Second Divisional Court*. 13 March 1916.

Friedman, J. (1987) *Planning in the Public Domain: From Knowledge to Action*, Princeton, NJ: Princeton University Press.

Goheen, P. G. (2000) 'The Struggle for Urban Public Space: Disposing of the Toronto Waterfront in the Nineteenth Century', in Murphy, A. B. and Johnson, D. L. (eds.) with the assistance of Viola Haarmann, *Cultural Encounters with the Environment: Enduring and Evolving Geographic Themes*, Lanham, MD: Rowman & Littlefield.

Habermas, J. (1962/1989) *The Structural Transformation of the Public Sphere: An Inquiry into a Category of Bourgeois Society*, Cambridge, MA: MIT Press.

Kingwell, M. (2008) 'The Prison of "Public Space" ', *Literary Review of Canada*, 16 (3): 18–21. Online. Available HTTP: http://reviewcanada.ca/essays/2008/04/01/the-prison-of-public-space/ (accessed 31 May 2009).

Klein, N. (2000) *No Logo: Taking Aim at the Brand Bullies*, Toronto: Knopf.

Lofland, L. (1973) *A World of Strangers: Order and Action in Urban Public Space*, New York: Basic Books.

Low, S., Taplin, D., and Scheld, S. (2005) *Rethinking Urban Parks: Public Space & Cultural Diversity*, Austin: University of Texas Press.

Rahe, P. A. (2008) *Against Throne and Altar: Machiavelli and Political Theory under the English Republic*, Cambridge, UK: Cambridge University Press.

Smith, C. (2004) ' "Whose Streets?" Notes on Urban Social Movements, and the Politicization of Urban (Public?) Space', *The Canadian Association of Culture Studies Second Annual Conference CULTUREPOLES: City Spaces, Urban Politics & Metropolitan Theory: Proceedings of the Second Annual Canadian Association of Cultural Studies Conference*, February 2004. Online. Available HTTP: http://www.culturalstudies.ca/proceedings04/pdfs/smith.pdf (accessed 14 April 2009).

Social Centre Stories. (2008) 'Squats and Spaces Solidarity Day: The Globe as a Temporary Autonomous Zone'. Online. Available HTTP: http://socialcentrestories.wordpress.com/2008/04/29/squats-and-spaces-solidarity-day-the-globe-as-a-temporary-autonomous-zone/ (accessed 29 April 2008).

CHAPTER 20

Urban agriculture in the making of insurgent spaces in Los Angeles and Seattle

Teresa M. Mares and Devon G. Peña

In this chapter, we consider two case studies of urban farms in the United States: the South Central Farm in Los Angeles, California, and Marra Farm in Seattle, Washington. These two spaces and the local and global politics and processes in which they are embedded reveal a great deal about current food systems and struggles for justice. Here we devote attention to the conscious strategies that immigrant and diasporic communities utilize to make place in these contested urban sites; we do this in order to argue for analytical practices grounded in subaltern experiences that focus on *how space is continuously reinvented as place* over time through the formation of place-based resistance and project identities (see Castells 1997, Peña 2003). This allows us to consider how public spaces are infused with memory and how identities are anchored in conscious strategies for "dwelling" in and reinhabiting transformational spaces.

The work of Henri Lefebvre (1974/1991), and especially his theory of *espace veçu* or lived space, provides a set of useful concepts for a political ecological understanding of urban space for food cultivation.[1] Over the course of a given city's history, the organization of urban spatial forms continuously shifts in rhythm with the cycles of social conflict and social movements experienced by shifting communities in everyday life. The political economy of the city is not just an invention of top-down neo-liberal governmentality and its managerial spatial imperatives. The struggles toward alternative use of space through place-making practices that promote self-reliance, community, and autonomy constitute spatial practices that are both counter-hegemonic and revealing of unplanned-for outcomes and uses.

As an urban land use activity, agriculture often presents itself as oddly out of place, despite the long history of urban cultivation in municipalities across the world. To many, it seems wholly incompatible with the management of space under the rule of the commodity form in the global city with its astronomical "ground rents" and inflationary real estate markets. Because of this, the full value of urban land for cultivation is often misunderstood or underestimated in relation to its value for development; a miscalculation that has repeatedly spelled disaster for the tenure of urban farms and gardens.

Nevertheless, urban gardens often embody a pattern of resistant uses and the recodification of space wherein local neighborhoods and communities assert control of places for communal uses that lie outside the purview or control of the market. Both Marra Farm and the South Central Farm reveal the promising connections between urban agriculture and struggles for food sovereignty,[2] a concept that combines the rich notion of community food security with the idea that food sources should be consistent with cultural identities and involve community networks that promote self-reliance and mutual aid. Although there are very real differences between these two sites, they are illustrative of the possibilities of urban agriculture for subaltern and marginalized communities who seek to create both a sense of place and transformative food systems.

A commonly told history of urban agriculture in the United States

Mainstream histories of urban agriculture in the United States trace the practice of growing food in cities back to the end of the nineteenth century. Historians, including Sam Warner (1987), note that urban agriculture was pursued both to feed and to control the poor in American cities in the midst of international crises, economic depression, and US military engagement. Not unlike the community gardens of today, these wartime gardens were located on vacant lots of urban land where the security of tenure was dependent upon the financial interests of the owner and value of the land for development. Known as war gardens, liberty gardens, victory gardens, and relief gardens, these urban spaces of food production were intimately tied to larger processes of human migration, militarization, and economic transformation.

US involvement in World Wars I and II brought a greater need for domestic food production and a more explicit connection between urban agriculture, American patriotism, and the obligations of US citizenship. Urban dwellers who were "formerly thought of as poor people in want of food and instruction . . . became full-fledged patriotic citizens" as they contributed to the war efforts as producers of food for civilians to consume (Warner 1987: 17). The National War Garden Commission worked at the national level to promote patriotism through urban agriculture and, following the end of World War I, war gardens were triumphantly renamed victory gardens, a new incarnation of urban agriculture that continued through World War II. At one point in 1944, "victory gardens produced 44 percent of the fresh vegetables eaten in the United States" (Hynes 1996: xii).

It is often noted that, following World War II, urban gardens declined in both number and political significance. Although the reasons behind this are varied, some scholars link this to a greater scale and degree of the centralization of food production and distribution (Saldivar-Tanaka and Krasny 2004). However, we challenge this interpretation as shallow because it overlooks an alternative subaltern history of "home kitchen gardens" among working-class and immigrant families. This is a tradition with roots in the rural origin communities that are the sending areas of immigrant and diaspora peoples today. The Mesoamerican ancestral civilizations – Maya, Toltec, Mexica (Aztec) – all shared a concern for maximizing the availability of public spaces for horticulture and agriculture in urban environments. This preference for shared food-producing open spaces in the urban contexts thus has deep roots in the ethnic cultural heritage of Mexican-origin and other Latin American peoples. This is especially the case among indigenous diaspora peoples.

Historians trace the next major wave of urban agriculture to the late 1960s and early 1970s. Rather than being prompted by food shortages due to national crises, this wave was motivated by the grassroots emergence of the civil rights movement, the environmental movement, and reactions to increasing urban decline (see Saldivar-Tanaka and Krasny 2004, Schmelzkopf 1995, Warner 1987). With these new motivations came a new politics and culture within urban agriculture, linked more explicitly to demands for justice and struggles against social, economic, and racial marginalization and injustice. This new generation of urban gardeners sought to create insurgent public spaces, often in direct opposition to local and regional governmental interests. It is within this new set of politics and culture that we locate South Central Farm and Marra Farm.

South Central Farmers Feeding Families: Los Angeles, California

South Central Farmers Feeding Families (SCF) is a grassroots organization in Los Angeles, California, that exemplifies a new multiethnic and transnational Latina/o ecological rationality. The farmers created this collective organization in September 2003 in response to a threat of eviction intertwined with city land-use politics and development interests and an elite-dominated regional food bank. In a collective fashion, the farmers democratically managed a landscape filled with native row crops, fruit-bearing trees and vines, and medicinal herbs, creating a vibrant space filled with social life and buzzing with an ethic of conviviality. In June 2006, after an intense and global campaign to save the farm in the face of encroaching development (Figures 20.1 and 20.2), bulldozers moved in and destroyed this urban oasis. The farmers have recovered from this tragic outcome by acquiring eighty acres and irrigation rights in Button Willow, California, where they are now producing even more produce for their "Food for the Hood" project.

Figure 20.1 Rufina Juarez, a South Central Farmer, at Immigrant Rights March, May 1, 2006. Photograph by Devon G. Peña.

Figure 20.2 "No
Human Being is Illegal."
South Central Farmers
at Immigrant Rights
March, May 1, 2006.
Photograph by Devon
G. Peña.

Organizations such as SCF have been and continue to be pivotal sources of resistance to the enclosure of community spaces and they are now redefining the nature of community-supported agriculture (they prefer the term "community-based agriculture"). The South Central Farm was established in 1992 and demolished after a three-year campaign by the farmers and a global coalition to prevent eviction and enclosure by a private developer. At fourteen acres, ten of them intensively cultivated, it was one of the largest urban farms in a core inner city in the US. The farm site is located in an area of South Central LA zoned for industrial and residential uses; however, the site itself is today surrounded by warehouses and wrecking yards. One of the nation's principal railroad lines, this one linking the Port of Los Angeles to regional freight transit hubs, and a six-lane arterial viaduct frame the site on either side (west and east). Comprising 360 families, SCF included US-born Chicana/os and people from indigenous diaspora communities originating in Mexico and Central America. For thirteen years, the farmers – including families of Mixtec, Nahua, Tojolobal, Triqui, Tzeltal, Seri, Yaqui, and Zapotec descent – relied on a rare piece of urban space to grow food while becoming self-reliant and building a sense of community. While creating a veritable Mesoamerican agroecological landscape in the inner city, they collectively developed a system for local food sovereignty that fostered a strong sense of place and community mobilization.

Los Angeles is a dynamic city where the ancient heirloom seeds of landrace *maíz*, *calabacita*, and *frijol* have found their way up north with their cultivators from Oaxaca or Chiapas. These seeds trace back 5,000 years to the heart of Mesoamerica and have come to meet the hot pavement of the straitjacketed networks of freeways and arterials of the US, growing and thriving in vibrant inner-city cultural landscapes. At South Central, family plots are perhaps best understood as attempts by diasporic people to replicate the *huerto familiar* or hometown kitchen gardens in Mexico, Central America, Puerto Rico, Cuba, or the Dominican Republic. A quick comparison of the classic Maya kitchen garden and the typical modern family plot at South Central reveals that Mexican gardeners were still growing the familiar sacred trinity of maize (*Zea mayz* L.), beans (*Phaseolus vulgaris* L.), and squash (*Cucurbita pepo* L.). They also were growing avocado (*Persea americana*), banana (*Musa sapientum* L.), and the traditional aromatic and medicinal herbs that are mainstays of the classic Mexican *hortaliza* or herb patch. In many cases, farmers reported that the plants they have used for generations in Mexico are now grown only in urban farms and kitchen gardens in the US. Indeed, many indigenous diaspora families that were involved at South Central are no longer farming in Mexico. The heirloom landrace cultigens are therefore being preserved only because the diaspora is seed-saving, planting, and cultivating in the US.

The struggle of the South Central Farmers was an important example of an emerging, grassroots restoration ecology that produced formidable resistance to neo-liberal enclosure and privatization of urban common spaces. As such it represents an important turning point in the history, organizational forms, and terrains of struggle of the US environmental justice movement. The SCF represents

Figure 20.3 *Ofrendas,* "offerings," beneath the maple tree that served as the sit-in site at South Central Farm. Photograph by Devon G. Peña.

an example of a grassroots ecological democracy based on the integration and use of both material practices and biotic baggage from point-of-origin communities and the reproduction of village-based forms of community self-organization. It represents a transnational diaspora people who were not only reshaping urban landscapes but also challenging the politics of urban planning and policy (Figure 20.3).

In the Latina/o urban core, vernacular foodscapes such as those created at South Central are expressions of "thirdspace" dynamics – they are results of communities appropriating spaces to support urban agriculture, a pattern that is particularly important for low-income immigrant communities (see Pinderhughes 2003; Peña 2002; Soja 1996). Urban kitchen gardens, as well as more collectively organized community gardens, are impressive for their scope, vigor, cultural significance, and role in struggles for more "sustainably just" cities. *El jardín* (garden) is a space for the charting of individual "autotopographies" – self-telling through place-shaping. This is certainly true of the classic home-based kitchen gardens that were grown at South Central Farm, and those that continue to spread across the urban US. These *jardincitos* are spiritual and political symbols of a process involving nothing less than the *re*-territorialization of place as a home by transnational communities.

In interviews with gardeners at South Central about why they garden, many replied with the same set of reasons: to supplement the family food budget; to grow ingredients for traditional recipes; grow organic (meaning to grow one's own food in order to know where it comes from and that it is fresh); to visit with friends and family members and learn about traditional foods from elders; to feel more at home; and to grow herbs and vegetables to supply family businesses. These kinds of gardens that are appearing across the west coast are the seeds of resistance in spatial politics: These struggles emerge through the process of autotopography and unfold in these newly forming communal spaces that nurture conviviality. One gardener at South Central, a thirty-year-old Zapotec woman, described her involvement in this way: "I planted this garden because it is a little space like home. I grow the same plants that I had back in my garden in Oaxaca. We can eat like we ate at home and this makes us feel like ourselves. It allows us to keep a part of who we are after coming to the United States."

Local autotopographical spaces such as the *huertos familiares* at South Central are constructed in conscious opposition to the global commodity chains that constitute the dominant food system. But this process is both internally heterogeneous and highly contested. In the case of South Central, which until its destruction was still officially administered by the regional food bank, one example of the contested nature of a communal space was seen in the challenges of managing a few acres of urban land to support the food production activities of some 360 families. The result at South Central was the division of the limited acreage by family plots of fairly uniform size (each approximately 200–260 square meters). These were divided from each other by a maze of lower-grade chain-link fencing that has been improvised over time.

A particularly remarkable feature of the South Central Farm was the profusion of cactus corridors or cacti fencing emerging and growing alongside the chain-link fencing, perhaps presaging a transition to a more culturally appropriate division of the space through a permaculture feature similar to the *nopal* (cactus) fences that are more common traditional fixtures of the vernacular landscape across rural areas of northern Mexico and especially Chihuahua, Sonora, Coahuila, and Tamaulipas. One gardener reported that many people wanted to bring down the chain-link fences altogether and were beginning to replace them not just with cactus but with sugarcane, banana, avocado, and other fruit-bearing trees and shrubs. Others were using vines to cover the fencing. In all these cases, the effort was to create a more natural set of boundaries that were both enjoyable and useful to the gardeners. Their approach was to make the "fence" part of an edible landscape.

The issue of management was not really about making a choice between *nopales* and chain-link fencing – the answer is obvious. There was, instead, a deeper conflict. How the South Central gardeners managed their space was by necessity a collective and adaptive process that sought to respond to the needs of a diverse community. However, the regional food bank organization and the City of Los Angeles seemed not to respect this process of autonomy in the management of a significant, and rather rare, urban cultural landscape. The South Central Farmers were at the center of a widening conflict over an urban commons that arose from the political economic context of contested urban land use politics. The overvaluation of urban spaces for commercial/industrial uses is the deeper cause of this conflict. The community garden workers faced a crisis embedded in the contested legal status of the land as property, which defined it as a space that should be developed for commercial and industrial uses, but which erroneously discounted the economic, ecological, and cultural value of this place to the community.

Marra Farm: Seattle, Washington

In Seattle, Washington, the provisioning of gardening space, expertise, and other needed resources to underserved communities and families comes together at a four-acre site, Marra Farm. This organic farm houses four community gardens coordinated by non-profit and governmental organizations and serves as an urban commons where people from diverse backgrounds grow food both for personal consumption and for redistribution through food banks and informal exchange. Unlike in South Central, the four acres into which Marra Farm now extends its roots have been cultivated since the city was settled. This land was first planted by the Marra family, Italian immigrant truck farmers who were one of the first family farmers to supply the Pike Place Market with local produce. The land remained in the Marra family from 1908 until it was sold to King County in 1970. In the 1990s, the land was purchased with funds from the Open Space Bond with the intent that the site would remain in agricultural production. Currently, the relationship between the farm and the city of Seattle is in a period of significant transition as the farm is transformed into a city park.

Upon first sight, Marra Farm stands out as a green parcel of intensive cultivation against the industrial backdrop of South Seattle. It is a collective space divided into smaller plots and managed by non-profit groups and individual farmers – a group as culturally and ethnically diverse as the fruits and vegetables they grow (Figure 20.4). Each summer, towering stalks of corn pierce the air in sporadic rows, dwarfing the

people who have come to tend and harvest them, as enormous squash rest on the ground in bright hues of yellow, orange, and green. Rows of apple trees line the northern farm boundary, and a creek where salmon habitat restoration efforts are under way also flows nearby. While walking through Marra Farm, one might almost forget that one is in one of the most contaminated areas of Seattle. The South Park neighborhood where the farm is located has long been plagued by environmental hazards and pollutants from nearby industrial production and shipping. In 2001, the Environmental Protection Agency placed the section of the Duwamish River that flows along the eastern border of the neighborhood on the federal Superfund Cleanup list because it contained an excessive level of polychlorinated biphenyls (PCBs), heavy metals, oil, mercury, arsenic, and raw sewage. Located fewer than five miles from Boeing field, the solitude and peace of the farm is periodically interrupted by the roar of planes and by the sounds of breaking glass at the recycling plant on the other side of the hill.

Spatially contextualized by this pollution of air, water, and land, the farm is a vital green space in one of the more economically disadvantaged, yet culturally diverse, neighborhoods in Seattle. The demographic differences between the residents of South Park and those living in the other sections of the city are stark. With a population of just over 3,700, 37 percent of South Park residents are Latina/o, compared with 5.6 percent in the Seattle Urban Area.[3] Roughly one third of South Park residents are foreign born, of whom 64 percent have entered the United States since 1990. This compares with 13.6 percent of Seattle's residents being foreign born, with 47 percent of the foreign born entering since 1990. Considering the median household income of $30,917, South Park residents earn far less than the rest of the city as a whole, where the median household income is almost $51,000. The effects of these neighborhood economic conditions can be seen in the condition of the housing, and the limited availability of food and other services. Unlike most other neighborhoods in Seattle, one would be hard pressed to find a cup of coffee from Starbucks anywhere within a few miles of the farm.

The Starbucks absence is ironic given that the burlap sacks laid down as pathways through the raised beds have been donated by the corporate behemoth that makes its home in Seattle. Because of this, there are always a few spare coffee beans that were grown by farmers in Costa Rica or Columbia scattered among the local varieties of tomatoes and chard. This seminal commingling is richly symbolic of the dynamic interplay between the local and the global that manifests itself in the farm in culturally fascinating ways. As in South Central, transnational and diasporic flows of people and cultures are materially present in the blue and red corn varieties grown by families from Mexico and South America, and the gigantic cucumbers and squash grown by members of the Mien community. This space allows people from opposite ends of the earth to maintain and negotiate a sense of place and identity in a city very far from home.

Throughout the year, Marra Farm is a hub of social and cultural activities. In the northwest corner, the Lettuce Link Program grows fresh produce to donate to the neighborhood food bank. The Lettuce Link children's garden also provides an area where children from the neighborhood schools and community centers learn how to grow their own produce and take part in on-site cooking demonstrations and nutrition classes (Figure 20.5). To the south of the Lettuce Link garden is the Seattle Youth Garden Works garden, where from early spring to late fall it is common to see a group of adolescents tending beds, weeding, and preparing produce to sell at a local farmers' market. The youth crew is usually accompanied by one or two mentors, energetic and supportive adults guiding the youth in horticulture and entrepreneurial development. Also present is the Mien community garden, which is rich in ethnobotanical diversity and produces an abundance of food. The gardeners here work the land for their own consumption, and multilingual signs surrounding the garden encourage people to not steal or vandalize the plants. The Mien people who cultivate this section of the farm possess horticultural skills and knowledge that deeply impresses the other growers in the farm, perfectly summarized by a lifelong farmer from South America: "*Sí, ellos saben cultivar*" ("Yes, they know how to grow").

This South American farmer grows his own plot in the P-Patch garden located on the opposite end from Lettuce Link.[4] The Marra P-Patch houses twenty-eight garden plots that measure approximately nineteen square meters each, and is almost a second home to many Latina/o families who have recently moved into the area. Corn is more abundant and varied in the P-Patch garden than in other sections of the farm, and, reminiscent of the routes that led to South Central, is often the result of transnational seed exchanges crossing national borders. These exchanges grow into the blue, red, and multicolored cobs that reveal a deep cultural significance for the Latina/o growers who cultivate them. In the corner of the P-Patch, one variety of corn stands nearly fifteen feet high, but doesn't have ample time to produce cobs as it does in its native climate. Despite this, the very fact that it continues to be planted is revealing of the efforts to recreate a sense of place in a new environment and the importance of connections between people and plants.

Figure 20.5 Children's
garden at Marra Farm.
Photograph by Teresa M.
Mares.

Figure 20.5 Children's garden at Marra Farm. Photograph by Teresa M. Mares.

The control over and uses of the farm's resources present an opportunity to make observations about both local and global processes and politics. As a self-proclaimed "Green City," Seattle clearly has a vested interest in the environmentally sustainable practices occurring at the farm. It is foreseeable that the city will continue to draw upon the environmental stewardship that occurs at the farm as examples of "green" efforts, raising important questions about how, and to what ends, the city is taming, harnessing, and harvesting both the labor and the identities of those working at Marra Farm.

The transition of the farm into a city park also raises questions about decision-making practices and the ownership and management of the land. The issue of ownership is complex and indicates the farm's nature as a contested space as

Figure 20.6 Shed and community mural at Marra Farm. Photograph by Teresa M. Mares.

competing interests have divergent views about the future of the farm. The farm is currently managed by the four organizations that make up the Marra Farm Coalition (MFC). Although the Coalition is negotiating with the Parks Department to clarify the roles and responsibilities of all parties involved, it is clear that the city government now has a greater say in the decisions that are made. Within the four acres, gardeners are growing produce for profit, for donation, and for personal consumption, though all of this takes place on land that the growers do not technically own. This is a problem given that many of the growers depend upon the produce from the farm for their livelihood and that of their families. The individuals and families at the farm who are involved are also providing a public benefit as they actively maintain one of the two substantial agricultural spaces that remain in the city. There is no doubt that much work is needed to ensure that the farm is a resource available to and representative of the local community (Figure 20.6).

Urban agriculture and insurgent space

The struggle for urban agriculture among diasporic groups and communities of color epitomizes an element of the environmental justice movement that seeks to link demands for open space, ecological protection, and food sovereignty with demands for fair and adequate housing, meaningful jobs with living wages, and the protection of the essential common spaces that neighborhoods and families require to sustain a sense of place and community. In this movement, there are exciting developments in sustainable food practices as urban growers become a progressive force for social justice, environmental self-determination, and food sovereignty. The emergence of these movements is a continuation of decades-long struggles by communities to control their own ecological and economic futures by creating sustainable and just neighborhoods. Against the surveillance grids, jacked-up ecological footprints, and fragmented echoes of failed suburbia that define the post-Fordist cities of neo-liberal dreams, inner-city urban forms are being reinvented and reshaped from the bottom up through the spreading multitude of heterotopias, the diverse shifting mosaic of cultural forms that everywhere transform space into place.

Community gardens around the world provide significant ecological, social, and economic benefits, which are consistently underestimated in the face of urban development.[5] As argued here, through the farming activities of indigenous migrants, urban community gardens can promote the *in situ* conservation of the genetic diversity of heirloom varieties and landraces and the environmental knowledge that is intertwined with this conservation. As genetically modified seeds continue to contaminate Mexican landraces in the wake of NAFTA and the continued domination of agro-corporations such as Monsanto, these conservation efforts and sets of knowledge demand our attention. Through our work at Marra Farm and South Central Farm, we hope to shed some light on the agroecological practices and underlying motives of the people farming and waging struggle at these important insurgent urban spaces. At stake in the struggle at South Central were the relationships between the farmers and the plants they cultivate, and their efforts to retain cultural identity and create community in a space that was not recognized for its true use value. What are currently at stake at Marra Farm are the issues of land ownership and stewardship in a site that, for some community members, has recently become overtaken by government bureaucracy. With this bureaucracy, however, comes a good chance of continued agricultural use, a chance that, despite their best efforts, was taken away from the South Central Farmers.

Most often, community gardens are located in contested space, involving the counter-claims of developers, speculators, planners, and even philanthropists. In this sense, urban gardens and farms are often a communal expression of a community's political power as asserted through the demand for space to support local families by encouraging conviviality, the intermingling of mixed generations and ethnicities, and the reproduction of original as well as hybrid identity formations and cultural practices through conscious placemaking. Urban farms such as South Central and Marra Farm are sources of plants for medicine and traditional recipes and are diverse agroecological spaces that biophysically and symbolically connect migrants to their origin community. These spaces have allowed for a *transnationalization of a sense of place*. They are the canvases for the telling of personal stories as well as a strategy to maintain cultural identity through the preservation of cultivars that resonate with one's foodways and knowledge systems. These communities constitute the multinational/multiethnic sources of a socio-cultural mosaic and are important forces redefining the basis of a sustainable urban ecology. Without essentializing their identities, we must acknowledge the wisdom of these growers' autotopographical interventions and adaptations to a new place.

"The garden is the smallest parcel of the world and then it is the totality of the world," wrote Michel Foucault (1986: 26). Both South Central and Marra Farm are small parcels of agricultural land in the urban landscapes that punctuate the topography of American cities. Each *huerto familiar* at South Central and each

P-Patch plot at Marra Farm is a site for the reconstruction of the gardeners' sense of place. This involves acts of autotopography in which urban farmers etch a story with elements drawn from the home world, the very plants and landscaping practices that allow them to produce a familiarized space. The survival of these heterotopias must confront the totality posed by their opposite – the capitalist market ever yearning to usurp and fetishize space as a merchantable good destined for consumption as fodder for the expansion of the neo-liberal grid city.

The United States needs hundreds more urban farms like South Central and Marra Farm. It does not need to destroy any more cultural treasures and replace them with more of the same: an impoverished, homogeneous landscape, a result of enclosure by privatization. The thirdspace human and natural capital created at South Central since 1994 must be valued as a model of grassroots urbanism. It is our hope that Marra Farm never faces the same threats that eventually destroyed the South Central Farm.

Inner cities across North America are being reinvented from the grassroots up in creative and hopeful ways. There is a sustainable urban ecology at work within the margins, and the farmers with whom we work embody this heritage of environmental self-governance. The process of revisioning a sustainable and just city must not be diminished by the encroachment of the heartless soul that is the post-industrial urban landscape of neo-liberalism.

Notes

1 Also see Soja (1996) who uses the term "thirdspace" in reference to this concept first proposed by Lefebvre.
2 See Dodson (2005) for an excellent annotated bibliography on food sovereignty.
3 These figures come from the 2000 US Census and we use the term Seattle Urban Area to reflect census categories. The South Park neighborhood is enclosed within census tract 112.
4 The P-Patch program is a community gardening program run by Seattle Department of Neighborhoods. This program coordinates over seventy gardens across the city.
5 The following sources offer helpful analyses of the benefits of community gardens: Armstrong (2000), Blair et al. (1991), Brown and Jameton (2000), Glover (2003, 2004), Hynes (1996), Landman (1993), Lawson (2005), Nemore (1998), Pinderhughes (2003), Saldivar-Tanaka and Krasny (2004), Schmelzkopf (1995).

Bibliography

Armstrong, D. (2000) 'A Survey of Community Gardens in Upstate New York: Implications for Health Promotion and Community Development', Health and Place, 6: 319–327.

Blair, D., Giesecke, C., and Sherman, S. (1991) 'A Dietary, Social, and Economic Evaluation of the Philadelphia Urban Gardening Project', Journal of Nutrition Education, 23: 161–167.

Brown, K. and Jameton, A. (2000) 'Public Health Implications of Urban Agriculture', Journal of Public Health Policy, 21: 20–39.

Castells, M. (1997) The Information Age: Economy, Society and Culture, Vol. 2: The Power of Identity, Oxford: Blackwell Publishing.

Dodson, S. (2005) 'Food Sovereignty: Annotated Bibliography', prepared for Professor Devon G. Peña in partial fulfillment of the requirements for the graduate seminar, ANTH 488 – Agroecology, Department of Anthropology, University of Washington.

Foucault, M. (1986) 'Of Other Spaces', *Diacritics*, 16 (1): 22–27.

Glover, T. (2003) 'The Story of the Queen Anne Memorial Garden: Resisting a Dominant Cultural Narrative', *Journal of Leisure Research*, 35: 190–212.

—— (2004) 'Social Capital in the Lived Experiences of Community Gardeners', *Leisure Sciences*, 26: 143–162.

Hynes, P. (1996) *A Patch of Eden: America's Inner-City Gardeners*, White River Junction, VT: Chelsea Green.

Landman, R. H. (1993) *Creating Community in the City: Cooperatives and Community Gardens in Washington DC*, Westport, CT: Bergin & Garvey.

Lawson, L. J. (2005) *City Bountiful: A Century of Community Gardening*, Berkeley: University of California Press.

Lefebvre, H. (1974/1991) *The Production of Space*, Oxford: Basil Blackwell.

Nemore, C. (1998) 'Rooted in Community: Community Gardens in New York City', *Urban Agriculture Notes*. Online. Available HTTP: http://cityfarmer.org/NYcomgardens.html (accessed 26 January 2005).

Peña, D. G. (2002) 'Environmental Justice and Sustainable Agriculture: Linking Social and Ecological Sides of Sustainability', policy brief prepared for the Second National People of Color Environmental Leadership Summit, Washington, DC, October.

—— (2003) 'Identity, Place, and Communities of Resistance', in Agyeman, J. Bullard, R., and Evans, B. (eds.) *Just Sustainabilities: Development in an Unequal World*, London: Earthscan.

Pinderhughes, R. (2003) 'Poverty and the Environment: The Urban Agriculture Connection', in Boyce, J. K. and Shelley, B. G. (eds.) *Natural Assets: Democratizing Environmental Ownership*, Washington, DC: Island Press.

Saldivar-Tanaka, L. and Krasny, M. E. (2004) 'Culturing Community Development, Neighborhood Open Space, and Civic Agriculture: The Case of Latino Community Gardens in New York City', *Agriculture and Human Values*, 21: 399–412.

Schmelzkopf, K. (1995) 'Urban Community Gardens as Contested Space', *Geographical Review*, 85: 364–381.

Soja, E. W. (1996) *Thirdspace: Journeys to Los Angeles and Other Real-and-Imagined Places*, Cambridge, MA: Blackwell.

Warner, S. B. (1987) *To Dwell is to Garden*, Boston: Northeastern University Press.

CHAPTER 21

When overwhelming needs meet underwhelming prospects

Sustaining community open space activism in East St. Louis

Laura Lawson and Janni Sorensen

Watching from her house a block down the road, Mrs. Drake saw the university van arrive at the Illinois Avenue Playground and immediately came out to talk. At eighty-seven years old, she could not walk quickly but her determined progress and hand gestures for us to wait let us know that she had a purpose in mind. Almost immediately upon coming into the park, she started to tell us what she wanted done: she wanted the sign repainted (Figure 21.1). Shifting our attention from the playground itself – the remains of play equipment, a few trash cans, and not much else – to the hand-painted sign on a piece of plywood, we could see the paint chipping away, making it hard to read the list of participants who helped make this park fifteen years ago. Mrs. Drake explained that all the other neighbors who had worked to create the playground had died or moved away and she needed help. Since we represent the University of Illinois East St. Louis Action Research

Figure 21.1 Mrs. Drake at the Illinois Avenue Playground sign. Photograph by Laura Lawson.

Project (ESLARP), which had assisted in its initial development, she was holding us responsible for its upkeep.[1] As we discussed not only how to fix the sign but also how to re-engage residents in the playground's care, she was clearly skeptical yet her pride in the creation of the playground and her desire to slow its decay provided a starting point for a renewed effort to reinvent the site.

About a mile away, Willie Beard could only meet with us briefly before heading off to her second job as a school bus driver. Her enthusiasm, however, did not subside as she met us at her door with exuberant hugs and greetings for everyone. For several years we have been working together to develop Pullman Porter Park on the 3.5-acre site that borders her neighborhood. When Willie bought her home on 41st Street thirty years ago, trees arched over the street, which was lined with well-maintained homes. By the mid-1990s, all the trees were gone, the street had reverted to a pot-holed gravel road, and many homes were falling into disrepair or abandoned. A group of residents formed into the 41st Street Neighborhood Action Coalition to conduct clean-ups, deter illegal dumping, and lobby for sidewalks, paving, and lighting. Buoyed by their successes, the group started the daunting project to transform the 3.5-acre privately owned lot into a community-

Figure 21.2 Willie Beard and Gene Spears at Pullman Porter Park, Photograph by Laura Lawson.

run park, which they have named Pullman Porter Park. Five years later, the lot shows encouraging signs of improvement, though far from the final proposed design they once discussed, and the group is regrouping to increase community commitment (Figure 21.2).

Underwhelming pictures of the Illinois Avenue Playground and the Pullman Porter Park belie the overwhelming commitment and action involved in their creation. The pervasiveness of empty houses, vacant lots, and crumbling streets in East St. Louis, Illinois, can sometimes obscure efforts underway by local residents to improve their neighborhoods. Community groups are actively resisting the tell-tale signs of deindustrialization, depopulation, and inadequate public services. These efforts – mowing vacant lots, blocking off sites prone to illegal dumping, neighborhood clean-ups, and creating new semi-public open space – are rightfully praised as self-help and community activism, yet community concerns about safety, education, economic opportunity, and health continue to require much more attention from the community and its supporters. Through two case studies – the Illinois Avenue Playground and Pullman Porter Park – this chapter explores the opportunities and challenges of community open space activism in a low-income community of color in the United States.[2] We focus on how efforts to reclaim vacant land by community groups must be looked at in terms not only of need but also of power. This perspective simultaneously highlights the importance of "grassroots" self-help and the imperative of broader public responsibility.

East St. Louis

East St. Louis illustrates many issues facing communities in America's "rust belt" cities: formerly vibrant industrial cities that are now mired with unemployment, depopulation, poverty, environmental degradation, and overburdened municipal services. Established in the 1790s as a ferry landing for goods and people to cross the Mississippi River, East St. Louis continued to grow as ferries gave way to railroads that then encouraged the development of industries, manufacturing, and warehouses. By 1910 it was the fourth largest city in Illinois and consisted of a diverse population. The city's urban development included neighborhoods of varying status, parks, schools, boulevards, and other civic amenities; however, local government maintained a pro-business focus that limited social reform and led to machine politics, organized crime, and minimal social reform (Edwards and Lawson 2005, Theising 2003).

During the early twentieth century, the city was affected by the rise and fall of industry in response to war and depression, but ultimately the deindustrialization that occurred throughout the eastern and midwest regions of the United States in the 1950s and 1960s put the city in severe financial and social distress. With the loss of businesses and residents, the city's tax base steadily declined, forcing the city to eliminate many services, including not only its planning department but also garbage pick-up from 1987 to 1992. While people with skills and opportunities followed jobs or moved to suburban areas outside the city, those who were financially unable to leave had few employment opportunities and failing social services. It was during the industrial decline that the population shifted from being predominantly white to African American. City population has continued to fall, so that between 1960 and 2000 it had dropped 61 percent. As of 2006, the total population in East St. Louis is approximately 29,500, of whom 98 percent are African American and 35 percent are below the poverty level (United States Department of Census 2009).

The physical city reflects the losses. Parks, boulevards, streets, and railroad corridors show signs of poor maintenance, neglect, and in some cases complete abandonment. Loss of industry not only reduced employment but also left behind contaminated brownfields that discourage any new investment and threaten public health. Throughout the 1960s and 1970s, city administrators applied for and received federal funds for urban renewal and revitalization projects; however, although money was spent on studies and site clearance, few final projects were realized (Judd and Mendelson 1973). Neighborhoods that had once been intact, some even overcrowded, are now pocked with vacant stores, schools, and homes.

With a financially strapped and overburdened municipal government that residents do not trust given a legacy of corruption and ineffectualness, neighborhood organizations have formed to address immediate concerns, such as illegal dumping, localized flooding, abandoned properties, and safety. Whereas the majority of neighborhood organizations are small volunteer-run groups, some have expanded into staffed organizations seeking grants to further economic and community development objectives. In addition, many churches and not-for-profit organizations provide social services and support community revitalization efforts. Residents and organizations also find support through the University of Illinois East St. Louis Action Research Project, which has a twenty-year history of engagement through research, courses, and volunteer service activities. Built on the empowerment planning model, ESLARP works on projects identified by community organizations (Reardon 1999). With staffed offices on campus and in East St. Louis and committed faculty and students from various disciplines, ESLARP is able to stay engaged on projects over multiple semesters and provide an array of technical and research assistance as well as hands-on physical labor. The two projects highlighted in this paper – Illinois Avenue Playground and Pullman Porter Park – are both projects in which community organizations have partnered with ESLARP faculty, staff, and students.

Illinois Avenue Playground

Prior to development of the Illinois Avenue Playground, the vacant lot at the corner of Illinois Avenue and 26th Street had concerned residents because of the loitering and drinking that took place there. Residents envisioned the site as a park to serve younger children who were often chased out of the city's few other parks by older children and young adults. The project was spearheaded by the Winstanley Industrial Park Neighborhood Organization (WIPNO), which had organized in 1992 to encourage neighborhood clean-ups and other revitalization efforts. Starting in 1993, the group began a participatory planning process facilitated by ESLARP students and faculty. The resulting design, which was basic and easily constructed, included a sandbox, a simple climbing structure, seating areas for parents, and some plantings.

Given that the neighborhood had substantial unwanted vacant land, the difficulty experienced in getting permission to use a publicly owned site for a public purpose was perplexing to the community activists. The county had taken ownership of the site on account of unpaid taxes on the property, yet seemed reluctant to grant the land to a community group. According to Ken Reardon, then director of ESLARP, the WIPNO representatives were held to a higher degree of scrutiny than other groups or communities and required to attend multiple council meetings to finally get approval (Reardon 1999). Rather than feeling elated at their final success in acquiring the site, the process left many feeling defeated and frustrated. As one resident leader noted, "it is a shame that we had to participate in nine hearings to secure property no one else wanted, on which less than $500 in taxes were owed, to build a playground for children who have no safe place to play" (Reardon 1995: 5).

On a sunny May weekend, over 100 residents and volunteers developed the majority of the site. Free railroad ties were used to distinguish different spaces, and old concrete pipes and industrial equipment served as play equipment. At the corner, a large sign announced the park and listed the key participants: Winstanley Industrial Park Neighborhood Organization, Concerned Citizens of Precinct 19, and the University of Illinois Departments of Planning, Architecture, and Landscape Architecture. On the back was a long list of contributors, including local nurseries, construction companies, and individuals from the neighborhood and university.

According to Mrs. Drake, the park was used and well maintained for about six years. Neighbors planted flowers under the sign and kept the park safe for children. However, as the key participants in the original organization got older and began to pass away, the park was again taken over by adults who drank and discouraged other users. The benches that once rested under shade trees have disappeared and the recycled railroad ties that were used to delineate various sitting and play spaces have decayed or been burnt to the point of being dangerous. All that remains of the play equipment is one forlorn concrete pipe. As the last of the community leaders who helped build the playground, Mrs. Drake has taken it upon herself to take care of the park by regularly picking up trash and calling ESLARP or the Park District for assistance in site upkeep.

Even as Mrs. Drake watched over the park to the best of her ability, the site was almost lost in 2007 when the county decided to put it up for auction and did not notify the neighbors. Fortunately, a county staff person who mistakenly assumed that the Park District was responsible for the park sent a notice to a recently appointed Park District director who, realizing the importance of the site as open space in this neighborhood, purchased the property. Considering that the Park District has difficulty maintaining its current obligations in some of the city's more established parks, this purchase did not immediately mean dramatic changes to its current condition. However it did increase accountability regarding maintenance, trash pick-up, and policing. It also catalyzed efforts to reinvigorate community involvement. In particular, the Park District began working with neighbors and ESLARP to develop an adopt-a-park program in which local organizations and churches take on core maintenance duties, look for donations for plants and equipment, and sponsor activities in the park.

Illinois Avenue Playground served as the pilot project for this effort, resulting in a local social fraternity adopting the park. A 2008 ESLARP-affiliated course began a participatory process to re-envision the playground's role in the community. Although Mrs. Drake is somewhat pessimistic about her neighborhood coming together to revitalize the playground, her face lights up at the thought of reviving the park with a freshly painted sign, some benches, and a safer play area. As a tell-tale sign of her ongoing sense of ownership for the park, when the Park District crew came to install a new Park District sign, Mrs. Drake would not let them remove the old sign (Figure 21.3).

Pullman Porter Park

In contrast to the situation at the Illinois Avenue Playground, when the 41st Street Neighborhood Coalition approached the railroad company to ask for the 3.5-acre site behind their homes, they were granted the right to use the site as long as it served a community purpose and the group maintained insurance for the site. With permission granted, the group started to develop the site through occasional clean-up events, making sure the site was mowed regularly, and discouraging illegal dumping by installing planters they made out of plastic trash bins at vulnerable entry points to the site. A couple of neighbors who enjoy gardening began to plant some trees and flowers in the area adjacent to their homes (Figure 21.4). Meanwhile, with the help of ESLARP student volunteers, neighborhood residents received flyers announcing the proposed park as well as a questionnaire to gather information about what neighbors wanted to see in the park. The resulting wish list included play equipment, a picnic pavilion, volleyball and basketball courts, paths, a community garden, and a small putting green.

Figure 21.3 Mrs. Drake's sign being repainted during a volunteer clean-up day. Photograph by Janni Sorensen.

With community interest raised, the next step was to develop a site design that would guide development. Working with students engaged in a 2005 ESLARP landscape architecture studio, community members reviewed various options put forward through several reiterations until a final design was developed. However, as the design process continued, debate arose about how developed and public the park should be. Some neighbors felt that a developed park might encourage "riff-raff" and teenagers into the neighborhood, whereas others wanted to redirect youth from delinquency by creating a legitimate recreational resource. Estimates on the cost and concerns about liability also raised skepticism in some participants about the ability of the group to succeed, especially given the pessimistic view that the city would provide little help. Explaining how the neighborhood had to supervise their recent sidewalk and street improvements to make sure debris was not dumped on the future park site or in people's front yards, resident Willie Beard voiced a common attitude when she stated, "You have to watch out. The city will come and run over you . . . or even if it isn't the city but someone else, they think 'they're just black people, they'll take any improvement. Any improvement is better than none.'" Concerns about the extended responsibility, along with some interpersonal conflicts, deflated the effort and led to an extended period of uncertainty.

Meanwhile, several residents have persisted in the effort to improve the site during the hiatus. Willie Beard, current president of the 41st St. Neighborhood Action Group, is adamant to continue the effort. She and her neighbor Gene Spears have continued to improve the site by picking up trash and planting dozens of trees and flowers. Ms. Beard regularly calls the railroad company to mow the site during

Figure 21.4 Pullman Porter Park, as it looked in 2005, showing a few recently planted trees that are intended to deter illegal dumping. Photograph by Laura Lawson.

Figure 21.5 Students and volunteers planting and installing a walking trail at Pullman Porter Park in 2008. Photograph by Laura Lawson.

the spring and summer months. Her dedication is strong and ongoing, even to the point of risking her own safety. One of her most frightening experiences was hearing a woman's screams as she was attacked in a car that had pulled into the park site, and having to argue with the police when she called and they did not seem concerned. She has also received somewhat threatening notes after calling to report excessive garbage around homes or other code infringements. Taking on this responsibility, and as a result realizing potential personal risk, is a burden that one person should not assume alone, and Ms. Beard hopes it will be temporary.

Even though the burden falls on her right now, she knows the importance of community participation, offering the advice, "don't try to do it all yourself." She is hopeful that community interest will rekindle with the success of smaller projects directly linked to residents' needs. For example, given that several of the seniors in the neighborhood like to walk for exercise but must currently drive to a nearby track, Willie Beard has worked with ESLARP to install a walking trail around the site (Figure 21.5). This effort has involved constant solicitation to the Park District, local quarries, and construction companies for donations of gravel, plants, and equipment, Ms. Beard hopes that neighbors will see and appreciate the improvements to the park site, start using the path for exercise and relaxation, and as a result become involved in its ongoing development. She envisions a reinvigorated 41st Street Neighborhood Action Coalition that engages residents and pulls in new partners that have access to labor, materials, and funds to build the park, and through this effort expand the safety and sense of pride in her neighborhood.

Framing the contradiction: open space, civic activism, and the reality of power

Although the futures of both Illinois Avenue Playground and Pullman Porter Park are unclear, the stories of their evolution both reaffirm the benefits associated with community open space activism and raise concern about the vulnerability of such efforts due to limited community resources. In a low-income community facing myriad social and environmental problems, the prospect of transforming a vacant lot into a park or playground is immediately satisfying in its tangibility and obvious benefit to the community. When public agencies are unwilling or unable to address a neighborhood's safety concerns, recreational needs, or other objectives, residents can come together to clean up trash, plant trees, and build benches. Multiple examples buoy a belief that the process of planning, designing, and building such spaces encourages a sense of community control and ongoing civic activism (Hester 1975, Fox et al. 1985, Francis et al. 1984, Hou and Rios 2003). Further evidence suggests that the resulting parks and open space, when well maintained and actively used, are effective tools to reduce crime, increase property values, attract investments, and encourage active living (Bonham et al. 2002, Crompton 2001). However, whereas the demanding effort to create community spaces has been acknowledged, less attention is paid to their sustainability, particularly when their status remains semi-public and volunteer residents – already overburdened – are responsible for ongoing maintenance and care. The resulting open spaces are not finite at the point of creation; it is their ongoing care and evolution that assure their performance as community resources.

Even as we celebrate the potential to reclaim and revitalize through grassroots efforts, we must also recognize the structural inequalities that both create a disproportionate need (versus desire) for civic activism in low-income communities of color, as well as an unequal access to public resources and support for their sustainability. Whereas in most American cities parks and open spaces are typically the responsibility of public agencies – park and recreation departments, planning agencies, and utility companies – recent trends towards "public–private partnerships" acknowledge the limited resources within municipalities that in turn seek additional funding, volunteers, and programming opportunities through involvement of corporations, not-for-profit organizations, and others (Project for Public Spaces 2000, Harnik 2000). In many low-income communities, residents face a shortage of park space and other public services while bearing the burden of large areas of derelict vacant land and environmental hazards. Given the struggle to maintain services amid reduced tax revenue and few prospects of attracting external investments, not only are parks and open spaces often neglected but the prospect of revitalizing vacant land remains a dream unless residents and community groups assume leadership and ongoing care.

The compulsory nature of some community action underscores a societal philosophy of personal responsibility for improving one's community, even when the problems being faced extend far beyond it. Often, residents in low-income communities of color must take responsibility for vacant land that has been abandoned by others, ranging from individual residential lots to large brownfields left over from industry or vacant land cleared for urban renewal (Bowman and Pagano 2004). Residents are compelled out of immediate threats of crime and danger associated with living next to unclaimed and uncared-for open space. Discussing the opportunities to reclaim unmanaged land in Philadelphia, the authors of *Old Cities/ Green Cities: Communities Transform Unmanaged Land* acknowledge the burden placed on residents by past industries and governmental policies, noting, "For the foreseeable future, it would be naïve to suggest that any but the most draconian policy initiatives could reverse the effects of urban decentralization and blighted neighborhoods – trends that were born over half a century ago" (Bonham *et al*. 2002: 5). In his discussion of a broader spectrum of community initiatives, Robert Halpern (1995), in *Rebuilding the Inner City*, criticizes the ability of neighborhood initiatives to achieve goals when faced with conditions of community neglect and exclusion and a lack of political leadership to address these concerns.

To assume that grassroots activism is a form of "community empowerment" often ignores the pervasiveness of structural inequalities and unequal access to resources; in other words, power. The process of engaging in community activism is often referred to as empowerment of participants. As such, "empowerment processes, if properly carried out, should result in actual shifts in power as symbolized by individuals' engagement and participation in making decisions in which they previously were minimally involved or uninvolved" (Miller and Campbell 2006: 298). However, distinguishing whether the dynamic is "power over" – domination of one person or group over another – or "power to" – associated with personal empowerment – has implications at the level of the individual, interpersonal, organizational, and societal relationships (Yoder and Kahn 1992: 381, Malhotra *et al*. 2002). Power can also be understood in terms of visible power, hidden power, and invisible power (VeneKlasen and Miller 2002). Visible power is grounded in laws and policies that might serve one group over others; hidden power is often maintained by powerful people who make decisions, set the agenda, and control access to voice; invisible power is maintained through socialization and culture that perpetuate exclusion and inequality, often denying access to information, which can lead to self-blame and feelings of powerlessness. When combining the obstacles of invisible and hidden power dynamics, low-income communities of color encounter not only practical obstacles, such as inadequate access to funding or inflexible regulations and procedures, but also limited access to information and the formal decision-making arena. Sometimes difficult experiences leave a residue of distrust that nurtures skepticism not only about the process but also about the residents' own ability to effect change.

When structural inequality and the hidden/invisible power are not acknowledged, processes meant to build "power to" (be empowering) can leave participants and their organizations feeling disempowered because the complex interconnection among environmental, economic, and social concerns affecting low-income communities of color has been ignored. The two opposing perspectives that often flavor discussions of community activism in low-income communities of color – one of apathy and the other of action – are not as opposite as one might think. In their book, *Derelict Landscapes*, the geographers John Jakle and David Wilson note that "people trapped in poverty have little basis for community bonding . . . attempts at community building fail because of fatalist and defeatist attitudes" (Jakle and Wilson 1992: 280). They write about anomie, not community, due to "unemployment, underemployment, blockage of aspirations, inadequate education, and the effects of institutionalized racism." But this is not the case in East St. Louis. We have seen community spirit, pride of place, pride in history, and an amazing perseverance in the face of obstacles. The real problem seems to be lack of resources to make and sustain change and too much responsibility without formal power and influence.

Although it is inspiring to witness community activism through claiming vacant lots or open space, there is also an environmental justice argument to build on community action with public investment. In their book *Public Space*, Stephen Carr, Mark Francis, Leanne Rivlin, and Andrew Stone note that self-help alone cannot address all concerns, "Significant investment of public resources in less affluent neighborhoods will be needed. This will most likely come as part of a renewed political movement to address the larger social inequities of which inadequate open space is a symptom" (Carr *et al.* 1992: 360). Until this movement materializes, however, activists in the field rely on building partnerships that bring resources from governmental agencies, not-for-profit organizations, universities, and others. The ease with which such partnerships grow depends on context, with some communities having access to organizations and institutions that may have a vested interest in the work and others having to start from scratch.

Most community leaders in East St. Louis understand their responsibility to nurture local organizations, build membership, and direct actions to help the community. There is also a clear need for partnerships that bring in outside resources that the community organizations can rely upon. At both Illinois Avenue Playground and Pullman Porter Park, university involvement through the ESLARP program has provided some useful technical assistance and enthusiastic student involvement, but it is limited by distance – the campus being roughly 175 miles away – and institutional limitations on actions such as political lobbying and fund raising. New hope has emerged with a proactive park director, but given her limited budget she, too, looks to residents, churches, schools, and others to improve and maintain parks and open space. The next step is to seek responsibility from a range of public agencies – local, regional, state, federal – as well as interest groups addressing social, environmental, educational, and other needs. Attracting these resources is difficult since East St. Louis has little left to offer to outsiders. Possibly, with social awareness that the poor conditions in East St. Louis are the legacy of exploitive industries and ongoing racism, the larger public will realize that their civic activism is needed, not only in their immediate community but also extended to communities such as East St. Louis as well.

Notes

1 For information on the University of Illinois East St. Louis Action Research Project, please refer to the ESLARP website: http://www.eslarp.illinois.edu.
2 Community open space refers to "any green place designed, developed, or managed

by local residents for the use and enjoyment of those in the community" (Francis *et al.* 1984: 1). These spaces may be publicly owned and maintained or developed on privately owned land or land held in trust by a not-for-profit organization.

Bibliography

Bonham, J., Spilka, G., and Rastorfer, D. (2002) *Old Cities/Green Cities: Communities Transform Unmanaged Land*, Chicago: American Planning Association.

Bowman, A. and Pagano, M. (2004) *Terra Incognita: Vacant Land and Urban Strategies*, Washington, DC: Georgetown University Press.

Carr, S., Francis, M., Rivlin, L., and Stone A. (1992) *Public Space*, New York: Cambridge University Press.

Crompton, J. (2001) *Parks and Economic Development*, Chicago: American Planning Association.

Edwards, M. and Lawson, L. (2005) 'The Evolution of Planning in East St. Louis', *Journal of Planning History*, 4 (4): 356–382.

Fox, T., Koeppel, I., and Kellam S. (1985) *Struggle for Space: The Greening of New York City, 1970–1984*, New York: Neighborhood Open Space Coalition.

Francis, M., Cashdan, L., and Paxson, L. (1984) *Community Open Space*, Washington, DC: Island Press.

Halpern, R. (1995) *Rebuilding the Inner City*, New York: Columbia University Press.

Harnik, P. (2000) *Inside City Parks*, Washington, DC: Urban Land Institute.

Hester, R. (1975) *Neighborhood Space*, Stroudsburg, PA: Douden, Hutchinson, and Ross.

Hou, J. and Rios, M. (2003) 'Community-driven Place Making: The Social Practice of Participatory Design in the Making of Union Point Park', *Journal of Architectural Education*, 57 (1): 19–27.

Jakle, J. and Wilson, D. (1992) *Derelict Landscapes: The Wasting of America's Built Environment*, Savage, MD: Rowman and Littlefield.

Judd, D. and Mendelson, R. (1973) *The Politics of Urban Planning: The East St. Louis Experience*, Urbana: University of Illinois Press.

Malhotra, A., Schuler, S., and Boender, C. (2002) *Measuring Women's Empowerment as a Variable in International Development*, n.p.: International Center for Research on Women and the Gender and Development Group of the World Bank.

Miller, R. and Campbell, R. (2006) 'Taking Stock of Empowerment Evaluation: An Empirical Review', *American Journal of Evaluation*, 27: 296–319.

Project for Public Spaces. (2000) *Public Parks, Private Partners*, New York: Project for Public Spaces.

Reardon, K. M. (1995) 'Community Building in East St. Louis: The Illinois Avenue Playground', *AICP Planners' Casebook*, 16: 1–8.

—— (1999) 'East St. Louis, Illinois: Promoting Community Development through Empowerment Planning', in Keating, D. and Krumholz, N. (eds.) *Rebuilding Urban Neighborhoods*, Thousand Oaks, CA: Sage Publications.

Theising, A. (2003) *East St. Louis: Made in the USA: The Rise and Fall of an Industrial River Town*, St. Louis: Virginia Publishing Company.

United States Department of Census. (2009) 'State and County Quick Facts: East St. Louis, Illinois'. Online. Available HTTP: http:/www.quickfacts.census.gov (accessed 23 November 2009).

Yoder, J. and Kahn, A. (1992) 'Toward a Feminist Understanding of Women and Power', *Psychology of Women Quarterly*, 16 (4): 381–388.

VeneKlasen, L. and Miller, V. (2002) *A New Weave of Power, People & Politics: The Action Guide for Advocacy and Citizen Participation*, Oklahoma City, OK: World Neighbors.

Index